I am the Monkey!

How to successfully manage and
live in foreign cultures

Dr. Jürg Wittwer
with Joanne Cackett

Once upon a time there was a great flood, the waters of which swallowed up two creatures – a monkey and a fish. The monkey, being agile and experienced, was quick enough to scramble up a tree and escape the raging waters. As he looked down from his safe perch, he saw the poor fish struggling against the swift current. With the very best of intentions, he reached down and lifted the fish from the water.

The result was inevitable.

Don Adams, *The Monkey and the Fish*

4

To Naomi, Joel and Cornelia

Content

Introduction 9

PART I: A MONKEY IN THE ZOO 13
1. A Visit to the Zoo 14
  Accept, Adapt and Adopt 21
  Awareness 37
  Action 40

PART II: AWARENESS 43
2. How Human Beings Learn Culture 44
  Primary Socialization 45
  Unconscious Learning 52
  Frame of Interpretation 53
3. What is Culture? 58
  Values 62
  Norms 68
  The Baobab (or the Theory of the Iceberg) 71
4. A Journey through Cultural Differences 83
  Seeing 84
  Touching 90
  Smelling 95
  Family, Sexuality and Love 100
  Management and Leadership 106
5. Building Blocks of Culture 112
  How important am I? 118
  Are laws more important than friendships? 129
  How important is punctuality? 137
  Does fate define my career? 145

6. The Trap of Ethnocentricity 153
    Ethnocentrism and the Workplace 156
    Ethnocentrism and Communication 158
    Breaking Down Barriers of Ethnocentricity.......................... 162

PART III: ACCEPT, ADAPT, ADOPT 165
7. Learning to Accept 170
    Don't judge 171
    Accept Ambiguity 175
    Active Tolerance 179
    Explain Yourself 184
8. Learning to Adapt... 187
    Seeking the "Why" 188
    Creating Analogies 197
    Using Stereotypes Wisely... 204
    Changing Perspective
    (or putting yourself in someone else's shoes)....................... 209
9. Learning to Adopt 216

PART IV: ACTION... 217
How to Learn about a Foreign Culture 218
10. The Learning 224
    Language 224
    Religion.. 231
    History 236
11. Sharing... 244
    Making Friends... 245
    Sharing Food 255
    Look for your Zookeeper.. 257

Epilogue: Do we really need all this? 263
Acknowledgments... 270
Notes... 272

Introduction

Over the last two decades, about two billion people have entered the world of markets and trade. The global economy has grown by more than 40% during the first ten years of the millennium. Emerging markets account for half of this global growth and for over 40% of the world economy. The time when mainstream US companies dealt mainly with European companies and vice-versa is long gone, as the global market expands and becomes increasingly competitive. The tallest building in the world is now in Dubai, UAE. The home country of the wealthiest man in the world has alternated between America's Bill Gates and Mexico's Carlos Slim. The American company, Apple, is still the largest public trading company, but China National Petroleum, founded in 1988, is coming up fast at number four. Russia claims the biggest airplane – the cargo plane, Antonov AN 225 Mriya. Reliance Industries, the world's leading oil refinery, is located in India, a nation that also boasts the world's largest movie industry, Bollywood. China has the greatest number of factories, and the world's largest mall is located here. All of this demonstrates that the major participants in business are growing more diverse every day, making multicultural skills all the more essential.

I am the Monkey! will enable you to deeply understand how culture affects our behavior, our perception and the way we interpret the world around us. It will also help the reader identify differences between cultures and guide you in processing these differences pragmatically. The final chapters are dedicated to helping you realize your own distinct methodology regarding acclimating to and accommodating any culture.

You will find many books available to you, discussing how to behave in other countries; bookstores at airports have plenty on hand. Many of these will inform the reader of a specific country's behavioral habits. From these books, you learn to give a firm handshake in Germany, to drink wine in France and to avoid using the left hand in African countries. These books will help you avoid the most obvious misunderstandings by providing you quick and simple advice. However, *I am the Monkey!* will take it one step further.

This book ventures far beyond these basic behavioral rules and into the deeply entrenched cultural avenues of society, so as to understand how culture can affect the minutest of details in day-to-day life. We'll examine why people with various cultural backgrounds behave differently and discuss why it's okay that they do. Culture influences individual and group ideology and perception of the world, leading to very different interpretations of the same facts. While examining these various cultural perceptions, you may diverge from your old way of thought and arrive at a new perception about your own culture and its underlying beliefs. Certain behaviors of which you were previously unaware will be brought to the surface and challenged. Certain behaviors you'd believed were universal will be revealed as subject to cultural perception. This is what the book *will* do: it will banish the smoke and mirrors of your previous worldview.

There is one thing this book *will not* do: it will not make a good manager out of a bad one. International management is challenging in its complexity. Cultural sensitivity is an important management skill today, but it is nowhere near the most important. An exceptional manager will seldom fail, no matter which cultural environment he works in. His empathy, his people skills will help him get by, even in an environment with which he is unfamiliar. However, knowing how to successfully manage across cultures may just give him an edge in a highly competitive workforce. Let's illustrate this with two famous athletes: Roger Federer and Rafael Nadal.

In 2007, Federer and Nadal had made it to the finals at the All England Championship in Wimbledon, the most prestigious tennis tournament in the world. After competing for 3 hours and 45 minutes, Federer beat Nadal by 7 points, winning 165 to 158. In 2008, the two champions again stood against each other in the final. This time the match lasted 4 hours and 48 minutes. Nadal beat Federer by five points, winning 209 to 204. Federer lost Wimbledon due to a measly 5 points, and this is because tennis is a highly competitive sport. In today's business world, being good is not enough. A manager must be excellent, because that little bit of edge can mean the difference between winning or losing to your competition.

Alfred Zeien, the now retired CEO of Gillette, stated that globally literate leaders were his company's scarcest resource.[1] He is not alone. In a survey of Fortune 500 firms, having competent global leaders was rated as the most important factor for business success. In the same survey, 85% of executives stated that they don't think they have an adequate number of cross culturally fluent leaders, and more than 65% believe their existing leaders need additional skills and knowledge before they can meet or exceed the challenge of global leadership.[2]

If you're an international manager, the information in this book may just give you the bit of edge you need to win in a globalized economy.

WITTWER

PART I: A MONKEY IN THE ZOO

1. A Visit to the Zoo

How about a trip to the zoo? But not a short, breezy Sunday afternoon visit. You're not a spectator today; rather, this is your home. You, yourself, are an animal in the zoo. You could be an elephant, a lion or any other animal, but for the purpose of this book, let's say you're the monkey. Every day visitors enter the zoo, and they come to see you. Parents stroll through with their little munchkins. Whole families stand around the cage to point and stare. Monkeys are a favorite for many guests; their cages are often surrounded by spectators. Not because they're the biggest, nor the most dangerous. Their popularity stems from their behavior; they behave similarly to humans and, yet, they're animals. So when people watch monkeys, to some degree, they're looking into a bizarre mirror and, for right or wrong, they interpret what they see through their human foundation. They imagine that the concepts of "love" or "friendship" are demonstrated through two apes hugging each other. A young monkey's playtime reminds them of their own children. Every move is reinterpreted, contextualized through human perspective, and adapted to align with the framework of human behavior.

When you pictured the caged monkeys, you more than likely placed yourself, mentally, into the role of spectator, standing at the cage and looking inside. This is normal. You are human and, thereby, will automatically choose the perspective that's most familiar to you. In doing so, you may have recalled a memory – the time your parents took you to the zoo as a child. It comes naturally to look at the world from one's own perspective, the one you're familiar with, the one to which you've adapted.

But let's return to our experiment and change all that. Really concentrate on placing yourself into the shoes – or the skin, so to speak – of the monkey. *You* are the monkey. *You* are caged, *you* are the spectacle, *you* are the center of attention. Imagine sitting on your branch and observing what's happening around you. You see dozens of strange creatures – these humans – watching you. They don't look like normal monkeys. Their skin is odd and hairless. Instead of a nice fur, they wear some hanging colored fabric, which either grows on the skin or is placed over the body, you can't tell. Whatever the case, they definitely look strange, unusual and not very attractive to you. But even stranger is their behavior. They seem particularly interested in your clan of monkeys. They're pointing right at you with their fingers, and they're constantly making strange noises with their mouths. Some actually even go so far as to throw peanuts at you. Where are their manners? And they're not very bright, either. You see an adult caressing a child, running her hand through her child's hair, and you think, "What an odd way to check for lice. This species is definitely none too skilled."

This is a rather radical mind game, placing yourself in another's perspective and, particularly, in another specie's perspective. And what we learn from this game is that perfectly normal behavior can be interpreted as odd, strange or unnatural by an observer from another background or from another culture. These moments of astonishment, misunderstanding and perplexity when faced with some unknown behavior in a foreign culture are what I call "I am the monkey" moments.

When I moved to the US as a young insurance manager, I, myself, had a distinct and memorable "I am the monkey" moment. Switzerland is one of the wealthiest countries in the world, and being Swiss but growing up in Africa, I'd always belonged to the exclusive, rich, upper tier of society and was always treated as such when traveling abroad…that is, until I arrived in America. I remember, vividly, my first day in the company. A couple of colleagues approached me and said, "You must be very lucky to work in the US. You'll be able to send money home to your family." These spectators saw the world through their own rose-tinted goggles and, to them, I was the monkey, a foreigner who came from another country and, thus, must belong in a lower social tier. This is something I wasn't at all used to.

Another of my personal monkey moments completely opposes this one. I was standing in line at the immigration police in Spain, because I wanted to buy an apartment in this marvelous city on the Mediterranean. I looked around me, and it was obvious that the other people in the queue were looking for work, while I was the only white-skinned person in a tie and suit. Again, I was the monkey. In the US, I was the poor monkey; in the immigration queue in Barcelona, I was the rich monkey. In both cases, I was the strange, foreign, exotic animal, appearing and behaving differently than all other species around me.

"Monkey" moments may be less pronounced, but they all have one thing in common: you are, all of a sudden, starkly different from those around you and are very much aware of the fact. In these moments, you may contrast so highly with those surrounding you that, in effect, if you stood in a line according to what was considered "normal" in the dominant culture, the locals would be clustered at one end, while you'd be alone on the polar end of the spectrum. And more importantly, you consider *yourself* to be the normal one and the others, the exotic, strange animals. In reality, through the eyes of the majority, *you* are the exotic. *You* are the exception. *You* are the monkey, and you don't even know it. Let's look at some specific "monkey" moments in a cultural context.

Peter, a German CFO, moved to Paris to work at the headquarters of an international company. In the whole of his department, he was the only foreigner – and he was the boss. This, alone, is not an easy position to be in, and to make it even more difficult, this was his first assignment abroad. Unfortunately, his story does not have a happy ending. His French team never accepted him, and after a year, he returned to his home country. At the time, I happened to know a couple of people on his Paris team, and I asked them why it hadn't worked out. Their answer: "Peter never adapted to our culture. We are French, not German. Look, every day when we went to the restaurant downstairs, he ordered a coffee with milk. He was the only one." Of course, how you take your coffee is not relevant to your job performance, but to his French colleagues, this represented Peter's lack of interest in local customs and the ultimate failure of his cultural integration. The way he took his morning coffee made Peter the monkey; it made him stand out. The worst thing about this monkey moment was that Peter remained completely oblivious to the fact that he was the monkey.

If you're managing people in a foreign culture, then you will have plenty of monkey moments. Ensure that you are self-aware and try to identify these moments, so you can alter your behavior wherever you can. For example, if you're the company boss in an egalitarian society, you may choose to do your own photocopying. Completing this simple chore yourself is humbling; it demonstrates that you don't think you are above such a task, thereby putting yourself on the same level as your employees. In a hierarchical society, however, you'd be considered a total "monkey" if you were to perform menial tasks as the company boss. Your employees may even think that by performing the tasks of a subordinate, you are threatening their jobs and suggesting they are expendable. They may also read your actions as inappropriate, inexperienced and weak, none of which are characteristic of a successful leader and, needless to say, all of which are misrepresentative of your intentions. Is this the image a boss would like to present to his new subordinates and colleagues?

Another example of a monkey moment comes by way of a simple handshake. A normal French handshake is weak-gripped; not strong and firm, like the German grip. So when a French manager offers this weak grip (also termed by the Germans as the "fishy" handshake, because the hand is limp), the German business partner assumes his French colleague will be a weak negotiator.

Monkey moments are not only individual; they can extend to entire corporations. This may lead to quite embarrassing hits to said corporation's reputation on the global stage. In the late 1990's, Walmart – the largest and most successful retail chain in the world – decided to take their business to the next level and expand internationally. They bought 95 superstores in Germany and announced the pending opening of 50 additional stores, exporting their highly successful, streamlined, low-price strategy into the biggest market in continental Europe. German competitors were frightened. Everyone expected a fundamental shift in the German retail market. But no shift occurred. Eight years after the investment, on the verge of insolvency, Walmart's German business unit was sold. The European adventure cost Walmart billions of dollars, and their surprising failure became a case study in cross cultural management.

So what happened? When it comes to catastrophe, multiple failures often contribute to the collapse of the greater whole; but the cultural insensitivity of the first CEO certainly played a central part in Walmart's dramatic failure. This CEO experienced a number of monkey moments, all of which accumulated until they'd become detrimental to the success of international expansion. And most of these moments occurred without the CEO realizing his own cultural insensitivity.

For instance, upon his arrival to Germany, he forbade flirting in the workplace. This regulation makes perfect sense in an American workplace, with the country's strict sexual harassment laws and a culturally entrenched separation between work and private life. But in Germany, flirting in the workplace is more than acceptable, and such a regulation would be regarded as a restriction of one's personal rights. The Walmart CEO had unknowingly become the monkey, the animal in a cage, acting strangely and completely oblivious to his strangeness. In his own eyes, he did everything right: complying with company regulations and protecting employees from unwanted sexual advances. But to the German employees, especially those unaware of American culture and the litigious nature of sexual harassment in the States, this regulation was unpopular, to put it mildly, and was considered an infringement on their personal freedom.

Shortly after taking up his position, the CEO also declared that the official company language would be English. This declaration could have been acceptable. Big international German companies – Allianz or Siemens, for example – have opted for English as the "company language" without lasting issues. But what really made a monkey out of the CEO was his complete disinterest in learning German. Even when *he* was the animal in the zoo, he believed himself the spectator, watching, pointing, and laughing at the animals and their silly "language." He didn't notice that they were pointing at him. He was no longer the king of the jungle, he was the exception and had now made himself the outcast. The others were "normal," and he was "odd."

"Normal" behavior is not how you behave but, rather, how the majority around you behave. What seems unfamiliar is not necessarily unnatural. Let's look at it from the monkey's perspective again. If you are the monkey, then you may wonder why this strange species of human flocks to your living space and throws peanuts at you all day long. Of course you like the peanuts, but still, what is the point? Every day, you receive plenty of food from the zoo ward (who, by the way, seems to be the only individual of this strange species that makes any effort to understand you). You are not hungry at all. You have not demonstrated any desire to eat. You were actually just hanging in the tree, trying to take a nap when, all of a sudden, these strange, hairless apes started throwing peanuts at you. They're insolent creatures – these humans – and, judging by their actions, they must be stupid too. Certainly, they aren't rational, or they wouldn't be standing and gawking all day, chucking peanuts.

Evolution reveals that man's closest relation is the monkey; this is the species with which we most relate, biologically. The physical appearance of this species is most like our human appearance; therefore, it's natural to expect likenesses in behavior as well. This concept can be applied to cross cultural management, the correlation being that, though we relate to foreigners in appearance, we don't necessarily relate in behavior. And still, both sets of behaviors can be natural and "normal" to our individual species or cultures.

The common bond we may feel with the big apes make monkey moments inevitable. Apes are like humans, only hairier. When we look at elephants, which are starkly different from humans in appearance, we expect different behavior, so an "elephant moment" wouldn't confuse us. No major consequences occur if you've misinterpreted an elephant's actions, as you don't expect to relate to this giant creature with a trunk, who looks nothing like you. The closer we relate to another in physical appearance, the less tolerant we are regarding different cultural behaviors.

The Germans and the French are physically similar. They are neighboring countries, and both belong under the banner head of "Western culture." Still, between these two nations and their business cultures, cross cultural conflicts abound nearly as much as business relations between Americans and the distant Japanese. There is a simple reason for this: because of the proximity and similarity in features, French people expect more conformity from a German manager than they would from an American manager. And they expect more conformity from an American manager than they would from a Japanese manager. The degree of intensity in regards to the monkey moment always depends on the expected degree of conformity.

My greatest cultural issues in management occurred when I returned to Switzerland from America. All of my managerial experience was essentially gained in the States, rather than in my home country, but when I became the CEO of a Swiss company, all the employees expected me to behave like a Swiss manager. Even I expected my managerial style not to conflict with cultural expectations, as I considered myself Swiss and didn't anticipate any cultural dissimilitude. But before long, I'd experienced enough monkey moments to be labelled "the American." This illustrates how anticipated sameness can end in conflict in cultural environments which seem to be similar enough to your own – and even in your own culture if you've been trained or deeply integrated into another culture at one point or another.

It's obvious that monkey moments do not aid assimilation. Instead of being a spectator, you must become part of the zoo, and you do this by making efforts to arrive at a common objective. Ignoring your need to assimilate creates misunderstanding and friction and decimates teamwork, altogether. A successful cross cultural manager will focus on improving two essential skills: 1) recognizing his monkey moments, and 2) once aware of them, correcting his own behavior through the appropriate strategies.

Before we discuss these strategies, let's take one last look at our zoo. When in contact with another culture, remember that *you* are the monkey; you are the odd one out. The "normal" see your behavior as contrary to their own norms and maybe even see your actions as offensive. You and all that you do will be watched through the lens of a culture you don't know or understand and dissected with tools of which you, yourself, have no concept. But there are ways to gain access to these tools and better assimilate yourself through acceptance, adaption and adoption.

Accept, Adapt and Adopt

Faced with unfamiliar behavior, humans often react in one of three ways: by rejecting it, by being curious about it, or by ignoring it completely. If the foreign behavior seems unnatural, then a person's initial reaction to it may be intensely strong and emotional, maybe even violent. Wars have been waged over cultural differences. Throughout history, scores of people have died due to this initial aggressive rejection of another's culture and beliefs. We will discuss the reasons why cultural differences may provoke such strong reactions in the next chapter. For the moment, let's take a quick look at the reactive behaviors, themselves.

Though the initial reaction to cultural differences may be negative, the positive aspect to come out of this reaction is you've realized that there are distinct differences between you and "the other." Even when you choose to reject or consciously ignore, at least the first step towards cultural understanding has been achieved: you've recognized you are different, and you've maybe even caught a glimpse of yourself in the mirror and identified that you are the monkey. But once you've arrived at this conclusion, the question is what are the appropriate strategies to becoming a human being, instead of the one who stands out in a negative way?

Certainly, to ignore the differences doesn't work. This was the strategy of the failed Walmart CEO. Rejection never leads to understanding, nor does it improve communication.

Is curiosity the answer, then? As a curious traveler, you may decide to further investigate and satisfy your curiosity. You might read and observe and begin to understand the foreign cultural behavior surrounding you. But once your questions have been answered, you'll still be faced with the same issue: how do I deal with this behavior which seems so odd to me?

FIFA, the world governing body of soccer, held the 2002 World Cup in Korea. America nearly boycotted the game, due to a significant cultural difference in the eating habits of the two countries. Koreans eat dogs. For Americans, dogs are considered "man's best friend" and are a common household pet. Eating a pet dog would be akin to eating a family member. The controversial dietary habits of the Koreans had been called into question many years before the World Cup, and as a result, the Koreans, themselves, had banned the sale and consumption of dog meat in the run up to the 1988 Seoul Olympics. Officials worried that South Korea's reputation would be cast in an unfavorable light.

By the time the 2002 World Cup rolled around, eating dog meat was only common among elderly people. It also continued to be sold in exclusive restaurants, which were at risk for having their licenses revoked in consequence for selling prohibited food. At the time, the Western world followed a simple two-point strategy in regards to this controversy: rejection and condemnation. Needless to say, this strategy didn't solve the issue and, in fact, exacerbated it. Months before the World Cup, emotions ran high on both sides. *The Korea*

Times quoted one of its readers, who summed up the sentiments of many Koreans in regards to the issue: "It is obvious ethnocentrism for some narrow-minded Westerners to denounce other people for eating certain meat which they don't consume. If they don't like a certain kind of meat then they shouldn't eat it and just shut up instead of sticking their noses into the eating practices of others."

In the midst of a major emotional conflict of culture, how should an American manager, dispatched to Korea, react appropriately to the situation? There are three acceptable strategies. Rejection, condemnation and ignoring are none of them.[3] Instead, reacting reasonably and with acceptance is much more appropriate, and you can do this in one of three ways. Accepting, adapting or adopting will allow you to appropriately accommodate the culture into which you're trying to assimilate. Let's call these three methods the "Monkey Methods."

Accepting

The first appropriate reaction is "accepting." You may feel very strongly about a cultural issue, whether it's broad or specific, like not eating dog meat. You may even believe it's your duty to change the other's point of view, as you regard the issue in a humanitarian light – in this example, you wish to protect dogs from being killed. But, still, you can respectfully accept that some people have different beliefs than you.

One way to move away from rejection and toward acceptance is to try and open up your own perspective. For instance, Hindus believe the cow is a sacred animal, as the animal's gentle nature represents the foundation of Hinduism and symbolizes the religion's teachings of non-violence. You are not a vegetarian. You eat meat. In fact, you love beef. So, what if a Hindu believer pointed a finger at you and told you that you are despicable for eating cows? How would you react? Perhaps you might respond that you've eaten beef since childhood; that this is acceptable in America and, anyway, that it's your right to choose what you eat. You would expect the Hindu to respect your culture and its ways, even if eating cows, in his view, is a sin. Now that you've placed yourself into the shoes of the accused, you know exactly how to react to the controversial issue of Korean dietary customs: primarily, to respect their culture and not cast the first stone.

As illustrated, the appropriate route to navigating cultural differences begins with accepting that there are reasons for unfamiliar behavior and acknowledging that they are usually good ones. Of course, accepting is easier when the behaviors in question do not strike an emotional chord or are not in direct contradiction to your own firm convictions and beliefs. For instance, it may be easy to accept that punctuality is important to Germans or a shared drink is the norm for Russians. The areas that are more difficult to understand are those that touch on morality.

Take, for example, the concept of "truth." Some African cultures do not base truth on what many would consider the "objective facts" but, rather, on what politeness dictates. For example, in some cases, a person may say whatever is required of them out of politeness instead of telling the god's honest truth, and doing so is not considered amoral; in fact, responding in this way is considered more moral than objectivity. This can be frustrating to foreigners and even disconcerting, as Western cultures base "truth" on fact.

Another instance of cultural faux pas may occur in regards to personal property. Property does not belong strictly to an individual in some cultures. Cultures with a strong sense of community believe that if you have no shirt and your neighbor has ten, then taking one from your neighbor would not be considered stealing. Again, this highlights how actions or behaviors that are considered morally "wrong" in one culture can be viewed as "right" in another. When you live in another culture, you'll find, in many cases, there is no universal "right" or "wrong."

In the following chapters, we will encounter and discuss a variety of behaviors, many of which may seem strange to those belonging to Western cultures. But never forget that *you* are the monkey abroad. When traveling or expatriating, *you* are the odd one out; *you* are the animal behaving strangely to those around you. So begin by treating everyone with respect and accepting differences. Some things may not look right or morally just in your eyes, but in order to be successful in a foreign culture, you must come to terms with cultural differences and understand that there are innumerable reasons – and good ones – for other people to believe and behave differently than you do. Accept that there are a litany of valuable worldviews, six dozen definitions of friendship, and innumerable codes of conduct regarding "appropriate" behavior at work. Simply accept this, and you'll be on your way to complete cross cultural integration.

Although accepting is the first step, it's easier said than done in some cases. As we've discussed, certain cultural behaviors may raise profound ethical questions. Should circumcision for girls, which mutilates their sexual organs, be tolerated? Are arranged marriages fair? Is the tying up of the feet of Japanese girls a tradition worth preserving, when it results in crippling? Indeed, there are limits to cultural acceptance.

Hurting members of society, mentally or physically, can never be justified by traditions or cultural heritage. Societies must evolve, and the evolution of a society means to break itself of harmful traditions and customs, those which are unworthy of humanity, itself. For instance, not many would argue that slavery was something to be proud of; rather, ownership of human beings is a stain on humanity's collective history. The American Civil War saw to it that plantation owners – or anyone else, for that matter – no longer had the right to own slaves, and most believe that ceasing slavery was just. Still, some southerners in America might claim the atrocity as an important part of their identity and heritage; they may even suggest it was God's will. Such worldviews result in continued racism and prejudice in America, highlighting the types of issues that may arise regarding differences in cultural behaviors and beliefs in a single country.

Another example of an ethical issue which divides individuals and groups is corporal punishment. Corporal punishment was overwhelmingly acceptable for centuries, but it has since been outlawed in many societies. Beating children at home or at school is no longer considered ethical. This demonstrates the evolution of societal ideology. Only when human life is at stake or harmed should cultural acceptance fly out the window. There's a line to be drawn between cultural acceptance and basic human rights, and cruelty is the line.

Fortunately, you will not often be faced with these deep and profound controversial issues in the business world. More or less, the cultural confrontations you'll experience in the workplace can be resolved through acceptance. Accepting that others behave differently and believe in and practice their own customs and traditions – in good faith and with their own rationale – would be a more than appropriate reaction when it comes to workplace integration and socializing with your colleagues.

Adapting

Sometimes you may feel that acceptance is not enough. While accepting will remedy judgment, criticism and disrespect towards others, in some cases, simply accepting and leaving it at that will not lead to connection and integration. In these cases, you must push it further and imitate your foreign friends, those with whom you'd like to connect and become integrated.

This brings us to adapting. Adapting to other cultures involves sharing in their behavior, and doing so requires that you become conscious of your own behavior. That which is normal to you may be abnormal to the culture in which you'd like to integrate. Cite the differences and determine the alterable behaviors to improve your chances at an easier and smoother integration.

Let's say a Swedish fellow is attempting to integrate into British culture. Cold and flu season comes along, and the Swede identifies a minor difference between his culture and the Brits'. Instead of blowing their noses, it's more common for Swedish people to sniff rather loudly. Someone raised in a traditional British household may find this habit quite disgusting. The Swede, upon immigrating to the UK, decides to adapt and start blowing his nose rather than sniffling or hawking. He realized that if he chose to continue behaving as he would on the streets of Stockholm, he may be regarded as rude or uncultured. On the other hand, the Swedes may regard a British person as arrogant, if she is unmovable in her ladylike manners while spending a weekend in a Swedish blockhouse.

When integrating into a new culture, the most important and obvious adaption is to learn the language. Learning a language does far more than to make communication easier; it also aids in the understanding of how a culture thinks and is a tangible and credible signal of your willingness to integrate.

Adapting to other cultures may also require alterations in your management style. A central element of business culture is hierarchy, which is often culturally established and followed. Geert Hofstede, a famous cross cultural researcher (we will learn more from him later in the book), summarized this cultural characteristic in the concept of "power distance." Power distance is the extent to which the less powerful members of a society accept and expect the unequal distribution of power. Individuals in societies that exhibit a high degree of power distance accept hierarchies in which everyone has a specific place, without the need for justification. Some are born kings. Some are born peasants. And that's just how things work. Societies with low power distance seek to share equal distribution of power. Every member of society must have equal rights. If there are differences, then they should be transparent.

Guatemala is a country with an extremely high power distance; 95 on Hofstede's index. On the other end of the scale is Sweden with only 31. The average Swedish manager in a Swedish company participates with his employees and is aware that external signs of hierarchy in dress, in office space, etc. are not good for company culture. He then assumes that treating all employees equally is better for the performance of his team and ultimately for business profitability. To put this knowledge about company culture into action, he insists on being reachable, keeping his door open, and picking up his direct line as much as possible. He sits in the cafeteria and chats with his employees on their level.

One day, he is promoted and sent to Guatemala to be the branch's CEO. To initiate the stages of cultural integration, he must choose either to assimilate his own managerial style into this new and very different culture or adapt to the managerial ways of the local culture. If he holds strong to his own cultural sense of equality in the workplace, he may be seen as weak by the locals. Societies with high power indexes expect superiors to make decisions and execute them – not to consult with lower-ranking employees. Bosses are expected to mark the hierarchical differences and treat their employees accordingly. And no one is bothered by the distance maintained between higher-ups and subordinates, because this is the culturally acceptable status quo; it's how their world works.

Cultures with high power-distances are like watches. In a watch, there are small wheels and big wheels. A watch with only uniform wheels won't work. To be successful in this new cultural environment, the Swedish CEO may have to adapt to the power distance of the culture. He'll adjust his management style and become the big wheel in the watch in order for it to keep on ticking. We'll learn more about power distance in the later chapters of this book, but for the moment, it's important to note that working in a different culture may mean adapting to the culture's managerial style.

As with "accepting," you must walk a fine line in the process of adaptation. If you don't adapt enough, then you may not be able to integrate or to manage in a successful way in the host culture. If you adapt too much, then you may lose your own identity or you may begin to feel remote from your actions and a distinct detachment from your sense of self. Your adapted behavior may be in direct contradiction with your own values, putting you under tremendous emotional and moral stress. In extreme cases, it may then be wise to quit the job and return to your country. Every person is different; every person has their strengths and weaknesses. But what is strength in one culture may be seen as weakness in another, as it was for the empathetic and participatory Swedish manager mentioned above. And, in his case, he may not wish to abandon his own strengths – whether innate or culturally valued – for the sake of a job in Guatemala.

To review, accepting cultural differences is the first step to successful management across cultures. It is, however, important to know where to draw the line – where the cultural practices not only contradict your own values, but perhaps those values shared by the whole of humanity.

Adapting to new cultural norms is the second step. Sometimes you'll have to change your own ingrown behavior, which may be difficult and uncomfortable. And, again, you'll have to find your own personal equilibrium – how far you are willing to adapt, without losing your identity.

Adopting

Cultural integration may not end at adaptation of behavior. In fact, it may lead to the adoption of the new culture as your own. Throughout the process, you may become convinced that the foreign culture in which you are living behaves in the "correct" way or a way that feels more comfortable and true to you than the one you were born into. You may have already adapted with your brain, but you adopt with your heart.

You know you've adopted a culture, when the cultural characteristics have become part of your own identity. You share more than simple everyday behaviors; you also share the values that drive them. You adhere to the norms out of your own conviction. When there is little or no contradiction with the values of your own culture, adopting can be simple; but if the new cultural habits and ideology go against your ingrained way of life, adopting may be truly difficult, maybe even impossible. You will, perhaps, never reach this stage when it comes to major conflicting cultural differences.

When values are in conflict with each other – yours and those of the new culture into which you are integrating – you begin to feel "the rub," so to speak. Your own upbringing has taught you that some behaviors and ideologies are right, while others are wrong. You may have learned that individual freedom and self-fulfillment is the foundation for an effective working society. If this is the case, then in order for a company to be successful, it must base its corporate ladder on merit, thereby making the natural aspiration of its employees the motivator for climbing the ladder, thereby benefiting both the employee and the company. The "American dream" is based on this belief, and it drives US business culture.

But if you're shipped overseas and are thrown into a company in the Middle East, you'll have to rethink your behaviors and motivators. In many Middle Eastern societies, individuals are not so much valued as the whole. Paramount is the survival of the group. Individualism, in most Middle Easterners' eyes, is a luxury; a luxury enjoyed only by those individuals of a wealthy and materialistic society, where old people die alone in their apartments. Most, therefore, feel a sense of duty to utilize their corporate power for the well-being of their kin. Family members are hired and placed in positions for which another more experienced candidate may have been better suited. In the West, we would call this behavior "nepotism" or "favoritism." In the Middle East, it would be viewed as familial support and solidarity.

As an American manager in a Middle Eastern culture, you would have a choice to make: will you accept your employees' cultural behavior? Will you accept this common practice of hiring family members?

The Middle Eastern employees also must choose between the values they've grown up with and the values you bring to the organization as a foreign boss. There is little doubt as to the choice they'll make: as you stick to your values, they, too, will stick to theirs. It's natural to do so. Without formal measures put into place to control nepotism, they will hire sisters, brothers, cousins and the cousins of cousins. Of course nepotism and favoritism also happen in France and in the US (and, for that matter, in all countries). The difference is that some cultures accept this as a positive behavior and even as a sense of duty, while others qualify it as negative.

Now imagine an American manager in the Middle East – let's call him Bob – has fallen in love with a local woman – let's call her Mirah. They meet at a local restaurant of which she's the manager. It's love at first sight. They start dating. Mirah studied at an American university, so she's been in Bob's place – a foreigner in America. She can help Bob better understand the local way of life, as she understands American culture. He slowly starts to develop a deeper connection with the local culture, its values and beliefs.

When the relationship progressed and love grew, they decided to get married. As the daughter of an influential local family – Mirah's father being an important entrepreneur – the lavish wedding ceremony lasted a couple of days. It was a marvelous time, and Bob felt welcomed into his new family.

A couple weeks after the wedding, Mirah's oldest uncle arrives at Bob's office at Bob's invitation. They sit at a conference table, and Bob's assistant brings them a tray of tea. Bob has learned that, in this country, the most important family member is the eldest one. As Mirah's grandfather died years ago, the oldest uncle is now the most prominent and is, moreover, holding the family together. The old man accepts the cup of tea, and he and Bob have a candid discussion. Bob is honored by the visit and, again, feels welcomed into the larger family.

Shortly before the old man stands up to leave, he says: "It is good that you are in my family now. You are an important man in this company, and my grandson needs a job. I will send him to you." With these words, Bob's situation has suddenly become significantly more complicated.

How would you react? Would you adapt your behavior and hire your wife's cousin? This is what the uncle expects. You are now part of his family. You are embedded in the social fabric of his culture and, in the Middle East, everyone looks out for family. Your family will stand up for you, as you stand up for them. Bob, after discussing his predicament with Mirah, decides to hire the cousin. He does this against all his learned managerial training and his own cultural customs. He does it against his own values, which tell him that everyone is responsible for his own fate, and career advancement should be based on merit. Nevertheless, though his values have not changed, he adapts his behavior. The result of this adaptation is a deep cultural conflict within himself.

The cultural significance of this adaptation becomes even more apparent, when Bob's own boss from America arrives a couple of weeks later. While reviewing the staff changes with his boss, Bob grows red in the face, his heart rate shoots up, and he begins to sweat. He hadn't informed his boss that the person he'd just hired was a cousin, and so his body reacts physically to the stress caused by the gap between his adapted actions and his Western-oriented values. When our actions contradict our values, our conscience begins to weigh on us. We feel guilty. And that's when it's perhaps time to initiate the last step to overcoming cultural differences: adopting.

When you truly adopt and embrace another culture's behaviors, conviction comes into play; your values change. And when your values are aligned with those of the culture, there is no longer conflict and, therefore, no nagging conscience.

Intuitively, many expats assume that whenever they experience this nagging conscience, those around them should experience it too. But, as previously mentioned, the concept of "truth" is not universal. In some cultures, truth is founded on politeness; in others, truth is whatever those in control wish it to be. This concept – exchanging truth for politeness – crosses into Western cultures, but to a lesser degree. For instance, we don't always respond truthfully when asked, "how are you?" And do we even listen to another's answer when we ask the question?

When it comes to cross cultural differences regarding "truth," the conflicts can be much more distinct. For example, if a European manager asks an Indonesian employee if a report will be finished on time, he may receive an affirmative answer, even if the employee knows perfectly well that there's no chance the report will be ready by the deadline. He will answer in the affirmative without bad conscience. He won't blush or sweat or show any signs of discomfort. He said what his superior wanted to hear, which is perfectly in sync with his cultural values. Only Western managers care about deadlines. But, when the report doesn't show up on the European manager's desk by the agreed upon deadline, the manager may view this employee not only as irresponsible, but as a liar, a person not to be trusted. This is, perhaps, the worst and most culturally insensitive assumption the European manager can make and, to take it one step further, he may thereafter regard all Indonesian employees are liars, which would be detrimental to the health of the company.

Let's return to Bob, our American manager in the Middle East. Not surprisingly, he suddenly finds himself in another pickle. Soon after hiring Mirah's cousin, the distant uncle returns. Bob suspects that he may be asked to hire more relatives. The pair sit at the conference table and drink tea together, like old times. And just as Bob is getting comfortable, believing his suspicions were unfounded, again the uncle mentions a distant cousin. Bob feared the situation would snowball, and so it has; this time, the uncle requests that Bob secure a major contract with this cousin. And so Bob's struggles continue.

His private relationships become increasingly entangled with the business. However, they do not result in the company's collapse, nor do they end his career; on the contrary, the company grows and makes a profit. Bob becomes more and more integrated into the fine, complex, multi-layered social fabric of the family and the community. He starts to discover the advantages of this familial system, a system that focuses on the benefit of the whole. In a country with virtually no social security, the family's bank account is pension fund, health insurance, unemployment insurance and so much more to each and every one of its members. The whole economy of this country is built on personal relationships. He slowly discovers the rationale behind the system and starts to adopt its values. Bob is still convinced that, in a Western context and for the sake of economic development, business shouldn't involve family connections or nepotism. But he is also convinced that, in a different context and society, different rules apply. Not only has he adapted his managerial style, but he's also adopted the underlying values of the local culture. He now understands the advantages of a typical collectivistic society. Of course, conflicts remain; but, suddenly, they are now between Bob and his American boss. The boss is someone who cannot see the value of family in a collectivist society and can't understand that what is good in the West is not necessarily good in another part of the world.

Adopting cultural values may take a long time, sometimes years. In some cases, you may never be able to adopt all the cultural values of your new home, at least not entirely. Sometimes the cultural conflict between your new home and your old one may produce a physical reaction; your emotions and your body may turn against you in a way, because you feel you're doing something wrong. Your heartbeat sky rockets. You toss and turn at night. These negative reactions may cause you to take ages weighing the pros and cons of adopting certain practices and behaviors. But, ultimately, if you are determined to live and succeed in another culture, you will adopt most, if not all of their values. In the next chapter, we'll discuss how we learn culture, and why it is so difficult to adopt values that are in conflict with our own cultural heritage.

Now that we know the differences between "accepting," "adapting" and "adopting," let's look at these concepts on a global scale. At an international level, a lack of practice in these areas has laid the groundwork for drama and violence in many emerging democracies. Unfortunately, democratic uprisings seldom work, despite billions of dollars in aid, popular revolutions and sometimes military intervention – from the invasion of Afghanistan to the popular social revolutions in the countries of northern Africa. Building democracies in cultures that are deeply ingrained in old ways seems to be a nearly impossible task. There are many reasons for the failure of establishing true democracy in these regions, but an important one is that working democracies require a change in deep-rooted cultural values. It's sensible to keep in mind that these changes happened in Europe and the US over two centuries and a couple of major wars…so let's not be too proud of ourselves, and let's not jump the gun; democracy may still prevail in these countries once the cultural values evolve, as ours did. Slowly.

When Blaise Compaore became president of Burkina Faso through a military coup, one of his first steps was to provide his hometown, Ziniare, with electricity. For many years, Ziniare was the only county in its province connected to the grid. Later he built an airstrip and then a zoo in the middle of nowhere. In 2014, after 27 years in power and a couple of rigged re-elections, he was overthrown by a popular revolution. Many issues led to his fall, but caring for his family, his village and his ethnic group were none of them. This is what is expected from the president of Burkina Faso. If family is the only security you have, then it makes perfect sense to vote according to family ties or ethnic groups.

In many regards, a functioning democracy requires a fundamental change in cultural values. Unfortunately, international aid agencies often forget this. Democracy comes so natural to Westerners, because we've grown up with it. But it is neither natural, nor universal. Too often, when our politicians promote democracy in a different country and culture a world away from their own, they are monkeys and are not even aware of it.

When managing in another culture, you must identify and recognize your monkey moments – the moments where you behave strangely in the eyes of your peers. In order to successfully manage and reach your objectives, once you recognize your "absurd" behavior, you can then choose an acceptable strategy to remedy it, and these strategies are accepting, adapting and adopting.

You must decide which aspects of the culture you accept. There may be parts into which you are integrating, and there may be unchangeable parts of your own culture for which you draw the line and will not compromise. Accepting doesn't mean to condone; it doesn't mean you are making a statement that something is "good." It only means that you accept the cultural difference, and you understand the rationale and believe there is good faith behind it. You may still stand morally against it or even find it personally repulsive, but you don't judge or condemn others for their differing beliefs.

Further, you will then have to decide which of the behaviors and values of the culture you adapt. These choices will alter your own behavior and may even result in your acting against how you've been raised or what you've been taught is morally "right." To manage in certain cultures, adapting to cultural norms may be unavoidable and necessary – for instance, wearing a headscarf as a business woman in some countries. If cultural values collide, adapting may create strong internal conflicts, which may eventually lead to adoption.

You may adopt some cultural values and behaviors, making elements of the foreign culture part of your own identity. After a couple of years, you may even adopt values, which contradict the cultural values of your home country. Arriving at the adoption stage of the integration process means that you have become fully integrated.

Ignoring, rejecting, judging or condemning cultural differences are not acceptable and respectful attitudes when dealing with other cultures. In the next chapter, we will embark upon a journey through culture: how culture is created, learned, and how deeply it influences our thinking. By embarking on this journey and following the evolution of culture, we will come to understand why these three strategies are so important to cross cultural management, and why our own monkey moments are so difficult to recognize. This awareness of our own cultural identity and cultural differences can help us keenly recognize when we are behaving like the monkey.

	HOW TO DO IT	DANGER
ACCEPTING	ACKNOWLEDGE THAT PEOPLE THINK OR ACT DIFFERENTLY, AND ACCEPT THAT THERE IS RATIONALE BEHIND IT. THERE IS NOT A "RIGHT" OR "WRONG" WAY.	EXCESSIVE CULTURAL TOLERANCE IN REGARDS TO BEHAVIOR AND NORMS WHICH ARE PSY-CHOLOGICALLY OR PHYSICALLY HARMFUL TO HUMAN BEINGS AND HUMANITY AS A WHOLE.
ADAPTING	ADAPT YOUR BEHAVIOR TO THE NEW CUL-TURE. LEARNING A LANGUAGE IS THE MOST IMPORTANT ADAPTION AND OFTEN A REQUIREMENT FOR SUCCESSFUL CROSS-CULTURAL MANAGEMENT.	CONFLICT WITH OWN VALUES AND FEELINGS OF DISHONESTY/HYPOCRISY. IF YOU ADAPT YOUR BEHAVIOR WITHOUT BELIEVING IN IT, THEN YOU WILL FACE SOME INTERNAL CONFLICT.
ADOPTING	ADOPT THE VALUES OF YOUR HOST CULTURE. TAKE YOUR TIME AND LET IT HAPPEN.	LOSING YOUR OWN CULTURAL IDENTITY.

Awareness

There are two different types of monkey moments: 1) when you're the monkey, and you know it, and 2) when you're the monkey but are oblivious to the fact. Obviously, if you want to work with foreigners and integrate into another culture, knowing you are the monkey is highly important. Only when you're aware that you're the monkey, will you be able to *Accept, Adapt, Adopt* and become integrated within another culture.

Cultural awareness is the foundation of communication. Awareness necessitates that we stand back from ourselves and look at our own cultural values, beliefs and perceptions from a distance. Why do we behave the way we do and not in any other way? How do we see the world? Why do we react to it with specific attitudes, while our neighbors to the north or south react to it otherwise?

People see, interpret and evaluate the world differently. What is considered an appropriate behavior in one culture may be inappropriate in another. And when you use your own cultural ideology to make sense of another's reality, misunderstandings arise.

For instance, an Italian will almost always perceive Americans as people who constantly work, discuss business over lunch, and drink their coffee racing from one place to another instead of enjoying it in a bar. What does this interpretation mean? Italians are lazy and Americans, hyperactive? That's not necessarily the case. Rather, the truth is simply that certain activities mean more to some cultures than others; people define all aspects of life differently and consider them significant or insignificant. Having lunch or dinner is an important event in certain cultures, while it's nothing but a menial activity to sustain life in others. In Italy, where relationships are highly valued, lunch, dinner or the simple pleasure of taking pause for afternoon coffee have a social connotation: people get together to talk and relax, to foster relationships. In the US, where time is money, lunch can be vital to closing a deal. Over lunch or coffee, business partners can share in a meal while discussing proposals and signing contracts. Meals can be events of productivity and can help foster business relationships.

Misinterpretations occur primarily when we lack awareness of the differences between our own behavioral rules and another culture's, and so we project our values onto theirs. In absence of cultural awareness, we tend to assume our values are everyone's values, instead of uncovering what, exactly, a behavior or activity might mean to the person involved.

Bringing awareness to our own cultural dynamics is a difficult task, because culture is so ingrained that we're not conscious of it. Since birth, we've learned to see and do things in specific ways without thinking about why. Our experiences, our values and our cultural background combine to guide our behavior. So, in order to recognize the impact our culture plays in our behavior, we must step outside of our cultural boundaries. To help us do so, one might gather feedback from foreign colleagues regarding the differences in his/her own behavior from the normal behavior in the local culture. This will help clarify one's own cultural traits from a foreign perspective and will open our eyes to the way these traits are viewed by others.

As mentioned, projected similarities also lead to misinterpretations. If we project similarities where there are none, we might act inappropriately in foreign cultures. Rather than assuming sameness, it is safer to assume otherwise until similarity is proven. Unfortunately, in cultures that appear similar to ours, we often act like a fish in water, instead of a fish out of water. Being as such, it's only when we splash-splash our way out of tank with a 'monkey moment' or two that we notice we're floundering in the first place.

In 2002 during the Iraq war, US Secretary of Defense, Donald Rumsfeld, made a speech which includes one of his most famous quotes: "Reports that say that something hasn't happened are always interesting to me, because as we know, there are known knowns; there are things we know we know. We also know there are known unknowns; that is to say we know there are some things we do not know. But there are also unknown unknowns – the ones we don't know we don't know. And if one looks throughout the history of our country and other free countries, it is the latter category that tend to be the difficult ones." This concept can be applied to cultural awareness: the most difficult issues to solve are the ones you don't even know exist. The irony of humankind is we never learn from our own history. Fundamental cultural misunderstanding is one of the primary reasons for the dramatic failure of American nation-building efforts in Iraq and, time and again, this is the case when it comes to foreign policy.

	STAGES OF CULTURAL AWARENESS
1.	UNCONSCIOUS INCOMPETENCE (BLISSFUL IGNORANCE)
2.	CONSCIOUS INCOMPETENCE (TROUBLING IGNORANCE)
3.	CONSCIOUS COMPETENCE (DELIBERATE SENSITIVITY)
4.	UNCONSCIOUS COMPETENCE (SPONTANEOUS SENSITIVITY)

There are different stages of cultural awareness, and the "unknown unknown" corresponds with the first stage: unconscious incompetence. A manager flung into a foreign culture without preparation may not even be aware that cultural differences exist. He is, therefore, unaware of making cross cultural mistakes. Worst of all, a manager in this stage of unconscious incompetence has no reason to distrust his intuition. Even if failures and misunderstandings arise, they'll be interpreted in his own personal cultural context. This is a stage of blissful ignorance about the depth and scope of cultural differences. Unfortunately, as the first months of America's presence in Iraq demonstrated, even highly competent executives flounder in this dangerous stage if they've not been trained accordingly. When unconsciously incompetent, the individual is completely unaware that he's a monkey in a zoo.

Once you're made aware of cultural differences, you will enter the stage of conscious incompetence. You now realize your behavior differs from that of other cultures. You know there are differences, but you're not sure why they exist or what the scope is. You start to doubt your intuition. You are a monkey, gradually coming to odds with the fact that you're in a zoo.

If at this stage you start to work on your cultural competence, you will progress into conscious competence. You know and recognize the cultural differences between people. You learn to accept that elephants behave a certain way, tigers behave a certain way, and even these humans – who look the most like you – behave differently. You accept that another's cultural behavior may differ from your own. You make attempts to modify your behavior to accommodate these differences. You adapt. You are in the process of replacing old intuitions with new ones.

Once you have not only accepted and adapted the other's cultural norms and beliefs, but you've also truly adopted them, you'll enter the stage of unconscious competence. You no longer have to think about what you're doing; you are naturally culturally sensitive. The other's cultural behavior is now part of you.

You can trust your intuition, because it has been reconditioned by what you now know and understand about cross cultural interactions. Experience shows that once you've gone through this process of cultural integration in one foreign culture, the steps will be easier and more quickly processed for your next cross cultural experience. You will more naturally become culturally competent whenever you enter into other foreign cultures, regardless of the scope of their differences, as cultural awareness is generic; while the cultures you encounter may be vastly different, the process is the same and will serve you when interacting with people all around the world. But where do you begin?

Action

The last section of this book will be dedicated to the process of action by which you can ease your integration. By taking certain actions, you may be able to influence your speed of growth and your adeptness at scaling the stages of cultural awareness. Yes, certain personalities may find the process of becoming culturally competent more achievable than other personalities, but anyone can improve this skill through understanding and action. With a willingness to step outside your comfort zone and the know-how and discipline to do it, you can improve your cultural competency and your ability to integrate into another culture.

This book will allow you to avoid experiencing too many 'monkey moments' by guiding you through the steps of leaving your cage and entering the zoo, where you'll encounter many other species and their behaviors. The five A's to keep in mind are: awareness, accepting, adapting, adopting, and action. These concepts will ensure easier integration and successful cross cultural management.

PART II: AWARENESS

2. How Human Beings Learn Culture

Culture is learned; it is not innate. Instead of telling you why, let's illustrate culture as a learned mechanism with food. Stefan Gates, a BBC journalist, travelled the world to discover and describe the strangest menus...strange from the perspective of someone who grew up in Europe, anyway. In China he ate deep-fried scorpions. This is actually a fairly common snack in Asian markets. The pincers and the poisonous sting are removed, the beast is speared on a stick and deep-fried in oil. The pincers are often used as tooth picks after the meal. Mr. Gates describes his eating  experience: "Very crunchy on the outside, yet smooth in the middle, and they smell of the rather elderly oil they were cooked in." Now ask yourself the following question: how long would you have to live in southern China to enjoy eating fried scorpions?

A few years ago I travelled through Tanzania along Tanganyika Lake. On the road I met a Swiss family, and as the road was dangerous, we decided to drive together until we reached a larger city. In the evening, we sat behind our cars and cooked spaghetti. The Swiss had twin six-year-old daughters with blond hair. In any Swiss alpine village, they would have blended in perfectly. As night fell, our lamps were quickly buzzing with swarms of insects. Very calmly, the girls approached the lamps, selected certain flying or crawling insects and shoved them into their mouths. Clearly these girls had been raised in Africa.

So why do we find eating insects repulsive? They are healthy, natural, rich in protein and, according to studies, they're probably the most ecological food on earth. In reality, whether we want to or not, we all eat insects on a regular basis; there are traces in our daily food – in ground pepper or salad, for instance. The US even regulates the percentage of insect matter permissible in ground pepper. Clearly, eating insects does no damage to our health. But somehow, if raised in a culture where insect-eating is not the norm, the gag reflex reacts pretty strongly at the mere mention of eating worms or locusts. If forced to do so, we can't swallow, we feel an urge to vomit, our body shakes, our muscles contract. So why do our bodies react so negatively to something so natural?

Our bodies do not tell us what is right or wrong. They react to what we have *learned* is right or wrong. From the very first moment we open our eyes, we learn culture.

Primary Socialization

From birth to roughly the age of seven, we learn the basics of surviving in the society into which we've been born. Actually, the human capacity for social learning develops so early in the first year of life that it's been necessary for developmentalists to design clever experiments to decipher what babies are learning months before language and precise imitation behavior exists.

It happens that one of the biggest dangers for an infant is anything related to the body orifices: the mouth, the nose, the genitals. This has to do with hygiene and, therefore, preventing sickness or poisoning is vital to an infant's health. But this prevention is sometimes difficult. Anyone who has raised a child knows there is no genetic predisposition against playing with poo. You have to teach the child that feces are potentially harmful and should be left untouched in the nappies. And by the same necessity, we teach children what to eat and what *not* to eat. There is no genetic predisposition against eating scorpions or insects. The only thing that prevents children from doing so is education. But because this teaching and learning occurs during primary socialization, abstaining from certain edibles is not about liking or disliking scorpions or any other food. It is about which food is taught to be "right" and which one is taught to be "wrong". Primary socialization defines the world for the infant, and this world will be their reference for the rest of their lives. In our Western world, this means insects are "bad" and need to be killed. The same applies to rats and snakes. Dogs are good, but they are man's best friend and should be treated humanely; they are never to be considered food.

Researchers at Rutgers University in New Jersey showed films of snakes and elephants to babies, aged between six and nine months. They measured their vital signs, including their heartbeats, and none of them demonstrated any fear of snakes. Similar tests have been done with baby chimpanzees born in captivity. None of them were afraid of snakes, but they learned to be quite quickly when they watched videos of elder monkeys showing signs of fear when encountering snakes.[4] Similarly to our preferred diet, no genetic predisposition exists when it comes to fear of certain dangerous animals. But consider this: when a child is potentially exposed to a poisonous creature, the parents will react strongly to their child being in danger. This strong reaction is imprinted in the child's mind. Thus, this fear of snakes becomes a norm in many cultures and is passed down and acquired subconsciously.

Moreover, what is considered "right" and "wrong" is not learned through an intellectual, rational process. Learning before the age of seven is very much an emotional process, and the stronger the emotion, the more clearly the experience is learned. When a child is told by his parents to avoid a hot stove, the emotional learning will come once the child reaches out, touches the stove, and burns himself. This moment of pain is seared in the mind, and thus, emotion proves to be a profound way of learning. Emotions are the central educational force for children under the age of seven, because emotions during these ages are generally extreme. Watch how often a young child's emotional state changes in a single hour. As the child grows, logic and rationale slowly start to direct the learning process. Primary socialization is, therefore, in large part an emotional learning of what is "right" or "wrong," which thereafter provokes an emotional reaction. At the core, this is one of the primary reasons different cultures have such different reactions to the same things.

An American child will grow up with peanut butter. Every morning, the child's mother prepares a peanut butter-and-jelly sandwich for her children, and so they come to emotionally associate this with motherly love and nurturing. I ate my first peanut butter-and-jelly sandwich at the age of 34 when on an expat assignment in America. My window of emotional learning had been closed long before, and so whether or not I liked peanut butter, no deeper emotion would drive such a strong association with the food. Of course, emotional learning is also possible as an adult, but the threshold of emotion must be substantially higher; emotional learning as an adult would require a serious accident or illness, a major professional upset or an event like September 11.

All values and norms learned during primary socialization are very deeply entrenched in a being's mental framework; and because primary socialization determines right from wrong, any contradiction to what has been categorized as such provokes strong emotions. As with the issue with eating dogs previously mentioned: America nearly boycotted the Soccer World Championship 2002 in Seoul, because the South Korean norm of eating dogs was utterly unacceptable to them. FIFA, the soccer's governing body, had to issue a statement that "eating dogs has nothing to do with football." Obviously any Hindu could feel the same about the American diet, as their holy animal, the cow, regularly ends up as steak in Western restaurants.

Understanding the principle of primary socialization is fundamental to understanding other cultures – and, of course, it influences more than just food. As stated, any norms related to the body orifices and, therefore, an infant's or toddler's survival, are deeply rooted in our subconscious. Therefore, anything which relates to these deeply rooted values and norms – such as health habits, like blowing or wiping your nose, where and how to use the toilet, and all things associated with human sexuality – should be respected when attempting to integrate into another's culture.

During primary socialization, we also learn about the basic societal structures relevant to our distinct culture. What is family? Is it – as in Western culture – a heterosexual couple and their children? Or is "family" considered the lineage of at least three generations, with the highest authority being the eldest man? In many traditional cultures in Africa, the eldest uncle holds more authority over the children than even their biological father. This may sound shocking to Westerners, because our primary socialization teaches us that parents hold the ultimate authority over their children. But traditional societies don't offer the elaborate social security, pension funds and retirement plans of our Western societies. Multi-generational families ensure better survival for all kin in some African cultures. And in Africa, you won't find old people being stowed away in a rest home or passing away in their own homes without anyone noticing.

What some societies consider to be "normal" can push the limits of what we may consider acceptable. Are arranged marriages acceptable? "Arranged marriages," as opposed to "forced marriages," require an agreement between the man and the woman to be wed with the proposed husband or wife. Usually the partnership is arranged by the parents, but in traditional societies, the grandfather or the eldest uncle can also make the arrangement. Anyone who grew up in a Western society will condemn arranged marriages on instinct. I did – until an Indian woman raised her hand during a lecture I gave at an American university. Her husband was chosen by her parents. She met him only once before the wedding, and while most Western marriages end in divorce after a couple of years, she was still happily married after six years. She explained the advantages of arranged marriages to the skeptical audience.

"My parents raised me, and in India, where we still get married at a very young age. I think my parents know far better which man suits me best. They have more life experience and their judgment is not as emotional as would be mine. I trust them to act in my best interest."

A scientific study conducted by Robert Epstein, the Harvard-educated Senior Research Psychologist at the American Institute for Behavioral Research and Technology, supports this student's point of view. Epstein studied arranged marriages, interviewing more than 70 people from various backgrounds. According to Epstein, feelings of love in arranged marriages tend to gradually increase as time progresses in the relationship, whereas in so-called "love marriages," where attraction is based on passionate emotions, a couple's feelings for each other typically diminish by as much as fifty percent after only eighteen to twenty-four months of marriage. In fact, according to a study conducted in India, arranged marriages appear to surpass love marriages in intensity at the five-year mark and to be twice as strong as love marriages within ten years.

And if you dogmatically condemn arranged marriages and consider them to be possible only in faraway countries, consider that the blue blood marriages in various royal dynasties in Europe were, more often than not, arranged.

The point is that what we consider "normal" is not necessarily normal or advantageous. And what we consider "right" is not necessarily always right. Looking at these things objectively obviously raises questions about how far cultural tolerance should stretch. However, this topic will be covered in a later chapter. For the moment, we only need to know and accept that there are fundamentally different views in the world, and none are exactly "right" or "wrong".

AN AMERICAN CHILD LEARNS	A MIDDLE EASTERN CHILD LEARNS
IT IS GOOD TO BE AN INDIVIDUAL	IT IS GOOD TO PRIMARILY IDENTIFY WITH THE FAMILY
BE SELF-RELIANT ("STAND ON YOUR OWN FEET")	YOU CAN ALWAYS DEPEND ON OTHERS (EVEN AS THEY DEPEND ON YOU)
DON'T GO BEHIND SOMEONE'S BACK	NEVER CONFRONT A PERSON DIRECTLY
"WHERE THERE IS A WILL, THERE'S A WAY"	GOD'S WILL IS PARAMOUNT

For example, primary conditioning for an American child is vastly different from that of a child raised in a middle eastern country. The children are taught two different world views, thus they will behave quite differently in the same situation.

The American child learns that happiness is of one's own making. Each and every child is an individual, and if you work hard enough, if you stand on your own two feet, then nothing is impossible, the world is open to you. The American dream is waiting for you. Through American media, a child is exposed to many examples of successful individuals who became wealthy by their own merit. As they grow older, they will complete motivational trainings, which direct them in how to become successful. Most likely, the child's parents will tell them that life progress is made through hard work, discipline and building towards one's goals.

In the Middle East, a child will experience a very different world. The child will grow up in a big close-knit family. Nowadays, school is an important part of every middle eastern child's life, but the teachings learned at school are still widely regarded as inferior to the wisdom of elders. The child's purpose does not hinge on building a career but, rather, on building a family and bringing happiness to all kin. A child's dream may be to someday work in America, but this dream is not career-driven; the goal is to send money back home to support the family. Obviously, America will only be an option if it is

God's will; it's not possible to force destiny. So the right course of action may be to drink a glass of good tea and simply wait.

These different worldviews and values are where culture can clash. Ann, a teacher from England, earned a placement in Tunisia, teaching language in a primary school. During a test, she caught Ahmed passing the exam answers to his cousin Khalid, scribbled on a small piece of paper. At a meeting with Ahmed's parents, she raised the issue. She expected their understanding and support. Ahmed cheated. He didn't obey the rules of the school and, even worse, cheating would only prevent Khalid from learning. In Ann's point of view, Khalid needed to stand on his own, to be motivated to learn on his own, so that he would be successful in life. Ahmed won't always be around to help him.

But Ahmed's parents couldn't understand or agree with the arguments of the young English woman. "Ahmed helped his cousin Khalid. Isn't this how a society should work? We always stick together in our family," the father tried to explain to Ann. "And by the way, there will always be someone from the family to help Khalid. We are a big and important family in this village." The father left angrily, and Ahmed continued to help Khalid – or continued to "cheat" as Ann would put it.

This story demonstrates how a child's behavior in different situations is consistent with the culture the child has grown in; and the way in which others view these behaviors depends on our own cultural upbringing. If an American chooses to teach middle eastern children, cultural conflicts will arise. How should the teacher have handled the situation correctly? By acclimating to the values of the culture in which she works, or by forcing her own cultural values on her students?

During primary socialization, we learn behavior, norms and values which define what is considered "right," "wrong" or "normal" throughout the society in which we live. Two more characteristics of the primary socialization process are our unconsciousness of the learning process and the way in which it structures our lives. Without a conscious knowledge of primary socialization, we are not aware that we're learning or teaching behaviors. We are also unaware that primary socialization provides a distinct framework for our daily lives.

Later in life, secondary socialization processes begin. Adapting to a company culture is one of these. Companies may possess strongly specific cultural elements, and employees will invariably adapt to their business life and also to the norms and values of their company. But there's one major difference between primary and secondary socialization processes: people are perfectly conscious that company cultures are different. For instance, Google is famous for its strong, creative and open company culture, but none of its employees would assume that the Google culture is "normal" and the culture at IBM isn't. We implicitly accept different corporate realities. But when encountering different concepts relegated to primary socialization – like eating insects, for example – it's much more difficult to accept foreign preferences as "normal."

Unconscious Learning

Europeans traveling to the US are confronted with an uncomfortable reality: there is no decent toilet paper in the new world. From youth hostels to luxury hotels, the only available toilet paper is thin, low quality and tears apart way too easily. How is it possible that the most powerful nation on earth is utterly incapable of producing quality toilet paper? Some researchers investigated this phenomenon, inquiring why it is that Americans do not complain about their own paper. Digging deeper, they discovered that toilet paper is used fundamentally differently in the new world versus the old. Americans are crumplers. They take a couple of sheets, crumple them up and go about their business. Europeans, on the other hand, are folders. They carefully tear two sheets from the roll and fold them together, often refolding a second time. European toilet paper manufacturers tried producing double- or triple-layered paper, believing customers would stop folding. To no avail. It doesn't matter how many ply, a European will always fold his toilet paper. Obviously resistance against tearing is far more important for folders than for crumplers, and that is why Europeans find the toilet paper in the US to be substandard.

From a primary socialization perspective, the following is interesting:

- no one remembers how they learned to use toilet paper – neither the crumplers, nor the folders

- prior to the research, no one was aware that there were cultural differences regarding the usage of toilet paper

- all implicitly assumed that the whole world uses toilet paper the same way

Because we consider ourselves "normal," we are unaware how abnormal we are in the context of another culture's "normal." Primary socialization is so subtle that we are not even aware of what we've learned, how we've learned it, or why we do and believe the things we do. At school the learning process is conscious. You may clearly recall at what point in your education you learned certain theories, and you likely even remember the teacher who instructed you. Culture is learned in a far more permissive way. You're unaware that you've been taught a "right" way of doing things and, even worse, you're still adamant that it is "right," with no real evidence to back up this claim. The ignorance of our learned ways is what makes cultural clashes so dangerous. You only become aware of your own cultural norms when they are being contrasted against another's, as in the example of the English teacher and her middle eastern student. Ann discovered that cheating is far less important in this foreign culture than supporting family members.

Frame of Interpretation

Without conscious awareness of our values and norms, our cultural foundation provides us a frame of reference for daily life that's invisible to the naked eye, helping us to interpret and make sense of what happens around us and to us. This frame of reference varies from culture to culture and, therefore, interpretations of the world and the way it works vary, as well. In business we like to talk about facts, because we consider them objective, invariable and concrete. Anyone involved in cross cultural management knows from their own experience that conflicts often arise despite a common and accepted set of facts, and if the manager isn't trained in cross cultural management, this inconsistency can drive management crazy. Often, the reaction is to further insist upon or prove the validity of the facts, but doing so never solves the problem. Returning to our previous example of the English teacher in a middle eastern school, Ann tries to reason with both Ahmed and his parents by explaining the importance of a child learning independently, so that he can both have a fair understanding of his own abilities and be prepared for future professional life. She might also explain her views on the immorality of cheating, in general. But however clearly and directly she articulates her own cultural perspective, the parents will not understand. From their cultural perspective, supporting the family supersedes everything else. The teacher may insist on her own principles, only to be met with the parents' resistance, and vice versa. In the worst case scenario, Ahmed's parents may remove him from school. In a multi-cultural environment, do not assume that cold hard facts will be interpreted unanimously.

To illustrate this point, let's take a short detour into information technology. IT-specialists distinguish between data and information. 3, 121, 911, 1122; these are all numbers, and numbers are data. They have no further significance than their numerical value. Now consider, again, the third number 911. When we say "911 is the emergency phone number in the US" then the number becomes information and, actually, quite important information for locals or any tourist in New York needing urgent assistance. A completely different context for this data: 911 is a famous Porsche sports car. Again, the data has become information and, according to the context, a different type of information altogether.

Taking this a step further, consider the context of dates. For anyone living in the US during the terrorist attack on September 9th, 2011, the data "911" is symbolic of this tragedy and, for many, translates to unbearable human pain. Recollections of people jumping to their deaths from the flaming buildings of the twin towers, the World

Trade Center crashing down, collapsing into the streets of New York City – this devastation is what many Americans recall vividly when they hear the numbers 9/11. Data becomes information, and information is placed in the context of our life experience. The same number "911" can provoke associations as diverse as a terrorist attack for New Yorkers or an exhilarating driving experience for a Porsche driver.

Through culture, societies are provided a common framework to interpret the daily facts of life, including interpreting data as information. And the interpretations are vast.

Consider this small exercise, which I've developed for my students. One half of the class is shown a figure with three numbers 12, 13 and 14. The other half is shown a figure with three letters A, B and C. The whole class is then asked to identify the middle figure. One half will see a 13; the other half will see a B. Like culture, the figures on the left and the right set the frame of reference for interpreting the middle figure, demonstrating that one single fact can lead to two completely different interpretations.

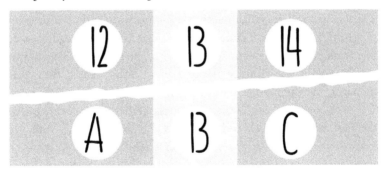

In the world of business, different frameworks may result in serious financial consequences. For example, a Swiss and a Russian manager are engaged in tough negotiations about a future collaborative project. The Swiss manager comes from a culture where conflicts are solved through calm discourse and compromise. This attitude and methodology permeates society in Switzerland up through the highest political level. The government is, by definition, composed of ministers from all major parties – unthinkable in most other countries. You will find a book on the win-win strategy in virtually every Swiss manager's office. Compromise is a symbol of goodwill for a partnership that will be mutually beneficial. Swiss managers, therefore, tend to offer concessions at an early stage in negotiations.

On the other hand, the culture of Russian management is far more confrontational. The win-win strategy is for losers. Winner-takes-all is the only way to go, as it demonstrates power and strength. Conflicts are usually resolved through direct confrontation, taking the proverb "may the best man win" to heart, and "best" in Russia usually means "toughest." An opponent's concessions are viewed as a sign of weakness and are almost never reciprocated.

The Swiss manager, unaware of the cultural differences in their approach to negotiations, will offer a concession early in the negotiation, as is his cultural norm. At the forefront of the Swiss mind is the long-term partnership, and so offering a true compromise at the beginning of the negotiations will project successful cooperation now and in the future. He will expect his Russian partner to recognize the goodwill of this gesture.

The Russian will most likely accept the concession and offer nothing in return. He will think either that the Swiss is a weak negotiator or in a weak position to negotiate. Either way, he'll believe that his own tough negotiation strategy resulted in a "win." Thus, the Swiss manager will then either be put in an unfavorable position or will feel it necessary to cancel the project altogether, as the outcome of the partnership is weakened. This is one reason why the Swiss are known for being very serious, very reliable…and very weak negotiators.

Alfred Adler, famous psychologist and founder of the school of individual psychology, made this point: "It is very obvious that we are not influenced by facts, but by our interpretation of the facts". And our culture sets the framework for these interpretation.

What we learned in this chapter:

- Culture is learned; it is not innate.

- Primary socialization teaches a child his/her culture's values and norms.

- We are unconscious of the fact that our behaviors are learned, thus we view them as "normal" and others' as "abnormal."

- Without consciously being aware of our cultural values and norms, our cultural background provides us a frame of reference for daily life, allowing us to interpret and make sense of what is happening around us.

3. What is Culture?

In the first chapter, we learned how we acquire the culture that makes us part of the society in which we live. But what exactly is "culture"? The word originates from the Latin "colere" with its root meaning "to cultivate." As the word is used today in social science and management, it no longer is relegated to farming and growing crops. The term was used for the first time in a non-agricultural context by the Roman orator, Cicero. He mentioned "cultura animi" which translates to "the cultivation of the soul." The term reappeared in the 17th century and was then used by the savants in Europe to refer to the refinement of individuals, especially through education. Only in the 19th century was the term applied to the commonalities of a group of people. First, it was connected to national aspirations and ideals; later, it emerged as the central concept in anthropology, to describe a group's distinct way of living.

Published in 1871, anthropologist Edward Tylor's work, "Primitive Culture," includes the first formal definition of culture: "Culture or Civilization...is that complex whole which includes knowledge, belief, art, morals, law, custom and any other capabilities and habits acquired by man as a member of society."

This first definition of "culture" in this context is already quite insightful. Tyler used the word "acquired." Culture is learned. As noted in the first chapter, this happens through socialization, particularly during an individual's childhood. Something which is learned cannot, by definition, be inherited or transmitted through genes. This is an extremely important distinction, which cannot be stressed enough. Culture has nothing to do with race or genetics.

First of all, we are all human. We all share the same genetic heritage. There are few elements truly common to all human beings, but they are all considerably important for the survival of our species. We all need food, shelter and nurturing. We all share the love for our children and grieve the loss of our loved ones. This is human nature.

On the other hand, we are also all individuals. Individuality is what makes each of us unique among the 8-billion-strong human species. Our individuality is partly genetic and partly learned, and includes our singular traits and personalities.

Culture is the layer in between humanity and the individual. It is what binds groups of people together, and all of it is acquired. There is no genetic input. Culture makes social life possible through learned behavior. We only understand each other, because we share common cultural elements, language being one of the most essential of these elements. It is clearly learned and not genetically defined, as is the way we dress, our understanding of family structures, our morals and values, etc.

Certain personalities play out better in certain cultures. A friend of mine had a maid in Africa who used to come on time, clean the house to the last corner and even rearrange all pots and pans so that they stood aligned like a Prussian army division. He used to joke that he came to Africa only to find someone more German than himself. This maid would have fit perfectly into German culture, while she was considered a little odd by her fellows in Accra, Ghana.

The differences between individual and culturally-conditioned behavior are fluid. We cannot change our genes. Someone born with blue eyes will have blue eyes for life. But anything learned can be un-learned, re-learned, rejected or simply forgotten. Therefore, even within a tight-knit cultural group, individual behaviors will always exist, but mainly within the confines of what is considered culturally acceptable.

Everyone makes their own choices. We all choose whether or not to behave similarly or differently from others, and when or where there is room to push the limits of cultural acceptability. Many Swiss are indeed punctual, many Germans are orderly, many Americans are outgoing and many Indians like to eat curry. But there will always be unorderly Germans, Indians who hate curry, Americans who are introverted and Swiss who are often late. There are even some Swiss who are less punctual than your average African; and if a "World champion of lateness" competition should exist, the champion could be a Swiss, but the probability would be low. Not only because Switzerland is a small country, but also because the majority of Swiss have accepted that punctuality is important to their society. Switzerland is a country where trains run on time and being late to a business meeting is considered disrespectful. The implicit societal message is that anyone who is not punctual is not reliable, and the Swiss accept this cultural norm and adapt to it. In fact, a survey found that punctuality is the most important value for Swiss people; "helping others" only ranked third in the same survey. So, again, though the probability of a Swiss earning the title, the "World champion of lateness," would be low, it wouldn't be impossible. Many Swiss are unpunctual; some because it's in their nature, others as a form of rebellion against social norms. Punctuality in whole societies, however, is related to the concept of time, an important cultural aspect, which will be discussed later in the book.

So, as with any cultural norm, we can say, "Swiss people are generally punctual," but we can never say, "Because this man is Swiss, he is punctual." Cultural values are standards used to assess a society, but they do not represent the totality of all individuals within a culture. We cannot draw conclusions about individual behavior based upon cultural values. In some cases, the bandwidth of individual behavior stretches wider than do cultural norms.

This brings us back to the initial question: What is culture? Tyler gave us the first formal written definition of culture in relation to societal values, but it was in no way the final word. Research in the 60s found over 300 different definitions of the term "culture." Many essays have been written on the subject. We will not deconstruct the discourse regarding defining culture "correctly." For the purpose of this book, we will adopt the following definition:

Culture is the shared values and norms of a group of people which result in characteristic behaviors.

Culture is always related to a group of people. Thus far, we've implicitly assumed that the groups in question are all country nationals: the Germans, the Indians, the Americans, the Swiss. This may be a useful simplification if you plan to vacation in these countries; however, the reality is far more complex. Within a single country, you will find different groups of people, with significantly different behaviors and mentalities. A New Yorker's perception will be different than that of someone who lives on the West coast, and the Westerner's different than a Southerner's. On the other side of the pond, Milano, the economic capital of northern Italy, is probably more comparable to Germany in its values and norms than it is to its kin in southern Italy. There are even cultural groupings within each city. New York's Soho is not like the Bronx, which is not like Harlem. Cultural groups shrink into subgroups, which may shrink even further. People working in the same company often develop their own culture, with their own norms and values. The management may even decide to proactively shape the company culture, promoting certain values and condemning others.

Any time people live or work together, any time people interact, any time people are grouped, they will develop a specific set of values and norms, in order to differentiate themselves from others and regulate the way group members interact. Culture creates behavior, producing in each of its members a feeling of attachment to something bigger than oneself.

In this book, we will concentrate primarily on national cultures. It is a simplification and certainly not always a wise one to make; but it is a simplification out of practicality. Our world is divided into countries, each with its own culture. We think in terms of countries, from the rankings at the Olympic Games to the structure of a travel organization's website. For many of us, our nation is the largest group of people to which we feel we belong. And our most exhaustive scientific studies about cultures lie within the bounds of national borders.

Values

The values of a culture determine what is important or unimportant, what is useful or useless, what is desirable or undesirable. In short, values distinguish good from evil, define the virtuous and the sinful in a culture's unwritten rule of law; they even quite often influence a nation's written law. Cultural values define what an individual wants or should want, and the order of priority they should want it in.

As we saw in the previous chapter, values are instilled in a society's members, firstly by parents, and later by society and the culture that provides its structural framework. As parents are a child's first role model, the values implanted by them can take root quite deeply in an individual, influencing a person throughout his entire life. These values are the most influential factor upon the stages of primary socialization. You'll see just how much weight a parent's moral compass carries through an individual's strict adherence to the direction in which it's been pointed; or to the degree of rebellious opposition to it. In some cases, the individual may also find some middle ground – a healthy mix of their parents' values and the values they've identified with personally through life experience, even if contradicting the original framework presented by parents. Whatever the case, an individual's spectrum of values is planted and watered at home; only then is it fertilized and cultivated by their culture. Once the child becomes more aware of the world around him, he starts to pick up on cultural values and feels pressured to adhere to them.

Cultural values are a ways and means by which a culture demonstrates what is most important to its society as a whole. These values direct everything from how individuals communicate with each other to the political structure of a nation's government.

Let's illustrate these cultural differences, along with the values they highlight for the individual and the group. "Individualism" and "collectivism" are among the most researched aspects of culture, likely because these philosophies divide the East and the West and highly influence the differences between Eastern and Western values.

Western cultures are often capitalist-driven democracies which idealize individualism and freedom of speech. These values lead

Westerners to communicate directly and concretely, without mincing words or dancing around the matter at hand. A Westerner will not often speak ambiguously. Instead, a Western person speaks directly his meaning and it is oftentimes clear how the speaker intends the meaning to be taken. Additionally, a Western listener will take their conversational partner at their word, without believing him to be dishonest (unless the speaker has previously proven otherwise). Openness and straight speech are the keystones of Western communication. In many cases, eastern cultures find this directness ill-mannered.

When crossing the divide between East and West, there's a marked difference in the way people communicate. In China, where communism is slowly evolving into a capitalist-communist fusion, the values of collectivism still reign supreme, and this contributes to the society's nonverbal and indirect communication. Collectivist values consider the harmony of the whole, creating a "don't-rock-the-boat" mentality throughout the constructs of Chinese culture and society. Thus, a person's spoken words may, at times, conflict with that same person's actions. This inconsistency is not always with the malicious intent of deception in mind, but rather, simply in order to maintain a balance or harmony, at least at the surface level. The East's contradictory approach to communication may confuse and frustrate Westerners, who expect meaning to align with action. However, easterners prefer that the relationship be preserved, rather than upsetting the balance by denying anyone anything. Furthermore, an eastern listener doesn't necessarily expect another's words to align with their actions; and they accept this. Inconsistency is anticipated, because the alternative – giving or receiving a direct "no" – is viewed as harsh and inappropriate. Speaking so directly, according to ingrained Chinese values, would make one lose face.

It's important to note that "saving face" is not a value restricted to Chinese culture. "Face" is, in fact, a universally valued concept, as preserving one's societal image and commanding respect has historically been esteemed across time and across cultures. But the values of each culture are what determine the composition of "face" and, therefore, how to "save" it.

The East and the West view this composition differently, thus they approach the creating and saving of face in different manners. In the West, one must first create a face for oneself, and the values prevalent in Western culture – such as individualism, independence, innovation – mean that a person creates this face by making waves, upsetting the balance, parting from the pack and standing out from the crowd. This setting oneself apart may be through status, wealth, personal achievement, professional success, etc. Once face has been created, maintaining its relevance and value often involves being assertive and vocal in one's opinions. That is what an American child would have learned at school. Stand on your own two feet, speak honestly and be proud. However, saving face in eastern cultures can mean quite the opposite.

Collectivist societies value a single communal harmony over an individual voice. This is because the betterment of the whole is viewed as more valuable than individual prowess. For instance, a student in China will receive lesser marks on exams or essays if his/her opinion contradicts that of the teacher's. In Western cultures, an opinionated, well-argued, detail-supported essay would receive high praise and high marks for individuality, whether or not the teacher agrees with its thesis; but in China it receives a failing grade. This is because individualism is not highly valued in China. Traditionally, asserting an opinion that may not align with the accepted collective view is radical (even if only moderate), and the individual who speaks out will be considered aggressive and unconventional, which damages their reputation and loses them face.

As demonstrated, the values of eastern cultures have produced a different "face" and, therefore, a different method of communication is needed to save it, the chief objective being to avoid conflict of any kind. And the values of Western culture have produced a "face" which, although too can be lost through conflict, can also be rewarded with values that are more highly esteemed in Western culture (i.e., success, drive, ambition, individualism). It can further be said that in Western cultures, if lost, "face" can be more easily repaired than in eastern cultures, where it's nearly impossible to rebuild one's reputation once it's been damaged.

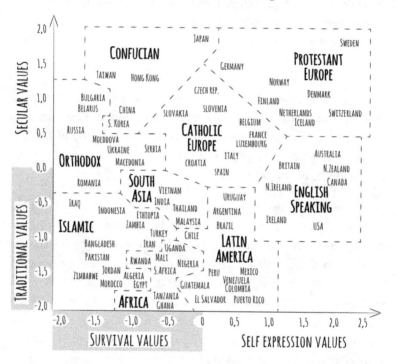

Cultural values in the East and West also differ when it comes to social power structures. The West's egalitarian structure contrasts with the East's hierarchical structure, each determining who in society is allowed to communicate with whom. The West is much looser when it comes to those participating in mutual conversation. CEO's can talk to janitors, multimillionaires can mingle with the lower classes. The homeless, too, have a voice and are more often heard. Most in Western cultures expect society to communicate freely with each other, without barriers of class, wealth, status or race. Again, eastern culture is different in this aspect.

Many of the East's communication habits are related to saving face, particularly when it comes to the hierarchical structure of Chinese and other eastern societies. CEO's don't often talk to janitors, multimillionaires aren't caught mingling with the lower class. The homeless are voiceless. This is deeply culturally and historically ingrained; thus, the hierarchical structure of Chinese society is not likely to bend at will.

To demonstrate this contrast between the East and the West's values, let's look at business culture. If a new company employee asserts oneself by presenting an innovative idea or acting on some task to great success, even without being prompted by upper management to do so, a Western company would see this behavior as forward-thinking and ambitious, each valued character traits in Western culture. However, if a new employee made the same assertions in an eastern company, he/she would be considered disobedient, and the individualistic and ambitious tactics would take the form of disloyalty to upper management. The top-heavy concentration of power in eastern cultures means there is much more face to lose when "rocking the boat."

Values are at the core of cross cultural research. Most categorizations of cultures are according to certain sets of values. The figure above is one example. The world map illustrates the values of secular-rational vs. traditional, and survival vs. self-expression. [5] Without further defining these concepts, we can already see that nations are not the only groupings with tightly knit values; larger geo-political subjects like poverty, political systems, religion, etc. all claim specific core values.

In later chapters we'll take a closer and more systematic look at the different values across many national cultures on this planet. Accepting the values of another culture – not only superficially but in your heart – is what *Adopting* is all about. This process, though satisfying, may be difficult and may not happen quickly, if ever. But when you've internalized the values of another culture, you can feel that you're truly becoming part of it.

Norms

Norms are directly related to cultural values. These are the expectations and rules accepted by the majority in any given culture, thus they are largely based on the majority's values. They guide behavior in various situations, influencing cultural customs and habits, and even at times dictating a society's written law. Norms appear in four sociological types: mores, folkways, taboos and laws.

Norms that are based upon morality are called mores, and these mores represent and direct a society's idea of "decency," which is often ingrained in deeply idealistic cultural values. Mores define what is *right* and what is *wrong*. For instance, public nudity in American culture is considered offensive or sexually-provocative, and so breaking this norm in any context is thought shocking by the majority. It is perceived as being *wrong*. However, in many European countries mores upon the subject are often more lenient. On certain beaches, for instance, no one will bat an eye if a woman chooses to go topless or a man swims in the nude, and nudity in European television programs and advertising is not nearly as censored as it is in the States. This freedom when it comes to nudity is not limited to Europe either. In the East, too, women and men visit separate (often same-sex) spas or saunas in the nude, and this is considered anything but shocking. And despite Africa's strong sexual mores, nude breasts aren't considered indecent in traditional Africa, as they aren't a part of a woman's sexual attractiveness. Breasts are functional; they're for feeding infants. Americans, however, largely find any situation of public nudity uncomfortable, because in their culture, nudity equates to sex; therefore, public nudity upsets their norm, making it one of the stricter mores in American society.

Folkways, on the other hand, are norms that are unrelated to morals but are still conventional standards or traditional customs that are socially acceptable by a culture. As mores distinquish between right and wrong, folkways define what is *right* and what is *rude*. Again, folkways are based upon cultural values. For example, when eating out at a restaurant with friends, many Westerners expect to pay their individual bill, rather than one host paying a group tab. This standard may be representative of the prevalent values of individualism and independence in Western culture. In eastern cultures – in China for instance –, it is customary for an individual to pay for the entire bill. In most cases, the man is expected to pay for the woman, the elder for the younger, and the host (or the person who invited another) for the guest. In fact, some may even put up a fight to pay the tab, as paying is considered an "honor," which as we saw previously, is a characteristic greatly valued in Chinese culture.

NORMS

FOLKWAYS	RIGHT VS. RUDE
MORES	RIGHT VS. WRONG
TABOOS	RIGHT VS. FORBIDDEN
LAWS	RIGHT VS. ILLEGAL

Even something as simple as a handshake can carry quite different folkways across cultures. For instance, in many middle eastern cultures, it is improper for people of the opposite sex to shake hands. Further, only the right hand is used in a handshake, as the left is viewed as "unclean." In Asian cultures, using only one hand when shaking is considered extremely rude or even a sign of superiority. Shaking with two hands shows formal respect. Western cultures don't have quite so many rules in regards to handshaking, though it is often said that eye contact and a firm grip is the key to a strong handshake.

Norms can also be so important to a culture's fabric that they ban certain behaviors, making them taboo. Now rudeness and wrongness are no longer in the equation; rather, the norms differentiate between what is *right* and what is *forbidden.*

Again, taboos vary widely across culture. In Muslim countries, many cultural taboos are based on Islam and are strictly forbidden. For instance, it is absolutely taboo that the prophet Mohammad be depicted. Of course, this contrasts greatly with other global cultures, who freely depict their religious figures – Hindu gods and goddesses, Jesus Christ or Buddha – in everything from art to advertising. The depiction of Mohammad is met with a death sentence. Restrictions on women, such as driving or leaving the house without a male relative, are also taboos in many Muslim countries, oftentimes being written into law...which leads us to our final set of norms.

Laws, of course, are the formally written and legal norms, enacted by the state. Similar to taboos, laws define what is and isn't acceptable, but this time the country's judicial system will enforce your compliance. While taboos are societally sanctioned, laws are nationally enforced. Laws define what is *right* and what is *illegal.* Nearly all taboos cross into law (i.e., laws prohibiting women driving or Mohammed being depicted in Muslim countries); however, not all mores or folkways hold such weight as taboos. For instance, whereas breastfeeding in public might be considered offensive by some Americans due to societal nudity mores, it is not against the law. Laws make up the most restrictive of a society's norms and are created to dictate conformity. Without conformity, cultural norms would not exist, and so laws put pressure on society to adhere to the accepted norms by punishing defiance with fines and imprisonment. In this way, cultures shape the infrastructure of their norms, and the accepted norms shape the individuals in the culture.

For a culture to exist, its individuals, its society must conform to norms, not only to allow society to function in the way its rule of law has determined it should, but to limit conflict between society members and to create a type of cultural harmony. Though values and norms may shift or evolve over time, a culture's foundational values and norms oftentimes remain securely intact. Members internalize their culture's values and norms, in order that they might be an acceptable and productive member of their society. Through primary socialization they are then passed on to their children and their children's children, sewing themselves more securely into the field of culture.

Adapting to the norms of another culture may be essential for integration or for the success of a business venture. You may accept many behaviors and leave it at that, but when it comes to norms, you'd better adapt. *Accepting* won't be enough for integration, as members of a culture are expected to comply with cultural norms. If the norm of a culture is to not breastfeed in public, then it is not enough to simply accept this norm; one must comply with it. If you are a young Swedish mother, for instance, it would be advisable for you to adapt to this norm in the US, in order to demonstrate cultural sensitivity and respect.

The Baobab (or the Theory of the Iceberg)

In the dry and wide savannah of Africa stand gigantic trees with huge trunks. These are the baobabs. They can grow up to 100 feet (25 meters) tall and can live for several thousand years. The baobab is leafless for nine months of the year then, when the rainy season comes, small leaves and sweet-sour fruits sprout on the high branches. The tree also stores water in its thick, corky, fire-resistant trunk for the nine dry months ahead. Sometimes the trunks are hollow. When they are, the common belief is that spirits live in them.

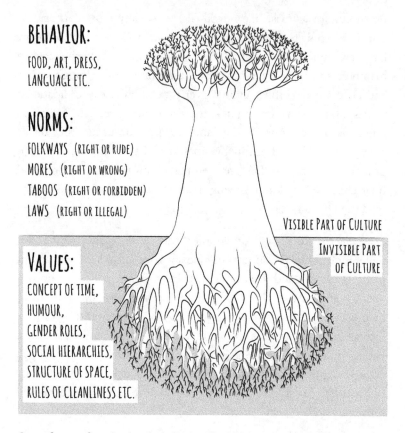

BEHAVIOR:
FOOD, ART, DRESS,
LANGUAGE ETC.

NORMS:
FOLKWAYS (RIGHT OR RUDE)
MORES (RIGHT OR WRONG)
TABOOS (RIGHT OR FORBIDDEN)
LAWS (RIGHT OR ILLEGAL)

VISIBLE PART OF CULTURE

INVISIBLE PART OF CULTURE

VALUES:
CONCEPT OF TIME,
HUMOUR,
GENDER ROLES,
SOCIAL HIERARCHIES,
STRUCTURE OF SPACE,
RULES OF CLEANLINESS ETC.

Seen from afar, the baobab looks like it has been picked out of the ground and stuffed back in upside-down. The trunk would be the tap-root, and the branches the finer capillary roots. In fact, the Arabian legend of the baobab is that "the devil plucked up the baobab, thrust its branches into the earth and left its roots in the air." Another legend related to the baobab describes what happens if you are never satisfied with what you already have:

"The baobab was among the first trees to appear on the land. Next came the slender, graceful palm tree. When the baobab saw the palm tree, it cried out that it wanted to be taller. Then the beautiful flame tree appeared with its red flower and the baobab was envious for flower blossoms. When the baobab saw the magnificent fig tree, it prayed for fruit as well. The gods became angry with the tree and pulled it up by its roots, then replanted it upside down to keep it quiet."

However the shape of the baobab came to be, the remarkable thing is that the roots of this tree are huge. They are actually often wider than the tree is high. And that brings us to the theory of the iceberg. Ever since the movie, *Titanic* – still one of the highest grossing box office hits of all time – most people know the physical characteristics of an iceberg in general: only approximatively one seventh of its volume is above the water line. The overwhelming mass of an iceberg lies hidden beneath the surface, a constant danger to ships navigating through cold seas.

Culture is often compared to an iceberg. There is a visible part – the behavior – but hidden below the surface is the bigger invisible part – the values. Now, I've never seen a monkey climb on an iceberg. So the baobab may be a more appropriate image for the purpose of this book. The canopy and the large trunk are the visible part of the tree and below the soil is a huge, invisible network of intertwined roots.

The visible part of culture is obvious, encompassing everything from the way people dress, the language they speak, the food they eat, their artistic expression, their architecture and their housing types, how they greet each other – with hands, kisses or no body contact at all – their body language, how they communicate while speaking – with direct eye contact, like in Europe, or avoiding direct eye contact, like in Africa, etc. These visible parts of a culture all fall under the general term, behavior.

Some of the behavior is regulated by norms. Folkways are not very strict norms. They are flexible. They are like the small but bendable branches at the outer edges of the canopy. Mores are stricter, requiring stronger adherence by society. They are like the thicker parts of these branches, as they reach toward the trunk. And finally taboos and laws require strict obedience by the members of a culture.

They are what keeps a culture cemented and grounded. They are strong and immovable like the large trunk of the baobab.

Most cross cultural business guides and books will focus on this visible part of the culture. Doing so is fine if you only plan to travel briefly to another country. It'll come in handy to know that the Greek language is extremely difficult, that their official working day finishes in early afternoon, and that formal events in the office are attended mostly by employees of the same rank. It'll also come in handy to know that in the UK, managers tend to be direct and decision-oriented. Most decisions are made in meetings where, despite their image of formalism, British people will call each other by their first name. And if you read a book on business mores of Portugal, you'll learn that the Portuguese address anyone suspected of having a university degree with the title, "Doutor" (doctor). Business relationships are usually based on personal relationships in Portugal, and formal dress is both required in the office and frequently worn for private functions.

These are only a few examples of the tip of the iceberg or the canopy of the baobab. You'll find that countless books on business cultures in European countries detail these behaviors, as they are the visible parts of culture. But far more important is the vast portion of culture, buried hidden under the dry African soil.

The parts invisible to the naked eye – the roots of the tree – explain *why* various cultures have developed certain behaviors. Until you understand the *why*, it is impossible to understand a culture and, if your goal is to integrate into a culture's social fabric, you must understand its underlying values. These values drive the behaviors and the norms of its people. If the Swiss are punctual (visible part of culture), then it is because of their concept of time (invisible part of culture). Americans like to promote their success (visible part of culture) because of the individuality engrained in their values (invisible part of the culture).

If you wish to sell products to another culture, then your pitch should be consistent with that culture's deeper layers. If not, your business will tank, as your marketing strategy will invariably fail. When you're introducing a new product or concept, you may be successful in altering some aspects of cultural behavior, but it's almost impossible to change a culture's norms or values.

We've already introduced some of what makes up the hidden part of the baobab: values like the concept of time, the importance of keeping face, the attitude towards life – whether one feels in control of life or subject to fate, etc. These are the deep, hidden parts of a culture. Educating yourself in these concepts will help you understand the rationale behind those behaviors, which may, at first glance, appear strange to you. Most people act quite rationally within their culture's constructs. The little boy, Ahmed, acted rationally when he helped his cousin, Khalid. Without strong mutual support, a family may not survive in a third world country. He acted in perfect harmony with the roots below his surface. Ann, the teacher, also acted rationally within her own cultural constructs. Convinced that individual success is paramount to happiness and economic well-fare, she wanted Ahmed to conform to the roots below her surface. Both acted rationally within the norms and values of their culturally-acquired framework.

In reality, the story of Ahmed and Khalid did not meet a happy end. The dispute between the teacher, Ann, and the clan of Ahmed had another, more tragic dimension. In accusing Ahmed and Khalid of cheating, Ann implied publicly that Khalid may not be smart enough to succeed at the exam. Being the source of such shame for his cousin embarrassed Ahmed and, moreover, he was accused of dishonesty in front of the whole class. He lost *face*. He pled with his parents to let him live with his grandparents, away from the city. And that is where he went – far away, leaving a good school and a good education behind him. Like the Titanic's demise, the source of potential friction lies below the surface, making catastrophe not so easy to predict.

How do the monkey strategies – *accepting, adapting, adopting* – relate to these components of a culture?

Managing or living successfully in other cultures always starts with accepting that culture as it is. You must accept that there are many ways to live, to organize a society, and even to manage a company. Accepting means to see the beauty in the baobab, from the roots up to the canopy. If you are not deeply convinced that your host nation's culture is beautiful and is *as good* as your own culture, then your colleagues will notice. Integration will be difficult to achieve and your managerial decisions will always be subject to a layer of mistrust. To manage successfully and be supported by your colleagues, you must fully accept your host's culture.

The baobab may not produce the thick foliage of trees you find in Europe or America, nor will the flowers compare with the cherry blossoms of Japan, and for many Westerners, its fruit, called monkey-bread, will not taste nearly as delicious as the apples and oranges we are used too; but accepting means to see the good in what we do not know, to search out the good in everything with which we are unfamiliar. Maybe you don't like the aesthetics of the baobab, but when you take some interest in the tree and discuss it with the locals, you'll discover the many ways in which the huge African baobab serves the community. The baobab's bark, leaves, fruit, and trunk are all useful; the bark is used for cloth and rope, the leaves for condiments and medicines, and of course, the fruit is eaten. Although it's not a juicy fruit favored in the West and is rather dry and sticks to your tongue, a great advantage "monkey fruit" has over apple and oranges is that it can be stored for months in the African heat without rotting. As with noting the beauty in something strange and different – something like the baobab, which didn't seem beautiful or useful at first glance – accepting a culture takes similar effort. You must endeavor to see the good in other cultures and accept behavioral differences without judgment or condemnation.

Of course, there will be aspects of a culture that you dislike or with which you disagree. We will discuss later how to react in these types of situations. But disliking or disagreeing with certain aspects of a culture is not a reason to refuse that things may be done or seen differently by other people.

This initial adverse reaction to another's culture may also be due to missing the comfort of home. The ease and familiarity of your own culture will make you nostalgic for the 'good ol' days' when nothing was new or surprising. While living in Japan, an American may miss his warm-hearted, jovial and informal relationships back home; and in America, a French person may miss the crusty bread; in Europe, the Chinese may have a hard time integrating into individualistic culture; and in Spain, the Japanese may loathe the loud and noisy restaurants. But missing something from home doesn't mean that what's right there in front of you is bad.

When growing up as child in Africa, I missed apples tremendously. I love apples. But missing apples does not make the monkey-bread of the baobab less appetizing. Accepting means you no longer categorize aspects of a culture as either good or bad. Instead, you accept differences and force yourself to see the good and the beauty in the unfamiliar and strange. And the day you truly open your eyes to watch the sun set over the African savannah, you will see the beauty of these huge trees against the horizon. You may even start to admire them.

Accepting the other culture is only the first step. You may also choose to *adapt* to some behaviors – how you dress, how you greet others, or what you eat, for instance. While *accepting* encompasses all aspects of the culture, *adapting* is specific to the behavioral aspects (i.e. the visible parts) of a culture.

Without adapting to some behaviors, integration will be impossible, but when it comes down to it, adapting to many local behaviors may be quite simple in the end. You may drink beer with lunch in Germany, wine in France or a Coke in the US. This is a fairly quick and easy way to integrate and become "one of the locals." Nevertheless, some situations may make adapting difficult or even impossible, because certain behaviors are complex. Speaking a language, for instance, requires time, patience and some language learning skills. For some behaviors, you may need to learn other special sets of skills, like the finger-snapping greeting practices in certain parts of Africa.

Moreover, in some cases, your body will not allow you to adapt to certain behaviors. For instance, in many ethnic groups throughout Africa, offering a visitor some water to drink is a common practice. If you're not used to drinking unfiltered water, then you may choose not to drink it for health reasons. Although you'll likely provoke a monkey-moment by declining the drink, the other culture will accept your decision if the reason is made clear that your health is prohibiting you from adapting to this custom.

You may demonstrate your acceptance of behaviors by explaining why you won't comply with certain local customs. You can also demonstrate your respect for their culture by complying with other cultural behaviors, for instance, attempting to learn the language. Greet the locals in their language – something that the Walmart CEO in Chapter 1 didn't do. These little demonstrations will show your new colleagues that you care enough about your culture to put the time in.

Sometimes behavior touches upon your own deeply entrenched values, and though you would like to adapt, you may just feel awkward and uncomfortable. From childhood, the Japanese learn not to touch other people in public. The Japanese don't shake hands, and they definitely don't publicly kiss. While living in Spain, at a language school, I met a Japanese woman, the wife of a diplomat, who was born into an aristocratic family. Imagine how difficult it was for this woman to adapt to the local Spanish habit of kissing instead of shaking hands. To adapt, she had to overcome her own values and deep physical discomfort. I have a great amount of respect for her decision to adapt, instead of just accepting.

Adaption becomes extremely difficult when certain behaviors are in direct contradiction to your own values. Though it's fairly easy to wear a headscarf – just tie it over your head and smile – , many Western women will refuse to adapt to this practice, because in their view, wearing headscarves should be a choice, not a requirement. It's not so much the behavior, itself, as the fact that the headscarf symbolizes values they reject. This is an example of a situation which may create profound cultural conflicts. If you feel you cannot comply with certain mandatory cultural behaviors, it's best to either avoid the situation altogether (i.e. don't travel to countries where the cultural norms require women to wear headscarves or a burka) or explain your rationale for rejecting this norm. The latter may be a gamble; your foreign counterparts may not appreciate or respect your rationale. But, if you can manage to explain yourself in a way that does not diminish and disrespect their cultural tradition, you may be given a free pass.

Not all adaptions are optional. If behavior is tied to cultural norms then you may be *required* to adapt. In these situations, acknowledgement and acceptance without behavioral changes will not be enough. In most cases, norms should be respected. Accepting should be followed by adapting your behavior – even if these norms are not in line with your own values. For instance, if one of the norms of your new culture requires you to be punctual, then you should adapt; if you don't, you will likely not be able to close business deals, because you'll be seen as disrespectful of other peoples' time.

Folkways are the softest form of cultural norms. You may choose not to adapt to them, but your behavior will then be perceived as rude or inappropriate. In the European business world, for instance, formal attire is far more important than in the US. An American manager may choose to attend meetings without a suit and tie. Doing so is not forbidden, although it may be perceived negatively.

But mores put even more pressure on adaption than folkways. These norms define the cultural right and wrong. A French businesswoman may dress in a way that other countries may consider too revealing, inappropriate or *wrong*, and the female manager will be pressured or explicitly asked to adapt her clothing.

Finally, adaption is absolutely mandatory when it comes to a culture's taboos and laws. Taboos define what is forbidden in a culture, while laws define what is illegal. There is no leeway here, and your behavior must change if you wish to thrive in another culture. If these norms require a woman to wear a headscarf, then you should adapt. Whether or not wearing a scarf is against your own beliefs and values, you accept that other cultures have other values and, if you've chosen to live in their culture, you must observe these values whenever possible. You will have to decide where to draw the line for yourself; it's up to you to choose which norms stand against your principles. But make no mistake, taboos and laws require adaption.

If you're confused about whether a behavior is a *norm* or not, the following will illustrate the difference:

In Iran, a woman must wear a headscarf. It is required not only by custom, but by law. On the other hand, in some ethnic groups in Papua-New Guinea, women go topless in public. Though this is not customary, it's not unusual, and it may be difficult for a Western woman to get used to or actually adapt, themselves. However, whereas the headscarf in Iran is tied to norms, going topless in Papua-New Guinea is not, and so neither society nor the law requires women to adapt this state of undress.

Components of a Culture	The Monkey Strategies
BEHAVIOR	ACCEPTING THE BEHAVIOR IS THE STARTING POINT FOR ANY CROSS-CULTURAL COMMUNICATION. ADAPTING IS USUALLY EASY, EXCEPT IN CASES OF CONFLICT BETWEEN YOUR NORMS AND VALUES AND THOSE OF THE CULTURE INTO WHICH YOU ARE INTEGRATING.
NORMS	ADAPTING IS REQUIRED. IF THE NORMS ARE TIED TO CONFLICTING VALUES, THEN A CULTURAL CONFLICT MAY BE INEVITABLE. IF ADAPTING IS NOT AN OPTION, THEN THE SITUATION SHOULD BE AVOIDED (E.G. DON'T TRAVEL TO COUNTRIES WHERE WOMEN ARE REQUIRED TO WEAR HEADSCARVES IF YOU ARE NOT READY TO ACCEPT IT).
VALUES	ADOPTING VALUES IS THE HIGHEST POSSIBLE LEVEL OF INTEGRATION INTO ANOTHER CULTURE AND THE MOST DIFFICULT PROCESS. ADOPTING MAY CHALLENGE YOUR OWN BELIEFS AND WILL LIKELY TAKE A LONG TIME.

Finally, to truly integrate into a society, *adoption* is necessary. Adopting means to make a certain behavior, norm or value your own. While adapting touches the visible part of culture, adoption is all about the invisible, deep layers of culture. If you truly adopt the values of your host's culture in your heart, then you enter the last stage of cultural integration. You will become part of a new culture, and the culture will become part of you. Just like any adoption process, this one will take time. How long might you have to live in Africa to actually enjoy eating termites? Once you've reached this stage, you'll truly be an global citizen. Not only will this global citizenship provide you with a deep connection with and insight into your new culture, but it will also allow you new insight into and freedom from your own culture.

What we learned in this chapter:

- What is culture? Culture is the shared values and norms of a group of people which result in characteristic behaviors.

- What are values? Values distinguish good from evil and determine what qualities a society esteems.

- What are norms? Norms are the expectations and rules accepted by the majority in any given culture; they guide behavior and are largely based on the majority's values.

- The visible part of culture encompasses all behaviors and norms, while the baobab below the surface is largely composed by a culture's values.

4. A Journey through Cultural Differences

One of the biggest dangers in cross cultural management is to assume sameness. From childhood to adulthood, we all grow into the limited cultural views of the society into which we've been born. The family, the house, the kindergarten, friends – the relative cultural structures of these concepts are often what we define as normal, and they serve as a reference for "normal" in all future experience.

In youth, we implicitly assume that our normal is the same as the rest of the world's. At around age 10, we start to discover the world, and autonomy begins to sprout within us and persists in growing and evolving. Parents may no longer be the main reference for normal. Friends become more influential, and we learn that normal is not a universally fixed concept – there are different ideas of normal not only throughout the world, but even within our own little communities.

We discover that human behavior may vary considerably from family to family, and our communication with and observation of other families within our society is perhaps the source by which we also make first contact with other cultures. At the same time, we begin to affirm our own personal identities, being made aware of how different we are as individuals. By the time we transition from the teenage years to adulthood, the foundation is firm – our basic views of the world are pretty well established. We've determined what is right or wrong, good or bad; we've learned how to judge what is socially acceptable and what isn't, according to our distinct set of criteria.

To be successful in a multicultural environment, the first and most important step is to let go of all these assumptions. Free yourself from your foundational views of right and wrong. Humanity is far more diverse than we assume. Your hometown, and even your nation, has only revealed to you a microscopic brushstroke in the enormous mural of humanity. The essence of human kind is much more elaborate, much more complex than a single brushstroke. This chapter will illustrate the extremes of cultural diversity and how these extremes deeply affect individual and group behavior and worldview. This journey will take us to the hidden roots of the baobab.

Seeing

To demonstrate how presumptuous we are about sameness across cultures, let's start with eyesight. Wouldn't we assume that the world visually appears the same to all human beings? In his book, *Looking Through the Language Glass*, Guy Deutscher tells the fascinating story of how human beings, through time and culture, have perceived and presently perceive colors.[6] In 1867 the philologist, Lazarus Geiger, discovered that old text used unusual color descriptions. Homer in his masterworks, *The Iliad* and *The Odyssey*, describes a wine-dark sea, violet wool sheep and green honey. None of these color descriptions would be our first choice. The sea is blue, wool is white or black, and who has ever heard of green honey? The Old Testament describes red horses, dove feathers covered with green gold, and according to Jeremiah, faces which turn green with panic. Apart from the Hulk, green faces of panic are relatively uncommon in the modern Western world. Hardly any of these are the color choices we would use today. Instead of chalking these descriptions up to artistic license, science decided to take a look at the evolution of eyesight.

The scientific reason behind this oddity took a whole century to thrash out. One of the first theories related the lack of correct color perception with the principles of evolution. During the evolutionary process, the human eye developed sensitivity across generations, starting with the ancient Greeks. The eye became more sensitive, as the perception of color became increasingly important in highly developed civilizations. This argument was seemingly supported by the complete absence of the color blue in many old texts. Whereas when it came to survival, it was unnecessary to be able to distinguish blue from other colors, distinguishing the color red was vital, as it signifies danger (blood) and sex (for instance, the female baboon's big red bottom). Being as such, the color red is present in most old languages. Red dyes were also the most common and least difficult to manufacture, while blue dyes were difficult to produce, as the color is extremely rare in nature.

In 1877 Alfred Russel Wallace, Darwin's contemporary, and co-discoverer of the principles of evolution by natural selection wrote: "Our present high perception and appreciation of color is a comparatively recent acquisition." In 1878 Ernst Haeckel, a biologist, wrote, "The more delicate cones of the retina, which impart the higher color-sense, have probably developed gradually only during the last millennia." The research was then extended to the use of colors in the language of traditional people – from the Nubians in Africa to the Klamath Indians in Oregon. They discovered that color descriptions were similar to that of the old scriptural languages.

As you may imagine, the research results had potential to be interpreted wrongly; and, indeed, for many years the scientific community largely assumed that the unusual use of language was an indication of the physical and intellectual inferiority of so-called primitive societies. According to popular belief at the time, "savages" were anatomically inferior to civilized people and, therefore, their intelligence must be inferior as well.

This raises a core question of cultural studies: what is genetic and what is acquired, learned behavior? For decades, the scientific community assumed that the so-called "inferior" vocabulary of color in primitive societies was directly related to genetic inferiority in terms of the ability to discern color. This was the accepted theory until 1969, when two researchers, Brent Berlin and Paul Kay, set out to analyze a systematic comparison of the use of color vocabulary. Dipping into twenty different languages of various ethnic groups, they used an array of colored chips to assess and collect the groups' color descriptions. They found that the identification of primary colors is nearly identical across cultures, which proved that the concept of colors in language has nothing to do with anatomy or the development of the retina. Progress in the evolutionary research also showed that the old Greeks and Hebrews had the same functioning eyes as we have today. The color use in the language is purely a cultural norm. However, depending upon the culture, the distinct boundaries between colors may vary substantially.

Take, for instance, the color spectrum from violet to red. If Russian scientists of the last century had investigated the British sense of color, they would certainly have concluded that the English language is somehow primitive when compared to the Russian language. The Russian language distinguishes between light blue, "goluboy," and dark blue, "siniy." Both colors are subsumed in English to one color. An English person would of course insist that there is, in fact, light blue and dark blue, but that these are "shades" of the same color. The Russian might argue that the British are not highly civilized, being that they cannot distinguish between these two obviously different colors. From a physics point of view, the Russian may have a point. The wavelengths of dark and light blue differ as much as light blue differs from green. So there is no physical reason to equate dark and light blue, lumping the distinctly different shades into one single color. However, whether or not we personally agree with the Russian color concept or the British one, this example reveals two important teachings about cultural assumptions.

The first and most important of these teachings is that "different" does not and should not equate inferiority. It is simply "different." Your own comparative cultural dissimilitude does not always indicate that another culture's norm is unnatural or less than. Realizing this is very important. Nothing in this book is intended to reflect positively or negatively upon any culture; this book's content is solely driven to help you identify and understand cultural differences and how to accept them. John Hooker, in his book, *Working Across Cultures*, said it best: "I have neither the wisdom nor the desire to pass judgment. For me every culture is a source of fascination, because it must encompass all of life and give it meaning."

The second important concept to take from this color research is that cultural conditioning influences how we perceive the world through our senses. Obviously the British can visually see the difference between light and dark blue, as they have exactly the same functioning optics as the Russians. However, it is also fair to assume, according to language, that the distinction between shades of blue is of lesser importance in British culture than it is in Russian culture.

Of course the perception of the world goes far beyond colors. In my classes, I like to show my students the following picture, allowing them a couple of minutes to memorize it. I then remove it from the screen and ask the students to draw the picture from memory on a blank sheet of paper. Over the course of nearly ten years teaching this subject, the success rate has been zero. No student has ever been able to draw this simple figure from memory.

Other figures like this one have been known to produce similar baffling results – for instance, the impossible triangle of Penrose or the infinite staircase of M. C. Escher. These figures confuse Western observers, as they try to interpret a two-dimensional figure as a three-dimensional object. The fork shown above is just a drawing with 3 circles, 6 horizontal lines, 3 diagonals and 1 vertical line. But in school, Westerners are trained to recognize three dimensional projections on paper as replications of real objects. People who habitually ascribe three-dimensionality to pictures have far more difficulty in reproducing these figures than people who have not been socialized or respectively trained in such a way.

J. B. Deregowski tested Zambian children with this same exercise. Their performance was far higher than my university students' collective performance over the years.[7] An African with no academic education will reproduce this picture quite easily. On the other hand, if you show a geographical map to an unschooled African and ask him to direct you, he likely will not be able to transpose the two-dimensional image against the three-dimensional reality of his surroundings.

You will find a similar outcome in the perception of the right angle across cultures. People who live in "circular culture" – i.e. architecture that includes round huts and arched doorways – will not perceive 90 degree angles. Since right angles don't appear in nature, they are not incorporated in the architecture of traditional societies. They simply do not exist.

The visual world is not objective; instead, it fits into the framework presented by our culture. What we see through our eyes is equal parts reality and the interpretation of this reality. And the interpretation of reality varies starkly across cultures.

For instance, a Westerner often regards snow simply as snow. Descriptions may be ascribed to snow, particularly by those who are avid skiers. Hard snow, powder snow, fresh snow – these are all descriptive variables ascribed to snow by Westerners. The Koyukon, however, hold a much more complex view of snow.

The Koyukon are an indigenous group who live in northern Alaska along the Koyukuk and Yukon rivers. They are popular amongst anthropological society because of their 16 different terms for snow. For any of the following categories, they have a separate and distinct word:

snow
deep snow
falling snow
blowing snow
snow on the ground
granular snow beneath the surface
hard drifted snow
snow thawed previously and then frozen
earliest crusted snow in spring
thinly crusted snow
snow drifted over a steep bank, making it steeper
snow cornice on a mountain
heavy drifting snow
slushy snow on the ground
snow caught on tree branches
fluffy or powder snow

Imagine how colorful and diverse a snow landscape appears to the Koyukons when compared to Westerners who view snow as one and the same. Even something as simple as the picture of a stair may lead to diverse cultural interpretations.

For an American, the stair depicted below is a set of stairs ascending. For an Arabic person, the stairs descend. The interpretation is influenced by the Western style of reading from left to right, while Arabs read from right to left. This detail may seem unimportant, but the differences can carry with them quite significant potential for misunderstanding. For example, take organizational charts in America and Europe. The CEO appears at the top, and all other departments are aligned on the levels below, according to their order of importance. The most important and biggest department is always on the left, because that is where we've been trained to look for it. Obviously, such a chart may be organized very differently in other cultures, according to cultural standards regarding the order of importance.

A quite famous example along the same lines comes out of Japan. A Western pharmaceutical company launched marketing for a medicine to settle a bad stomach. Their advert ran, showing three simple pictures: the first displayed someone feeling ill, the second illustrated the person taking the medicine, and the last picture showed the now healthy and smiling man under bright sunshine. This comic strip obviously only works if read in the intended order. However, Japanese comic books, the so-called Mangas, are always read from back to front. So, according to a Japanese reading of the advert, a smiling, healthy man appeared to become sick after he took the medicine; the opposite message of what was intended.

Touching

Body contact and personal space is one of the most discussed and sensitive topics when it comes to cultural differences. As a young manager, I was relocated to Madrid, Spain. Negotiations often took place over long lunches, which frequently last until late afternoon. The real deals started after dessert. This is when a potential business partner might put his hand on my arm, which would be resting on the table. The intermittent body contact of a potential business partner resting his hand on your arm may at first be disturbing to one who is accustomed to a respect of personal space, especially when it comes to business.

During the same period, my wife attended a Spanish course, where she met the wife of a Japanese diplomat. The diplomat told us how difficult it was for her to adapt to the Spanish tradition of effusively giving kisses on the cheeks on any and all occasions. Raised in an aristocratic family, body contact with strangers, or even colleagues, was strictly forbidden. Touching the body of another is considered very intimate in Japan, and thus, is reserved only for intimate relationships. To grasp to what extend this Japanese woman had to overcome the values instilled by primary socialization, imagine that in traveling to an unknown country, someone greets you by rubbing their chest against yours. Being greeted this way would likely come as a great shock to you, but remember that the breasts in many cultures are not a sexual part of the body. Still, knowing as much would not make it any less uncomfortable. It is extremely difficult to overcome your own primary socialization and culturally accept another's. But you must in order to fully accept and be accepted by another culture. In this case, you would need to accept publicly greeting others in this way. Over time, you may even become comfortable with it.

Kissing, as a matter of fact, is one of the most overt tip-of-the-iceberg cultural behaviors, because it's so plainly visible. 90 percent of the world population practices some form of kissing; however, forms differ substantially across cultures. As mentioned previously, Spanish people frequently kiss each other on the cheeks; the gesture is commensurate with shaking hands. Nevertheless, it is strictly reserved for women. In eastern Europe on the other hand, kissing man-to-man is pretty common, like shaking hands between friends. Egyptians and Eskimos kiss by rubbing the nose. On the flipside, kissing is often prohibited in certain circumstances in some cultures. For instance, in parts of America, kissing has been made illegal in specific instances. Those in Cedar Rapids, Iowa are prohibited by law from kissing strangers, while women in Hartford, Connecticut are not legally allowed to lock lips with their husbands on Sundays. Obviously mores have changed in America since these laws were enacted; but as we saw previously, sometimes values become law, and the laws remain even if the societal values have evolved. Though these cultural laws and mores may seem bizarre to you, Margaret Mead's study on cultural differences related to kissing is even more astounding.

Margaret Mead was an American cultural anthropologist who became famous during the 60s and 70s through her reports on attitudes towards sex in some of South Pacific's traditional cultures. Her book, *Coming of Age in Samoa*, shed a scientific light on a society with considerably more sexual freedom than the Western world at that time. In Samoa, adolescence was not a time of "storm and stress" but, rather, a time of sexual freedom which allowed an easier transition from childhood to adulthood. Her theories were quickly adopted by the proponents of the 1960s sexual revolution. She remained a strong defender of broadened sexual mores all her life.

Long before her research in Samoa, however, Margaret Mead investigated an apparently conflicting difference in the courting habits of Americans and the British. During and after the second world war, millions of American GIs visited or were stationed in the United Kingdom. Human nature took its course and, naturally, young American men began courting young British women. This provided a unique opportunity to study direct human interaction between the two cultures.

One aspect of Mead's research involved the observation of differences in courting habits between the US and Britain. A paradox quickly became apparent. The US soldiers said that British girls were "too easy," while British women had the same complaint, claiming the Americans were "too fast and direct." Both genders felt pressured by the other and complained about a lack of consideration for each other's courting and mating habits.

To study the differences in courting habits, Mead categorized all the steps from first contact up to sexual intercourse. She discovered that in both cultures, the progress from a casual to an intimate relationship was split into 30 steps, more or less. However, though the number of steps was the same on both sides of the Atlantic, the progression of these steps varied significantly. One notable difference was the French kiss. According to Mead's research, in the US, the French kiss comes in at around step number five, because it is viewed as rather innocent. So in the eyes of a US soldier, it was natural that the French kiss should arrive early on in the courting process. On the other hand, a British girl considers Frenching as something very intimate. In the British courting process, the French kiss doesn't enter into the equation until stage twenty-five. After a nice candle-lit dinner, the American might quickly lean towards the

Brit and try innocently to kiss her. The girl would then have two choices: either she could spring to her feet in outrage, throw a glass of wine in his face and zip away, or she could jump 20 steps of her culturally ingrained ideas of courtship etiquette and accept the kiss, all the while feeling pressured to do so. In either case, she would have felt pressure. In the latter case, she would then have implicitly accepted, according to her culture, that the next steps were equally as intimate, and some even rather more so. She might then pressure the American to progress to these stages, which were the natural next steps to follow in her culture after a French kiss, but were much further along in the 30-step courting process in his. Being as such, the American is then given the impression that all British girls are "easy," while the Brit believes the American is "too fast and direct."

Mead's research illustrates the miscalculations that arise when we assume that another's cultural norms and values are (or should be) the same as our own.

We're all familiar with famous kissing scenes in films and art, and if you're from a Western culture, then you likely implicitly assumed that French kissing was a universal phenomenon. Scientist, Sheril Kirshenbaum, notes in her 2011 book, *The Science of Kissing, What Our Lips are Telling Us*, that kissing romantically is a global habit. But research shows otherwise. Recently a team from the University of Indiana investigated 168 ethnic groups on five continents. In 77 of these groups, romantic kissing was a habit, but in 91 of the groups, kissing was insignificant to the couples' love lives. The kiss, defined as a conscious and intimate touching of the lips between two persons, is prevalent in Europe, North America, the Middle East and Asia, but is not so prevalent in most cultures in Africa and Latin America. There, the touching of lips may even be regarded as repulsive and disgusting.[8]

Another major cultural difference in intimacy is found in personal distance. In any culture, when two people are talking to each other, they tend to stand a specific distance apart. Each person has an invisible boundary around their body – personal space – of which other people may not invade. If someone pierces this boundary, the person in question will feel uncomfortable and move away to regain their boundary. This preference for personal distance is not due to bad breath or body odor; rather, closeness lends a sense of intimacy that may be at odds with the relationship in question. Obviously personal distance varies within a culture from person to person, as well as when it comes to those one loves or specific circumstances (when in an elevator, for instance). However, personal space is generally a sensitive matter.

At around age 3 or 4, personal space begins developing and is later cemented by adolescence. Research shows that the circles of personal space are constructed and monitored by the amygdala, the brain region which triggers fear. When someone invades your personal space, the amygdala is activated. This elicits a strong – even if subconscious – emotional reaction when somebody gets too close.

Generally, Americans tend to require more personal space than other cultures. The American department of education even felt compelled to highlight this cultural norm in advice given to foreign students preparing to study in the US: "If you try to get too close to an American during your conversation, he or she will feel that you are 'in their face' and will try to back away. Try to be aware of this, so if the person to whom you are speaking backs away a little, don't try to close the gap. Also, try to avoid physical contact while you are speaking, since this may also lead to discomfort. Touching is a bit too intimate for casual acquaintances. So don't put your arm around their shoulder, touch their face or hold their hand. Shaking hands when you initially meet or part is acceptable, but this is only momentary."

American managers working in Latin America often utilize a little trick to avoid too much physical closeness with their employees. Instead of increasing the gap with a step backwards (which will inevitably be closed by the Latin American fellow, as he feels uncomfortable with a wide gap), they place a table or desk between the employee and themselves to create the gap for them.

Another example of cultural differences regarding touching has to do with the acceptable contact between two females in a culture, two males and male-to-female. While public affections are accepted between females in Europe, they are considered taboo in many cultures in Africa. On the other hand, in African cultures, two male colleague walking hand-in-hand along the street is often widely acceptable and carries no sexual connotations. However, in general, physical contact in Africa is rare in public. Couples will not even hold hands in public in many traditional societies.

The use of the left hand also varies across cultures. In regions where water to wash hands is not readily available, tasks are quite often divided between the left and right hand. Dirty tasks are usually done with the left hand so, naturally, it would be considered rude to touch or greet someone with the left hand, even if the right hand is busy holding a child.

The hand shake varies according to culture as well. In Germany the shake is usually firm and short, while in France a weak handshake is considered polite. German managers might call this polite French handshake "fishy." In Africa one might hold onto the hand for a long while or they might even take it up again after shaking, grasping it for the entire duration of the conversation.

Smelling

In our journey through cultural differences in terms of senses and how they relate to cultural perceptions of the world, we will touch upon a rather underestimated sense, at least in our culture: the sense of smell. The human species' sense of smell is feeble compared to that of many animals. No customs officer will ever be able to sniff drugs. However, our sense of smell is still quite sharp. Andreas Keller at Rockefeller University in New York recently conducted research which shows that the human nose is far more sensitive than the eye or the ear. We may not always be conscious of the diverse complexity of smell molecules, but the smell of a rose alone is composed of roughly 275 different elements. Keller came to the conclusion that the human species can differentiate between trillions of scents, while the ear may only discern between roughly 340,000 sounds and the eye will only see 2.3 to 7.5 million colors. Keller's 2014 study published in *Science Magazine* states that the human nose has evolved to the point that it can detect minute differences between smells. For instance, the nose can discern between fresh food and something that's just beginning to spoil. Consequently, the sharpness of differentiating between smells could be a matter of life and death. As Keller stated, "The human capacity for discriminating smells is much larger than anyone anticipated." Another interesting fact resulting from Keller's research is that women consistently out-perform men when it comes to discerning scents.

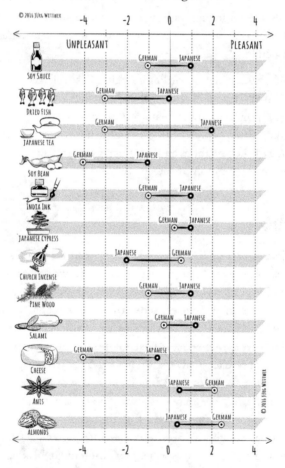

Smelling results from basic brain functions, and emotion plays a huge role in associating smells with items and memories. Hence, perfume makers and marketing specialists play on consumer emotions to attract them to certain fragrances. Fragrances can also be aphrodisiacs, arousing sexual desire, they can create a positive mood, and experiments even show that when a work environment is pleasantly fragranced, productivity increases. The strong association between emotion and scent may induce vivid memories connected with daily life. This is because the olfactory receptors in the nose are directly connected to the limbic system, the most ancient and primitive part of the brain and the brain's seat of emotion. Smell sensations are then relayed to the cortex, where cognitive recognition occurs, only after the deepest part of our brains have been stimulated. By the time we correctly identify a particular scent – for example, "rotten fruit" or the perfume of teenage love – , the scent has already activated the limbic system, triggering more deep-seated emotional responses.

According to "The Smell Report" by Kate Fox, director of the Social Issues Research Center, smell is probably the most undervalued of the senses in Western culture. But this was not always the case. The current undervaluation of smell is a result of a revaluation of senses by philosophers and scientists of the 18th and 19th century. The intellectual elite of this period decreed eye-sight to be the superior and most important sense. Sight was considered a civilized sense, one based on reason, while the sense of smell was deemed to be of a considerably lower order, "a primitive, brutish ability associated with savagery and even madness."

The emotional potency of smell, due to the physiological properties described above, was, for a long time, believed to threaten the rational detachment of modern scientific thinking; hence its demotion. This demotion of smell has had a lasting effect on academic research, resulting in a lesser knowledge about our sense of smell than we have about more "civilized" senses, like vision or hearing. This lack of knowledge is also what spurred Andreas Keller to conduct his research. For decades, experts had claimed that people were capable of detecting only 10,000 different odors. This number comes from a discredited early 20th century theory, which asserted that there are four primary smells, similar to the concept of primary colors. "And I found that so interesting and ridiculous," Keller said, "that I thought it would be time to do an experiment and test how many odors there really are."

The indifference to smell in Western culture is reflected in our language: colloquial terms for "nose," for example, are almost all derogatory or, at the very least, disrespectful, and large or distinctive noses are considered ugly. On the other hand, all other senses have positive associations in everyday language. We may speak of a person as "visionary," "keen-eyed," "having a good ear," etc. Equivalent terms for our olfactory organ are nonexistent.

However, the sense of smell is appreciated to varying degrees in other cultures around the world; in some, it is even the most esteemed of all the senses. For the Ongee of the Andaman Islands, the universe and everything in it is defined by smell. Their calendar is constructed around the scents of flowers which blossom at different times of the year. Each season is named after a particular odor. Personal identity is also defined by smell in this culture. To refer to oneself, one touches the tip of one's nose, a gesture meaning both "me" and "my odor." When greeting someone, the Ongee do not ask, "How are you?" but, "Konyune onorange-tanka?" This means, "How is your nose?"

The Bororo of Brazil and the Serer Ndut of Senegal also associate personal identity with smell. For the Bororo, body odor is related to the life force of a person, while the Ndut believe that each individual is animated by two different scent-defined forces. One is physical, associated with the body, the other is spiritual. This is how the Ndut can determine which ancestor has been reincarnated in a child, by recognizing the similarity of the child's scent to that of the deceased person. In the Batek Negrito tribes of the Malay Peninsula, sexual intercourse between people of similar odor is prohibited. Even sitting too closely to one another for too long is considered dangerous.

In India, the traditional greeting of affection, equivalent to that of a Western hug or kiss, is to smell someone's head. An ancient Indian text declares, "I will smell thee on the head, that is the greatest sign of tender love."

The differences in the role and importance of the smell-sense between cultures will also strongly influence scent preferences. If you fly to Africa and visit a local market, the first thing impressed upon you are the scents. All unfamiliar. All very strong. Western notions of pleasing fragrances are by no means universal. In Western cultures any natural body odor is considered bad. And in Africa, I was told that white people smell like dead people, which we may rightly assume is not a pleasant smell.

Another difference in smell preference is related to urine. To the cattle-raising Dassanetch of Ethiopia, no scent is more beautiful than the odor of cows. The association of this scent with social status and fertility is so strong that men wash their hands in cattle urine and smear their bodies with manure.

For the Dogon in Mali, the scent of onion is by far the most alluring fragrance for a young man or woman. They rub fried onion all over their bodies for perfume. And while Western men use deodorants to hide any potential natural body odor, Arab men effusively use perfumes, such as rose and aloewood behind their ears, on their nostrils, in their beards and in the palms of their hands.

Even within the more familiar first-world cultures, we may find significant differences in the range of preferred fragrances. Americans generally like the smell of wintergreen, whereas the British do not. The Germans like the smell of marzipan, whereas the Japanese believe marzipan smells like oil or bee's wax.

Japanese researcher, Saho Ayabe-Kanamura, conducted an extensive study, published in 1998, about the differences in perception of everyday odors between Germans and the Japanese. Some of the results of this study are detailed in the chart above. One of the conclusions drawn was that people tended to rate odors of food which they consider to be edible as preferred fragrances. That comes as no surprise, as what we eat is usually a deeply acquired part of primary socialization. To illustrate this, I once dined at a fine French restaurant with an American senior manager. We wanted to get acquainted with French dining culture, so we ordered some escargot for an appetizer. When I asked him how the dish tasted, he answered: "For you, these are escargot, for me they will stay what they have always been: slimy snails." For the American, they have always been slimy snails, due to his culture's primary socialization.

Family, Sexuality and Love

I will go on in this cultural journey with the differences regarding family, sexuality and love. These subjects are quite thoroughly researched within the science of anthropology, the very origin of all cross cultural studies. Anthropology is the study of humankind in the past and present. It is a broad field of study, encompassing such diverse sciences as archaeology, ethnology and linguistics. Discussing concepts of family and sexual mores may not be important in a corporate context. Nevertheless, I'll spend some time upon these subjects for two reasons:

1. Family structures are weaved into the social fabric of all cultures, and if you want to understand and integrate into a society, you need to understand the values and norms relating to family.

2. Sexual norms are socialized very early and often enforced with social and religious taboo. Consequently, our own cultural mores are likely to clash most with sexual norms, resulting in the strongest emotional reactions. It's important to remember that what is unfamiliar is not necessarily unnatural.

In the Western world, the concept of an ideal family is fairly straight-forward: a man, a woman, preferably married, and children, all living in the same household. Sexual commitment between the parents should involve exclusivity. In recent years, this ideal concept of the nuclear family has been called into question. As divorce becomes more common, we see the emergence of so-called patchwork families, where the children do not necessarily live under the same roof as both of their biological parents. They may even alternate households every other weekend and integrate into another family for a couple of days. In their second family, they may eat at the table with the children of their stepmother or their stepfather. Even the traditional concept of the nuclear family's parental composition being that of a man and a woman is subject to emotional and political debate. In many Western countries, homosexual couples have been lawfully permitted the right to marry and, moreover, to adopt children. The modern concept of family is changing rapidly...or maybe this concept is not so modern after all. As we will see, patchwork families have long existed in traditional societies, as have families with same-sex parents. Furthermore, the Western concept of sexual exclusivity between the parents of a core family is not at all a universal concept.

One of the most famous examples of what we might call today "alternative" life styles can be found amongst the Inuit and Aleut people living in the northern areas of Greenland and Alaska. Arthur J. Rubel published a summary of various findings in the anthropological papers of the University of Alaska in 1961: "Among the Komallik Eskimo, wives are exchanged but for seldom more than one night at a time. (…) Among the Eskimo around the Bering Strait, it is a common custom for two men living in different villages to agree to become bond-fellows or brothers by adoption. Having made this arrangement, whenever one of the two men goes to the other's village he is received as the bond brother's guest and is given the use of his host's bed with his wife during his stay. (…) On St. Lawrence Island, this wife-exchange pattern was always formally thought a special ceremony which involved various aspects of the religious system. This ceremony, called the kaezivas, implicated the closest kinsmen and their wives. (…) On the last day of the ceremony, all the men and women who had danced together had sexual relations with each other." The article includes many other examples from various field researches, the oldest dating back to 1888.

It's important to note that one must be careful in interpreting anthropological studies. Often they've been written through the lens of Western mores, thus sexual habits may be exaggerated. The lending of wives to perfect strangers did occur, but the behavior has since been proven not to be as widespread a custom as it was presented. The spouse exchange often had a purpose or was directly associated with religious rituals. For instance, if a Labrador man wished to pass a season fishing for salmon, and another man wished to spend the season hunting game, but the wife of the former was more adept at cleaning hides than at the preparation of fish, then the fish specialist would spend the season with the fisherman, and the fisherman's wife with the hunter. More recent research actually established that without some form of extra-marital relationships, the genetic pool in these remote villages would not have been sufficiently renewed.

Of course the mores of our modern world are far and away from the mores and habits of traditional societies still surviving on hunting and gathering. However, some modern societies' concept of family might not correlate with the Judeo-Christian values of the Western world. In Japan, marriage is based far more on economic advantage than in Western society, for instance. For those shocked by this, remember that until the beginning of the twentieth century, it was considered normal to marry in Europe according to which man or woman would ensure the survival of the farm. By Confucius custom, love comes secondary to economic advantage. In Japan the wife is in charge of the household, including the handling of finances. The husband's responsibility is to bring home the money. Until recently, the custom of visiting a Geisha was generally acceptable. These Japanese female entertainers would perform music, songs, dances and also sensual services. Men were not bound by the constraints of remaining faithful to their wives, as long as the sexual relations were with a Geisha. A long-term relationship with a non-professional concubine would not have been permissible, as it would have jeopardized the husband's main task: providing a steady stream of financial income. The result of this conception of marriage leads to a much lower divorce rate in Japan; only half that of America's. Only 2% percent of Japanese women and 8% of Japanese men acknowledge guilt when having an affair, compared to 25% in the

Western world. According to the study, 84% of Japanese women even believe that affairs positively impact their marriage.

Now, what happens if a husband in Japan loses his job? In the Western conceptualization of a loving relationship, the wife should stand by her man. She should comfort him, and together they will try to overcome the crisis. In the stereotypical Japanese marriage, the man is hit triply by disaster. He loses his job and his social standing, and he may also lose his wife. A Japanese man would not expect support. He is no longer able to fulfill the task for which she married him. In this context and considering how powerfully Japanese feel shame when they lose honor, it may come as no surprise that many men who lose their jobs resort to suicide. This also explains the reluctance of Japanese companies to fire staff. In order not to shame employees, they'd rather keep their workforce on the pay roll than to get rid of ineffective staff. Workers who aren't performing may receive smaller offices, sometimes offices without windows or air-conditioning, but they'll still have a job.

In neighboring China, marital prospects are taken seriously by parents. In Shanghai, parents present the advantages of their daughter or son on a piece of cardboard in what is called the "marriage market" in the city's People Park. The selling points may read "Born in the year of the dog/171cm/12.000 Yuan salary" or "Own apartment/76sqm/188cm." Clearly the currency for what we in the Western world would consider a "successful" relationship is love; but in China, it's not love but income, home ownership and the horoscope (as being born in the right year is essential for happiness). A Chinese mother expressed it this way: "First you build your life, and only then also your love."

In the West, love belongs to life. Love is needed to construct a happy life. Wlada Kolosowa, a journalist for the German Magazine, *Spiegel*, writes "American love is French kissing, laughing and occasionally some emotional disputes. Chinese love is rather a team sport somehow, as you would get a life-long roommate to help you raise your children. In the Western world, love is a matter between two individuals; in China it is a union between two families".[9]

In his article on "Partnership and wife-exchange among the Eskimo and Aleut of northern North America," Arthur J. Rubel references anthropologist, Nelson Edward, from the Bureau of American Ethnology, who wrote in 1896: "When the visit is returned the same favor (i.e. the wife exchange) is extended to the other, consequently neither family knows who is the father of the children... but the children know each other by a special term and the two men also separate their relationship and mark it with a unique term." This is an entirely different concept of family when compared to our Western nuclear family. The children do not know who their biological father is and, in fact, the information is actually of no importance to them.

Many other societies have similar familial structures. In the Mosuo society in southwest China, paternity is so low and inconsequential that men help raise their sister's children as their own. The Mosuo are a matrilineal, agricultural people, passing their property and family name from mothers to daughters. So the household revolves around the women. A Mosuo girl has complete control over who steps through her private door. The only strict rule is that her guest must be gone by sunrise. This model has some advantages for survival. The children can roam at will and visit house to house and village to village without fear for their safety. Every adult is responsible for every child, and every child, in turn, is respectful towards every adult. If you presume this type of society is rare, Christopher Ryan and Cacilda Jetha in their award-winning book, *Sex at Dawn*, compiled a list of traditional societies in South America with alternative paternity models: the Aché, the Araweté, the Bari, the Canela, the Cashinahua, the Curripaco, the Ese Eja, the Kayapo, the Kulina, the Matis, the Mehinaku, the Piaroa, the Priaha, the Secoya, the Siona, the Warao, the Yanomami and the Ye'kwana. All societies from Venezuela to Bolivia.

Obviously these societies have values and social norms which are drastically different than those of Western cultures. In business, we most likely will never directly deal or negotiate contracts with remote populations whose concepts of values and norms diverge so much from our own. Nevertheless, it is important to realize that values and norms that are fundamentally different from what we've experienced do exist in the world, and there isn't a correct or superior way of living; there are only different ways of living. As we have seen, most cultural values and norms serve a purpose – be it to promote genetic diversity or to ensure the safety of children, etc.

Additionally, as mentioned, the modern patchwork family in Western cultures is evolving. As the renowned anthropologist, Marvin Harris, wrote, "In view of the frequent occurrence of modern domestic groups that do not consist of, or contain, an exclusive pair-bonded father and mother, I cannot see why anyone should insist that our ancestors were reared in monogamous nuclear families and that pair-bonding is more natural than other arrangements."[10]

Anthropologists also make a distinction between two-generation families and extended-generation families. Most Western modern societies live in two-generation families. The nucleus consists of two generations: the mother, the father and their children. The one-parent family, divorced or unmarried parents are also two-generation families. When our politicians defend family values, the "family" is always relegated to this two-generation concept.

On the other hand, extended families consist of at least three generations: the grandparents on both sides, the mother, the father and their children, the aunts, the siblings, cousins, nieces, nephews and other kin of the wife and husband. This extended concept of family is actually the prevalent form for a majority of the people on earth. It ensures a larger social cohesion, a certainty of being cared for in old age, an interconnected community to better ensure sharing and survival. Later in this book, we'll discuss the direct link between the prevalent definition of "family" in societies and the underlining cultural values that determine it. But for now, you can assume that individualism is typical for two-generation societies, while extended families build on collectivist values.

Language, as well, will reflect the importance of larger families to a culture. For instance, in Western culture, knowing what blood-line your cousin is from is not that important. The Yanomani would consider our language poor in this regard, as the word "cousin" lumps together no less than four distinct relatives: amiwa, the daughter of a paternal uncle or a maternal aunt, eiwa, the son of a paternal uncle or a maternal aunt, suwabiya, the daughter of a maternal uncle or a paternal aunt, and soriwa, the son of a maternal uncle or a paternal aunt. There are even more complex systems of familial vocabulary, such as the "Crow system," as it's known to anthropologists. In this system, the same word is applied to both one's father and certain cousins. This vocabulary of differentiating relatives is often internally logic, but nevertheless, the structure diverges radically from culture to culture.

Let's return to the Chinese Mosuo people. In an example of cultural intolerance, their traditional lifestyle has since been destroyed. When the Chinese established full control of the southwest in 1956, government officials began making annual visits to the Mosuo to "convince" them to adopt "normal" marital customs. These officials even arrived one year with a portable generator and a film. In the film, actors were dressed as Mosuo, ill in the final stages of syphilis. The audience response was not what the Chinese officials expected: their makeshift cinema was burned to the ground. But they didn't give up. These officials ambushed men on the way to their lover's houses, dragged couples out of their beds and exposed them naked to their own relatives' eyes, a strong taboo in Mosuo culture. When even these severe tactics failed to alter traditional lifestyles and concepts of "decency," the Chinese cut off essential deliveries of seed grain and children's clothing. Finally, starved into submission, many Mosuo agreed to participate in government-sponsored marriage ceremonies. During the writing of this book, I met a women from southern China, and she knew of the Mosuo people. According to her, though they've changed their way of living in the cities, the old ways still prevail in the countryside.

Management and Leadership

Leading globally is a complex reality, and different cultures anticipate different attitudes for their leadership and constructs for their hierarchies, though management trainings do not yet broadly reflect this. All business administration curriculums teach the Maslow "hierarchy of need" as a model for human motivation. In a 1943 paper, the researcher, Abraham Maslow, categorized human needs in a pyramid. The lower levels comprise physiological needs, such as food, shelter and safety. Once these basic needs are satisfied, the human need to love, to feel esteem and to be self-fulfilled follow. "What a man can be, he must be," Maslow once said.[11] Most top Western managers implicitly use this simple model as incentive to motivate their teams. In doing so, the highest possible motivation – self-fulfillment – logically manifests in personal career development and power.

Though this model may seem intuitive to a Western mind, it hasn't stood the test of cross cultural validity. Studies have found that in certain countries, like Greece or Japan, security needs motivate employees more than the need for self-actualization. Employees of these countries often consider life-long job security as more important than being challenged on the job or climbing the career ladder. In countries like Norway, Sweden or Denmark, where the emphasis is placed on quality of life, social needs are also a stronger motivator in the workplace than building a career. Hofstede notes: "My interpretation is that this tells us more about Maslow than about the other countries' managers. Maslow categorized and ordered his human needs according to the U.S. middle-class culture pattern in which he was embedded himself – he could not have done otherwise."[12] Additionally, the second most widespread motivation theory – Herzberg's two-factor theory, which states that satisfaction and dissatisfaction in one's job are not dependent on each other – didn't withstand cross cultural tests either and can only be applied to Western culture, for which it was invented.[13]

So to what extent do cultural differences influence management styles? In 1991, Robert J. House, professor at the Wharton School of the University of Pennsylvania was asking himself this very question. At that time, a substantial amount of research had been published on the importance of charismatic leadership. House read studies on the topic from India, Singapore, the US and the

Netherlands, and he wondered if the behaviors of charismatic leaders were indeed universally favored and effective. And, thus, GLOBE was born.

GLOBE stands for Global Leadership and Organizational Behavior Effectiveness. It's become one of the premier cross cultural research programs of all time. In the ten years that followed, 170 investigators from 59 countries processed information from interviews and focus groups with 17,300 managers from 951 organizations for this project. What they discovered about a culture's influence on management was astonishing. The results of this massive research clearly indicated that organizational cultures reflect their societal cultures.[14]

Leadership was defined as the ability to motivate, influence and enable employees to contribute to the objectives of the company. The GLOBE project identified six leadership styles:

- Charismatic/Value-based: a broadly defined leadership style based upon the ability to inspire, motivate and expect high performance outcomes from others, grounded in firmly held core values.
- Team-oriented: a leadership style emphasizing effective team-building and the implementation of a common purpose or goal among team members.
- Participative: a leadership dimension reflecting the degree to which managers involve others in making and implementing decisions.
- Human-oriented: a leadership style promoting supportive and considerate leadership, including compassion, generosity, modesty and sensitivity to other people.
- Autonomous: a leadership style which has not previously appeared in business literature and refers to independent and individualistic leadership.
- Self-protective: also a new procedural dimension, focusing on ensuring safety and security of the individual or group member, with an emphasis on status consciousness and face saving.

The study found that a charismatic/value-based leader is indeed universally desirable. How could one not like a visionary, self-sacrificing leader who inspires and is performance-oriented? But the other styles were often culturally contingent. For instance, to be ambitious is "good" in some cultures and "bad" in others, and the results reflected that. Overall, the charismatic/value-based leader is particularly appreciated in Anglo-Saxon countries, such as the US, the UK and Australia, while this was the least favored type in the Middle East. Team-orientation is highly favored in Latin America, while human-orientation is high in South Asia and low in Nordic Europe. The autonomous leadership style is the highest in Eastern Europe, which is reflected in the cultural preference for strong political leaders, while self-protective leadership styles are highest in South Asia and the Middle East.

CULTURAL CLUSTERS AND DESIRED LEADERSHIP BEHAVIORS

REGION	RELATIVE IMPORTANCE (IN DESCCENDING ORDER)*					
EASTERN EUROPE	⬤ AL	✖ SPL	👑 CVBL	♣ TOL	👤 HOL	▼ PL
LATIN AMERICA	👑 CVBL	♣ TOL	✖ SPL	▼ PL	👤 HOL	⬤ AL
LATIN EUROPE	👑 CVBL	♣ TOL	▼ PL	✖ SPL	👤 HOL	⬤ AL
CONFUCIAN ASIA	✖ SPL	♣ TOL	👤 HOL	👑 CVBL	⬤ AL	▼ PL
NORDIC EUROPE	👑 CVBL	▼ PL	♣ TOL	⬤ AL	👤 HOL	✖ SPL
ANGLO	👑 CVBL	▼ PL	👤 HOL	♣ TOL	⬤ AL	✖ SPL
SUB-SAHARAN AFRICA	👤 HOL	👑 CVBL	♣ TOL	▼ PL	✖ SPL	⬤ AL
SOUTHERN ASIA	✖ SPL	👑 CVBL	👤 HOL	♣ TOL	⬤ AL	▼ PL
GERMANIC EUROPE	⬤ AL	👑 CVBL	▼ PL	👤 HOL	♣ TOL	✖ SPL
MIDDLE EAST	✖ SPL	👤 HOL	⬤ AL	👑 CVBL	♣ TOL	▼ PL

* SIX GLOBAL LEADERSHIP BEHAVIORS:

👑 CVBL	CHARISMATIC/VALUE-BASED LEADERSHIP	👤 HOL	HUMAINE-ORIENTED LEADERSHIP
♣ TOL	TEAM-ORIENTED LEADERSHIP	⬤ AL	AUTONOMOS LEADERSHIP
▼ PL	PARTICIPATE LEADERSHIP	✖ SPL	SELF-PROTECTIVE LEADERSHIP

Western cultures and the Middle East diverge the most in leadership style preferences. Self-protective leadership is viewed as less problematic in the Middle East than in other parts of the world, and charismatic/value-based or team-oriented leaderships were not favored as much there as in other regions. Additionally, the research discovered a local cluster of desirable attributes of leadership in the Middle East, which included family-orientation, humility and faithfulness. This calls into question whether these cultures may lose their inherent sense of warm hospitality and empathy in the export of Western management styles.

Because of the stark differences in desirable leadership styles the authors of GLOBE research also note that mergers and acquisitions between countries from Europe and the Middle East may be the most problematic.

Overall, the GLOBE project provides powerful insight into how cultures around the world perceive leadership and what expectations they have of global leaders, thus offering an outline for the favored leadership patterns in every culture. By knowing the cultural blueprint of leadership, an international manager can learn and apply different tactics accordingly. But more importantly, this research empirically proved there are different leadership expectations in cultures around the world. This means that, as an international manager, the management style you've learned at university may not be applicable outside of your country. What you expect from your boss may not be what employees from a different culture expect from you.

What we learned in this chapter:

- One of the biggest dangers in cross cultural management is to assume sameness.

- The seeming acuity of senses based on vocabulary and descriptions is not determined by genetics or cultural superiority or inferiority, but rather on cultural values and norms.

- What is unfamiliar is not necessarily unnatural.

5. Building Blocks of Culture

In the Mossi tribe of Burkina Faso, a village chief has the power of life and death. A visit to the chief is mandatory for many administrative tasks, such as matrimony, the purchasing of land or any legal dispute. The Mossi are also known for fatal poisons. The visiting ceremonial at the chief's house begins with a drink from a large wooden cup, which is then passed from one person to the other. Observe the chief. If he puts his thumb in the water after having taken some sips and passes the cup to you, then he may have decided to poison you. Only a Westerner would refuse to drink.

The Mossi operate on a radically different wavelength than we do. One cannot quite grasp their mentality and worldview unless he suspends some of his own deepest assumptions about society and human nature. What are the values behind such behavior? That is the question we will try to answer in this chapter.

Fortunately, business is seldom about life and death. During my stay in Africa, I've visited many traditional chiefs and spent hours waiting in the hot sun. Most of them were enjoyable encounters; sometimes a special brand of friendship even followed. The reality of interacting with the average Mossi chief was far away from the extreme (yet, real) situation described above. While some cultural behaviors are completely incomprehensible to those of another culture, we are still able to communicate relatively reasonably. We all belong to the human race, and what binds us together is far stronger than what separates us.

But sometimes a general understanding of the "other" is not sufficient. For instance, when negotiating a contract or managing a diverse staff, we may find ourselves in a situation where cultural values collide. In these cases, a good grasp on cultural differences and how to manage them is essential. It is, therefore, useful to bring some form of order into this wide field.

At the forefront of systematic research on cultural differences is a Dutch researcher, Geert Hofstede. He grew up and studied in the Netherlands, after which he entered the military. Nothing about his early career would have led anyone to believe that he would become one of the most influential researchers in the field of international cultural differences. In the late sixties, he joined IBM as the management trainer and manager of staff research. In this function, he became the driving force behind the creation of IBM's International Employee Opinion Research Program. Over a period of six years, he and his colleagues collected and analyzed more than 116,000 survey questionnaires, completed by IBM employees in 72 countries around the world. The questionnaire contained 183 questions about the work environment, asking employees to choose which option was the most important to them amongst several available options. For instance, one question might ask which was most important to the employee: "to have a job which leaves you sufficient time for your personal or family life," "to have challenging work to do – work from which you can gain a personal sense of accomplishment," or "to have considerable freedom to adapt your own approach to the job." His department was not involved in investigating culture at the time. They didn't even use the word "culture." But the data Hofstede and his team collected resulted in patterns of varying behavior and opinion from those of different cultural backgrounds. At the time, the team drew no conclusions from the data.

Hofstede went on sabbatical from IBM then left to teach at the IMD in Lausanne, Switzerland. Outside his usual line of work and engaged in academia, he had time to consider and analyze the findings of the IBM research. He realized the different themes of behavior discovered in the survey could only be accounted for by nationality.

To test his theory, he began questioning people outside IBM from various countries. The same cultural differences continued to emerge. It took a while for Hofstede to discover the immense scientific value of this research. Very few people were interested in cultural diversity from a business standpoint at that time. This is because, in the seventies and early eighties, the US was the dominant and unchallenged economic power. Cultural sensitivity was not necessary for economic success, at least not from the perspective of the thriving US economy; nor was the issue of cultural sensitivity any more significant in Europe. As Hofstede recounts: "In the 1970s I was living in Brussels when I started developing my ideas of culture and I approached the European Commission about this, but found myself initially directed to an official who was responsible for museums! Such was their idea of culture!"

The early 1980s saw the publication of Tom Peters and Robert H. Waterman's famous book, *In Search of Excellence*, and various other books about the "Japanese miracle." The Japanese had begun to out-perform the Americans, and it became clear that differences in culture perhaps influenced this upset. For the first time, culture became an important economic concept and everyone, from those specializing in social sciences to CEOs of big corporations, strove to understand the phenomenon. While many superficial books were published on the subject, Hofstede provided the first scientifically-founded analysis on cultural differences and their consequences for the work place.[15] His book, *Culture's Consequences*, published for the first time in 1980, had been cited over 2000 times by the end of the century, and no empirical work is more influential in the field of culture and psychology.[16] In this way, IBM was not only instrumental in the global presence of the personal computer, but also in the first truly global cultural analysis and the subsequent focus on its significance in every stratosphere of the business world.

In his original work, Hofstede discovered four cultural dimensions by which nations differ. Each dimension represents a value or a set of values on a scale from one extreme to the other. Between these two poles, each nation's values can be positioned according to the survey done by the nation's populous. Hofstede identified, for instance, the dimension of "Uncertainty Avoidance." This is the extent to which a culture programs its members to feel either comfortable or uncomfortable in certain situations. Such situations may be unknown, surprising or different from the norm. Once a the populous was surveyed, the question of whether or not and to what extent these situations produce stress are statistically answered. A culture that avoids uncertainty will emphasize an adherence to rules, laws and rituals, the last of which are an ancient device for managing stress. In other words, does a culture favor the innovators and the risk-taking entrepreneurs, or does the culture fear change and maintain tradition?

Hofstede discovered this dimension of uncertainty avoidance while examining the responses to the survey questions about work-related stress. One of these questions was, "How often do you feel nervous or tense at work?" with answers ranging from, "I always feel this way," to, "I never feel this way." The results of this question correlated with the results for a question about the importance of company rules. This question prompted whether or not company rules should be broken if doing so was in the company's best interest. Employees were further asked about their intentions to stay with the company in the long-term. The results of these questions were intriguing.

On one poll, Hofstede found that, when faced with new situations, some cultures were not affected by stress, and these cultures tended to like change. On the other end of the spectrum, some cultures avoided stress, relied on laws, bureaucracy and rituals, and held onto the past, keeping tradition alive and avoiding change. Latin American cultures are, for instance, considered "uncertainty avoiding" cultures. They often surround themselves with a protective layer of rules and procedures.

Robert Kaplan, an American journalist, provides a grim example in how bureaucracy and law can provide certainty in an uncertain environment. In his excellent book, *The Ends of the Earth*, he describes his experience in Rwanda. When he arrived at the Rwandan border with plans to report on the civil war there, he presented his passport to the control station, which was a small shack that sat in the middle of a scene from hell. Outside the shack, people were stacking human body parts in large piles for incineration. Inside the shack, functionaries examined every jot and title of Kaplan's visa to make sure he could enter. Kaplan marveled that Rwandans would care about such trivialities when their world was falling apart. But it was precisely because their world was falling apart that they cared. Bureaucratic procedure was the only vestige of predictability in a life reduced to horror and chaos.[17]

With more research, Hofstede increased the number of dimensions in culture from four to five. Many other researchers added even further dimensions. Let's take a look at some of these:

- Rule-based vs. relationship-based cultures: Is individual behavior governed by relationships or by rules and laws?

- High-power distance vs. low-power distance cultures (from Hofstede): Do subordinates accept their subservient position or is there a preference for all to have the same hierarchical position?

- Collectivist vs. individualist cultures (from Hofstede): Is individual loyalty primarily to the family or to oneself?

- Polychronic vs. monochronic cultures: What is the concept of time? Do people prefer to structure their schedule and perform one task at a time, or are they comfortable multi-tasking?

- High context vs. low context cultures: Is information transmitted explicitly or implicitly through cultural norms?

- Polite vs. rude cultures: Is the individual concerned with the feelings of others or does justice take precedence over courtesy?

- Shame-based vs. guilt-based cultures: Is the individual primarily motivated by the approval or disapproval of others, or is he, to a large extent, motivated by an internalized conscience?

- "Humor as amusement" vs. "humor as a joke": Do people find humor in the twists and turns of everyday life or do they find humor in irony and in the violation of rules and rationality?

- Masculine vs. feminine cultures (from Hofstede): Does the culture emphasize aggression and competition or nurturing and cooperation?

- Uncertainty avoidance vs. uncertainty tolerance cultures (from Hofstede): Does the individual prefer a stable environment and show a reluctance to risk-taking, or does the culture favor individuals with the ability to deal with unpredictable environments and the willingness to take risks?

- Internal vs. external locus of control: Do the individuals of a culture believe that they are in charge of their own lives or does fate dictate life for each individual?

- Apollonian vs. Dionysian cultures: Does the individual find security in equanimity and a well-ordered lifestyle or does he look for intense experiences?

- Long-term vs. short-term oriented cultures (from Hofstede): Does the culture program its members to accept delayed gratification of their material, social and emotional needs or must the gratification be instant?[18]

- Affective vs. neutral cultures: In relationships with others, do individuals show their emotions (in which case, do they expect an emotional return?), or are they neutral, subduing and controlling their emotions?[19]

This list in not exhaustive, and as the research on cross cultural management continues, inevitably we will find more ways to slice, cut and measure the values of a culture. Whatever their practical relevance, these building blocks of culture provide significant data about the differences in values from society to society. All of these dimensions have been measured and tested in several countries, though none on the broad scale of more than fifty countries measured by Hofstede. We'll now look deeper at four of these building blocks of culture.

How important am I?

In his book, *Figuring Foreigners Out*, Craig Storti asks the reader to complete a small exercise. A group of people is given an important project to work on, which involves intensive teamwork and cooperation. But as we've all experienced in our own lives, the time investment and effort of each teammate often varies considerably. Claudio works the most. He actually does 50% of the total, or half of the job, by himself. Paul and Lisa do some work, around 20% each. Finally, John is essentially partying during that time, and his contribution to the success of the project might be something like 10%, if that. The project is a success and the group is awarded a $20,000 cash prize. Now here's the big question: how would *you* split the award?

	CONTRIBUTION TO THE PROJECT	INDIVIDUALISTIC CULTURE	COLLECTIVIST CULTURE
PAUL	10%	5'000	5'000
LISA	20%	2'500	5'000
CLAUDIO	50%	7'500	5'000
YOU	20%	5'000	5'000

Typically, someone from an individualist culture would answer: "Split the award according to the contribution of the individuals. Paul should receive the biggest share, and John the smallest." This mentality is prevalent in many Western cultures, because it corresponds to what we believe is fair. Rewards should be directly commensurate with one's level of effort. On the other hand, someone from a collectivist culture would distribute the award differently: "We have all done this together. We are only strong as a unit. So dividing the spoils evenly, increasing the well-being of everyone in the group equally, is the fairest way to distribute the award."[20]

The social psychologist, Harry Triandis, argued that "perhaps the most important dimension of cultural difference in social behavior, across the diverse cultures of the world, is the relative emphasis on individualism versus collectivism."[21] The ideals of individualism versus collectivism are related to how individuals fundamentally live their social lives; whether they, on a deep level, think more as an individual or collectively as members of a group. Collectivist versus individualist thinking was one of the dimensions discovered by Hofstede in his aforementioned research: "Some animals, such as wolves, are gregarious; others, such as tigers, are solitary. The human species should no doubt be classified with the gregarious animals, but different human societies show gregariousness to different degrees. Here again then, we have a fundamental dimension on which societies differ: the relationship between the individual and the collectivity."[22]

Hofstede defines this dimension of culture in this way: "Individualism pertains to societies in which the ties between the individuals are loose: everyone is expected to look after himself and his or her immediate family. Collectivism as its opposite pertains to societies in which people from birth onwards are integrated into strong, cohesive ungroups, which throughout people's lifetime continue to protect them in exchange for unquestioning loyalty."

In an individualist society – often those of Western countries (the United States and western Europe, in particular) – the smallest unit of survival is usually the individual. The Commission of National Goals reported to President Eisenhower that the possibility of individual self-realization was the central goal of American civilization.[23] In this oft self-serving culture, people primarily identify with themselves, and their own needs are generally satisfied before those of the group. When dreaming the American dream, one wishes for one's own economic success and that of one's immediate family; not often does the dream extend to the success of one's third cousins.

Individualistic societies emphasize values such as independence, self-reliance and personal freedom. For any person joining an American company, the strong individualistic culture will be immediately visible and felt. Incentives and rewards for individual employee performance are common. In many company lobbies, photos for the "employee of the month" or bulletins recognizing individual achievement are displayed. When working in the US, myself, I started to appreciate the motivational effectiveness of such measures. After a couple of years, my assignment ended, and I returned to Switzerland. Always eager to apply successful business concepts, I introduced an "employee of the month" award at the Swiss company I managed at the time. The reaction of the staff was immediate and overwhelmingly negative. They told me that this is "typically American," that in Switzerland it's not good to single out specific persons, and that to be successful, we must work together. Though on one hand, "employee of the month" is viewed as a far too individualistic reward by the Swiss, they do allow for achievement-based promotion and pay-for-performance, because these assume that individuals seek to be distinguished within their group and that their colleagues approve of this.

Collectivistic cultural management is generally very different than individualist cultural management. Collectivistic cultures place a higher value in belonging to a family, a society or even a company than they do on the individual self. What is best for the group is best for oneself, and the group's overall well-being is far more important than one's own personal ambitions or goals. Therefore, one would sacrifice his own career or financial benefits for the sake of the group's. The principle is not simply that loyalty to the group entitles one to loyalty from the group; loyalty to the group is loyalty to oneself. Neglecting group members is equivalent to neglecting parts of one's body.

A manager in a collectivist culture would assume that if individuals are continuously taking care of their fellow human beings, the quality of life will improve for everyone, even if it obstructs individual freedom and individual development. Actually, this exact statement has been put to the test in an international survey. 70% of managers in Egypt, 59% of managers in China and 61% of managers in Japan agree with this statement, but only 31% of US managers agree.[24]

In collectivistic cultures, the primary group is usually the family, though, as previously mentioned, the concept of "family" differs between cultures as well. What some might consider "family" may diverge substantially from the two-generation core assumed by the Western world. In other cultures, the family may extend to a whole clan or village. Some indication for this is in the use of language. English uses one word for "uncle," while in a collectivist culture, the mother's brother often is termed differently than the father's brother, as specific terms distinguish all the roles in a group. One's identity is, in large part, a function of the membership and the role in the group. The survival and success of the group ensures the well-being of the individual, so by considering the needs and feelings of others, a person ensures his own well-being. Obviously, in this environment, harmony is highly valued, as is the interdependence of group members. All lives depend on each other, and the group only survives together, so children are socialized in groups to become interdependent. They work together and share with other members of the group, instead of being called out for their individual achievement. There is relatively little psychological or emotional distance between group members. For this reason, arranged marriages are often common or acceptable in a collectivist culture, as the family plays a major role in deciding who joins the group.

Knowing this theoretical background, we now also better understand the cultural clash between the English teacher and the Tunisian family presented at the beginning of the book. For Ahmed and his parents, it was perfectly acceptable, if not expected, that Ahmed help Khalid. The well-being of the group is far more important than a single individual's success. A dialogue (see figure below) between the teacher and the pupil demonstrates what could have happened, as well as the valid assumptions made on both sides. The teacher is worried that Khalid is setting himself up for failure; if he doesn't learn his lessons on his own, he may not be fit for the future. She is convinced that, ultimately, each of us has only ourselves to rely on; therefore, in helping Khalid, Ahmed is making him interdependent, which would significantly reduce his chances of success in society...or at least in the type of individualist society for which Ann is accustomed.

DIALOGUE	INTERPRETATION
ANN: KHALID WAS LOOKING AT YOUR PAPER.	ANN DISCOVERS THAT AHMED AND KHALID WERE CHEATING.
AHMED: HE WAS?	AHMED DOESN'T UNDERSTAND THE CONCERN, AS HE WAS HELPING HIS FRIEND.
ANN: YES. HE COPIED SOME OF YOUR ANSWERS.	ANN INSISTS ON HER VISION OF THE FACTS.
AHMED: PERHAPS HE DIDN'T KNOW THE ANSWERS.	AHMED IS EMBARRASSED, AS ANN IMPLIES THAT KHALID WAS DOING POORLY AT THE TEST. AVOIDING SHAME – ESPECIALLY PUBLIC EMBARRASSMENT – IS A PARAMOUNT ARAB VALUE.
ANN: I'M SURE HE DIDN'T.	ANN IS WORRIED THAT KHALID MAY NOT BE FIT FOR THE FUTURE, IF HE DOESN'T LEARN HIS LESSONS. ULTIMATELY EACH OF US HAS ONLY OUR OWN SELF TO RELY ON.
AHMED: THEN IT'S LUCKY HE WAS SITTING NEXT TO ME.	AHMED IS RELIEVED THAT HE WAS RIGHT TO HELP HIS FRIEND.

Ahmed's perspective is obviously the exact opposite. Life is not about Khalid or Ahmed. It is about the whole family, and therefore help by each member will positively impact the greater good of the whole. Later in life, whoever earns money will provide for the welfare of the entire family.

With all her best intentions, Ann stepped into a second and potentially even more dangerous cultural trap via the method of her approach. She called Khalid out in public, accusing him of not knowing the answer and doing so in front of the class. Saving face is a common value in collectivist culture. People often live in tight-knit communities, and therefore importance is placed on social standings.

There is no other place to go, to hide or to build up a new life. Feeling embarrassment and shame from the teacher's public remarks, Khalid lost face, and Khalid's parents resented this fact.

We have yet to discuss the following aspect relating to collectivist cultures: What is this "group" that we keep talking about – the group that a person identifies with in a collectivistic culture? In order to understand a society's values and norms, determining the group with which individuals have the closest identification is essential. An individual might most closely identify with their family, their clan, their company, their religion, their profession, their nation, etc. For instance, as efforts to bring peace to countries like Afghanistan and Iraq – both collectivistic cultures – have failed, one reason may be that the strong loyalty to groups prevents democracy from working properly; clan ties may be stronger than the concept of objectively voting for a candidate based on his/her political ideas, experience and ability to govern.

The point is that group identity is flexible; it is not necessarily tied to a clan of relatives or an ethnic group. In France, people often identify with France, "la grand nation," and the family. In Japan, people identify with their company and work place. In the former Eastern Bloc, they identify with their party and Slavic ideals. In Ireland, religion – the Roman Catholic Church – is the entity to which people are drawn. [25]

To summarize, individualist societies emphasize individual identity, independence, self-fulfillment and standing out. Collectivist societies emphasize group identity, interdependence, social responsibility and fitting in. In one culture, conformity is often viewed negatively, while in the other, uniqueness can be viewed as a form of deviance. These are the two extremes, but it is important to note that elements of both individualism and collectivism exist in any culture. As always, in the area of cross cultural research, cultural characteristics are not black and white, but shades of grey. Many graduations exist between the two extremes…and even some surprises.

A widespread belief persists, particularly in the US and Europe, that individualism is required for economic development. Since Adam

Smith, the West's standard economic model is based on the individual's initiative and motivation to build a career, earn more money and improve his/her social standing. This concept was shared by Max Weber, another of the West's economic freethinkers. The entrepreneurial spirit, the aspiration to build a career and the incentive to climb the social ladder are all values typical of an individualist culture, and these characteristics were once thought to drive economic success. But Japan has demonstrated that a collectivist-oriented culture can thrive. Many Japanese business models, such as the quality circle and the steady steps to improvement (Kaizen) are consistent with collectivist values and have proven outcomes; however, these models are often applied incorrectly in an individualist environment.

Let me illustrate this: a couple years ago, I was invited to a presentation of the Japanese luxury brand car, Lexus. The manager explained a peculiar manufacturing method to ensuring high quality in the production process. The cars are mounted in a big hall, the car body steadily moving along the assembly line. A worker is responsible for a specific task each step of the way, such as screwing or welding a piece to the car. At every stage, a string hangs from the ceiling. If a worker pulls on the string, the whole assembly line stops, and production is interrupted. This costs the company a lot of money, but it's important that the workers do this if they see a quality issue. Now what happens to the employee who stops the line? Is he punished for the costly delay? No, he's cheered. With the assembly line at a standstill, the team takes a step back and applauds the one worker who had the courage, for the sake of the team, to interrupt the workflow. No one is punished or singled out, which may be one of the reasons why Lexus is known to produce such high quality and reliable cars.

Since the seventies, Japan has shown that individualism is not necessary for economic development. While individualist cultures do have strengths, collectivist cultures have them as well. The assumption of a correlation between cultural values and economic success has led to research in this area, and rather than being wholly related to individualism or collectivism, the key factor for economic success seems to lie with whatever in-group may be driving worker motivation. If the in-group is the company or the country, then a collectivist culture could actually be a powerful driver for economic growth.[26] Whatever the case, adapting your management style to the values of the culture you're working in – be it collectivist or individualist – is necessary for success.

How does this cultural dimension translate into workplace management? We already saw the popular individualist motivational management method of awarding individuals for outstanding work in the Western world – praise or recognition, be they monetary awards or immaterial. But other cultures are not motivated in this way. If you manage teams in other cultures, the following are further methodological differences and motivational perspectives you may want to consider.

- In collectivist cultures, diplomas are more often seen as an opportunity to enter a higher status group and less so as a factor in gaining better career opportunities. Furthermore, they are certainly never sought after to boost self-confidence in one's own abilities.

- Occupational mobility is lower in collectivist culture, as mobility always implies some form of change in your in-group. Geographical mobility may force you to leave your family. Hierarchical mobility will not only affect your position in the company, but also your position within your in-group, and therefore needs to be consistent with the role given to you by your in-group. For instance, becoming a clan elder's boss may not be acceptable. The hierarchy in your clan will always prevail over the formal organizational authority in the company.

- In an individualist culture, one assumes that employees are "economic persons" who pursue the employer's interest if it coincides with their self-interest. In a collectivist culture, the in-group interest always prevails. While hiring a family member without the proper qualification would be regarded as morally wrong in Europe, doing so in a collectivist culture would be encouraged or even expected by family members.

- In an individualistic culture, hiring and promotion are ideally based on skills, rules and merit. On the other hand, in a collectivist culture, hiring may be guided by the interest of the in-group. This phenomenon can be observed in the hiring for government positions in many emerging democracies. To the exasperation of the aid agencies of Western countries, nepotism rules in these countries. The President of Burkina Faso, Blaise Compoare, comes from Ziniare, a small village about 50 kilometers from the capital city. Not only did he hire members of his extended family, he also built an airport and a zoo in his village and, for many years, it was the only village with electricity. What a Westerner would call favoritism created surprisingly little discontent in the country. In a collectivist culture, it is broadly accepted and even expected that you care for your in-group, and so the president did nothing morally wrong according to his culture. His actions demonstrated that he cares for his people, and this is a good thing. For the same reason, elections in these collectivist regions will always be determined by ethnic groups, and as Mr. Compoare belongs to the Mossi, the largest ethnic group within Burkina Faso, his reelection every four years was ensured, without requiring a rigged election. Until, that is, de- military deposited him in 2014.

- In a collectivist culture, the employer-employee relationship is basically moral, like a family link. This applies even if the company is not the in-group; society is simply programmed to think this way. Your in-group supersedes all. Whatever group you are connected to is expected to act according to the rules and values of your in-group. This concept may clash with the individualistic perception of the professional relationship, which is purely contractual.

- In an individualist society, organizational structures and hierarchies are constructed for the owners, employers and customers. Employees submit to this structure, because it's in their personal interest to do so. The relationship with the company is an abstract one, based on contracts, salary payment and hopefully some form of personal satisfaction. On the other hand, in a collectivist culture, organizations and companies are part of the social fabric. The members, themselves, give these organizations meaning and purpose. Often they are closely tied to a large family or clan, hence the hiring of kin. The growth and prosperity of organizations are not considered bonanzas for individual shareholders or gravy trains for top managers; rather, they are valuable ends in and of themselves, serving society and the clan.[27]

- All business administration curriculums teach the Maslow "hierarchy of need" as a model for human motivation. In a 1943 paper, the researcher, Abraham Maslow, categorized human needs in a pyramid. The lower levels comprise physiological needs, such as food, shelter and safety. Once these basic needs are satisfied, then comes the inner fulfillments: the human need to love, the need to feel esteem, and finally, at the top, self-fulfillment. "What a man can be, he must be," said Maslow.[28] Most top Western managers implicitly use this simple model as incentive to motivate their teams. In doing so, the highest possible motivation – self-fulfillment – logically manifests in personal career development and power.

Though this model may seem intuitive to a Western mind, collectivist cultures prove contradictory in motivation. Cross cultural studies have found that in collectivist countries, like Greece or Japan, security needs motivate employees more than the need for self-actualization. Employees of these countries often consider life-long job security as more important to satisfaction than being challenged on the job or climbing the career ladder. In countries like Norway, Sweden or Denmark, where emphasis is placed on quality of life, social needs are also a stronger motivator in the workplace than building a career. Hofstede notes: "My interpretation is that this tells us more about Maslow than about the other countries' managers. Maslow categorized and ordered his human needs according to the U.S. middle-class culture pattern in which he was embedded himself – he could not have done otherwise."[29] Additionally, the second most widespread motivation theory – Herzberg's two-factor theory, which states that satisfaction and dissatisfaction in one's job are not dependent on each other – didn't withstand cross cultural tests either and can only be applied to Western culture, for and from which it was invented.[30]

For these reasons, managers from individualist cultures may find operating a company in collectivist cultures particularly challenging. The motivational methods applied in one's own culture will inevitably fail, because what one considers right may actually be wrong in the opposing culture, and vice versa. So how does one manage in such an environment?

In managing across cultures, you absolutely must accept that there are no absolutes regarding management and motivation. If you don't want to end up a monkey in your office, as a Western manager, you must acknowledge that individual success is not necessarily the only driver for economic success or the only possible motivating factor for your employees. You will need to adapt your style. Instead of managing individuals, you must learn to manage groups.

The concept of self from individualist and collectivist perspectives has been extensively researched. In the chart, "Concept of Self," you'll find an overview of this research. Not surprisingly, the US is on the individualist end of the scale, followed by many major European countries, while most Asian societies are on the opposite end.

CONCEPT OF SELF

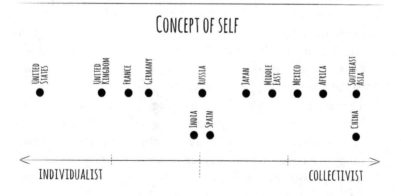

Are laws more important than friendships?

Imagine you are going out with a good friend. He picks you up, and he drives toward city center. The street is fairly crowded, and suddenly he hits a pedestrian. Despite the ambulance's quick arrival, the pedestrian dies. A couple of weeks later, you are requested to appear in court to testify in the lethal accident under oath. The speed limit was 20 miles per hour. Just before the accident, you noticed that your friend was driving at least 40 miles per hour. If you tell the truth, then your friend will go to prison. If you lie, your friend will walk away a free man. What would you do?

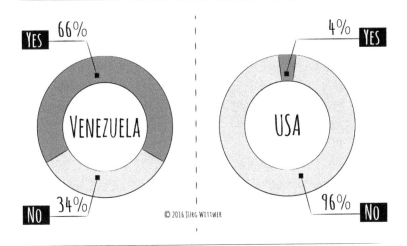

YOU ARE RIDING IN A CAR DRIVEN BY A CLOSE FRIEND. THE CAR HITS A PEDESTRIAN. YOU NOTICED, THAT YOUR FRIEND WAS DRIVING 40 MPH INSTEAD OF THE ALLOWED 20 MPH. UNDER OATH, WILL YOU TESTIFY THAT YOUR FRIEND WAS DRIVING 20 MPH TO PREVENT HIM FROM IMPRISONMENT?

YES 66% — VENEZUELA — NO 34%

4% YES — USA — 96% NO

© 2016 JÜRG WITTWER

If you grew up in a relationship-based society, you'll likely choose to protect your friend, while those from a rule-based society will abide by the law. Complying with the law will weigh more heavily than a friend's fate, and you'll testify that he drove faster than the 20 mph speed limit.

In a survey, people from Venezuela and from the US were confronted with this hypothetical scenario. Two thirds of

Venezuelans surveyed said they would protect their friend and lie under oath. Only 4% of Americans agreed. This example highlights opposing attitudes toward societal responsibility.

Most Western cultures are, to a large degree, rule-based. They are also called universalist, because in these cultures, established rules must be applied universally. Justice means all people are treated according to the same rules or laws. Rich or poor, friend or stranger, black or white, the same rules should apply. No one should escape justice. Everyone is equal in the eyes of the law.

The rules are not only equal for everyone, people also expect rules to be essentially permanent. What is right today should also be right tomorrow. These principles are engrained into the democratic process. Not even the president can change the rules from one day to the next. Laws also apply to him, and laws can only be changed through a lengthy process involving parties, parliament and often direct or indirect public opinion.

Nothing illustrates this severity of law in a rule-based culture better than the red light at a pedestrian crossing. Try to cross the street when the light is red in Switzerland or Germany. Even if there's no traffic, people will frown at you. If you're raised in such a strict, law-abiding society, you will wait for the green light even at 2 o'clock in the morning.

On the other hand, in relationship-based cultures, human existence goes beyond the individual by encompassing the extended family, the village or the tribe. Ostracism from the group is almost a form of death, because one does not exist apart from one's connection to others. In the Confucian ideal, for example, taking care of parents and grandparents comes first, followed by caring for one's children and, only then, oneself. This prioritization differs to the norms in Europe and the US.

In the Bantu cultures, an individual's welfare is identical to that of the village. The greeting ritual of the Shona people, for example, begins *Maswere sei* ("How is your day?"), to which the response is *Ndiswera maswerawo* ("My day is OK if yours is."). Because relationships are fundamental, social control is exercised through relationships. Certain figures must hold inherent authority over others to whom they are related, much as the head has authority over the body. Parents have authority over children, husbands over wives, older siblings over younger siblings, village elders over their neighbors, and so forth. This gives rise to a culture, in which the subordination of some people to others is accepted, even by subordinates, as natural and inevitable.[31]

On the opposite end, rule-based cultures regard human beings as autonomous individuals. Autonomy means, in part, that no individual has natural authority over another. For society to work, instead of delegating authority to any one individual, it is embodied within an abstract set of rules which are applied to everyone. Originally, the monotheistic theology of God and his Commandments heavily influenced the West, due to the godhead representing a lawgiver, the conception of which evolved into governance by universal rules of conduct. The Greek conception of individuals as rational beings reinforced this concept by allowing the rules to be understood as self-justifying, because they are inherently logical. [32] We find this logic also deeply engrained in our understanding of management. All students learn the principle of "homo economicus" and learn that logical and rational people are the fundament of a prosperous human society.

Behavior in rule-based cultures is based on respect for rules. This is not to say that rule-based cultures have rules and relationship-based cultures do not; both do. Rule-based cultures are distinguished by two characteristics:

- people respect the rules for their own sake, while in relationship-based cultures derive authority from the persons who lay them down;
- compliance with rules is often encouraged by feelings of guilt and fear of punishment if caught violating them, rather than shame and constant supervision as in relationship-based cultures.

The contrast between these two cultures can produce major mistrust in business relationships, as each culture will consider their ideas of fairness and justice as correct and the other's as corrupt and untrustworthy. A manager from a rule-based culture will say of his relationship-based counterparts: "They cannot be trusted, because they will always help their friends." Likewise, the relationship-based manager will not trust his rule-based counterparts, "How can we trust someone who would not even help a friend?"[33] This mistrust is how cultural misunderstandings form and destroy business relationships.

Again, the most important thing in cross cultural management is understanding. You should never try to change people or alter other's cultural values and norms when it comes to a business relationship. You must first educate yourself on cultural views and behaviors and then manage in a way that is considerate of differences in culture. Put yourself in their shoes. If you are from the West, and someone confronted you about the universality of your law and judicial system, you would certainly defend it. You wouldn't appreciate an outsider coming in and trying to change the way things have been done for hundreds and maybe even thousands of years. If you are in a management position in a cross cultural environment, you must instead acknowledge cultural differences diplomatically and not press upon touchy subjects that will divide you. Avoid cultural issues that cannot and will not be changed without the course of active social progress. You are there to do a job, which is to unite your cross cultural team, not divide it.

One way to unite is to build up relationships, particularly with leaders. When you manage in a relationship-based society, you are not managing individuals, but groups. The best strategy to unite a whole group in your favor is to identify the leader of the group or those persons who are already established and respected, and build up relationships with them, win their trust and respect, motivate and inspire, and thereby, win over all those who follow. It's a simple strategy: win over the leaders, and you win over the followers.

China is such a relationship-based culture. A familiar clause in Chinese contracts stipulates that if a problem arises, the parties will discuss it and possibly redraft the contract.[34] For a Westerner, this clause may appear strange. In a rule-based society, a contract is supposed to regulate all possible aspects of a business relationship in an unambiguous way. For instance, if the parties have a dispute, then the contract stipulates the city in which a potential court case may take place, and everything is based on established rules. However, this Chinese clause makes the concept of contractual agreements fundamentally different, as anything at any time is subject to renegotiation. The value of a contract in Chinese society is not what is stipulated, but rather that both parties agree to engage in a respectful, mutually beneficial business relationship. Based on the personal relationships of those involved, any potential future disagreements will be negotiated. Having worked often in relationship-based countries, I found that a signed contract actually marked not the end, but the start of the negotiation. Even prices could be subject to renegotiation a couple of days after signatures were drawn up. Still, the signing of a contract was important. Often accompanied by ceremonies and lunches, it signaled the two parties had agreed to enter into a relationship, marking publicly that the leaders are now friends and will treat each other with respect.

Companies and company decisions go beyond the frontier of the work place, especially in a relationship-based society. Employees in a relationship-based society will not usually separate business life from personal life. Concepts like "business relations" versus "personal relations" do not exist. Relationships dominate any company rule, especially if the employees yield to a family or a tribe. A business conflict with an employee will become a conflict with his family or with anyone considered his kin or in-group.

An example of this cross-over: an American company built a new assembly plant in a town in Eastern Europe. Aspiring to be "fair and generous," the company offered their new laborers four times the average hourly wage, which resulted in the disruption of the town's social network. The villagers were anxious about which families would benefit from these new lucrative jobs. The induced anxiety put the company in a precarious position. In the end, they decided to hire one person from each family unit, and so preserved the locals' social harmony. This illustrates how, in a relationship-based culture, company decisions easily influence life outside of the company.

The same family ties and personal relationships can qualify a candidate for any profession. For instance, an HR manager from the US may hire the candidate with superior skills and experience, while his Latin American counterpart may insist on hiring a less qualified person with impressive familial and political connections. This is because, in a relationship-based society, someone with strong personal ties may be able to better achieve company goals. In other words, "who you know" may often be more important than "what you know."

Business communication and negotiations work differently in rule- and relationship-based societies. US and European managers tend to be direct and straight forward in their communication. This makes perfect sense, as all agree on a certain set of rules. These rules are spelled out explicitly, and people observe them. Even a medium-sized American company has thousands of pages of written rules: the company's vision, the mission statement, strategies, expense regulations, HR handbooks, job descriptions, compliance handbooks, and much more. In any case, written regulations are assumed to have absolute priority over any personal preferences, and certainly no exceptions are allowed to favor relationships. Managers can rely on this set of rules in communication and therefore tend to communicate concisely and unambiguously. In a relationship-based culture, anything and everything may be negotiated, and the rules only exist as the person in charge dictates them. In communicating within these cultures, the complex network of human relationships has always to be taken into account.

This applies even further in negotiation. The direct approach in rule-based cultures results from an underlying confidence that rules have objective validity and can therefore serve as a basis for resolving disputes. The absence of such confidence in relationship-based cultures requires that all those in positions of power fall back on courtesy and face-saving. Negotiating in relationship-based cultures does not involve agreeing on clauses, but upon building and maintaining a relationship with the authoritarian business partner, which is a distinctly different strategy than what Western managers are used to. In a relationship-based culture, it's nearly impossible to negotiate in a tough manner and then go golfing like nothing happened. In America, doing so would be the norm. Business is about rules, about money, and thus, these discussions should not be taken personally. You can laugh together with business partners, eat a good steak, even talk about family life, and then, once negotiations start, the tables turn; dealings are aggressive, like no prior comradery existed. This will not work in a relationship-based society. These cultures draw no distinction between business and private life; the two are more closely interwoven.

Ambiguity is the most difficult aspect of cross cultural relations; a manager from a rule-based culture may feel the rules are ambiguous in a relationship-based environment, and vice versa. Traditionally, US management theory is fundamentally rule-based and seeks to provide clear advice relating to successful management. Students in American universities learn that organizations should not be organized "ad personam" but "ad res." In other words, organizations should be structured indifferently from the persons who work. You can change the names in the organizational chart, but the structure should be adapted to the business. A relationship-based culture is organized the opposite way. Organization, "ad personam," is considered correct.

When behaviors, values and norms all seem vague, the uncertainty leads to wrong assumptions and misunderstandings. As with anything, the first step to displace ambiguity is to seek understanding. This all goes back to searching out the rationale in your cross cultural compatriots. Identify the issue that conflicts with your beliefs and values and look at it from the standpoint of the other culture's perspective. Try to see the advantages of relationship-based managing. Look at it through their eyes, their worldview, their societal and familial upbringing. Look at it and find the logic. You may still not agree with the other's ideas of personal and social responsibility, but you may, at the very least, rid of the ambiguity through understanding of the other's logic and rationale.

If you're from a rule-based culture, when you try to understand the rationale behind a relationship-based culture, you may also discover important advantages to their methods. The individualistic and rule-based culture in the West has limitations when addressing today's global problems. Interestingly, the Western world is now seeking, through business research, to introduce new, more socially responsible, less individualistic concepts. One of these is the concept of social responsibility.

Social responsibility is an individual's or an organization's obligation to behave beneficially to society as a whole, while personal responsibility involves an individual moral code of conduct. Social responsibility, in particular, welcomes a balancing of economic ecosystems, be they material development or societal and environmental welfare. For instance, when an organization's productivity negatively impacts the environment, their social responsibility must be called into question. Environmental impact can destroy the health of a community by polluting the air and drinking water and can destroy biological ecosystems; in short, social irresponsibility can destroy our planet. This is something that reflects upon the business' culture, indicating its indifference to the society it's supposed to serve.

Social responsibility can also be active or passive. For instance, if you work in retail and are aware that many of your coworkers shoplift, you might stumble down the slippery slope, thinking, "Well, if everyone else is doing it..." However, if you refuse to engage in this unethical activity while keeping your mouth shut about your colleagues' theft, you are being passively socially responsible. Moreover, if you directly advocate for antitheft procedures – such as spot-checking all employees' bags before they leave for the day – , you are being socially active.

Corporate social responsibility is a new type of management strategy where, in the process of doing business, companies simultaneously seek to positively impact society. Corporate social responsibility can either be governmentally mandated or voluntary, but its primary objective often involves a two-tier motive: to improve quantitative and qualitative aspects of society. Quantitative aspects involve the company's societal impact, while qualitative aspects involve the efficient management of processes and employees. This newfound corporate social responsibility comes at a time where shareholders are more interested in the external ripple-effect of a company – how it impacts society and the environment. Instead of focusing wholly on maximizing profits, shareholders hold big corporations' feet to the fire, forcing them to be more socially aware of industrial repercussions. So, in some way, the relationship-based cultures – those based around collective societal responsibility – have found their place in the rule-based economic management theories of the West, the point being that we can always learn from other cultures and find value in their beliefs.

PERSONAL VERSUS SOCIETAL RESPONSIBILITY

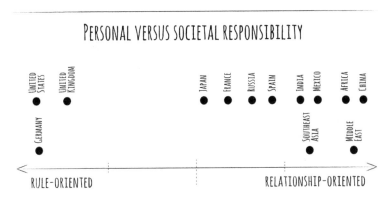

How important is punctuality?

If you've ever travelled or lived as an expat in another country, you may have noticed that the valuation of time differs across cultures. Some cultures consider time valuable and allow it to dictate their daily schedule, their goals and their decisions. Other cultures consider time of little value and don't think of time in a linear sense; they are of the mind that "things will happen when they happen." Thereby, these cultures are not ruled by a set schedule, and neither are their businesses and industries. The way time is conceptualized varies from culture to culture and correlates to the ways in which things are done, not only in business, but throughout every aspect of daily life. Whereas you might set your watch by the train in Switzerland, to do so in, say, Mexico could very well put you in a different time zone. This is why time can play a major role in cross cultural expectations in the workplace. When a colleague's time expectations are different and your expectations are breached, misunderstandings arise.

So let's first look at the basic concept of time. Think of time in terms of a line. At any point along the line, a person is participating in one activity, while at a separate point further along the line, he or she is participating in another activity. In this way, time is portioned off into intervals, each dedicated to a separate activity. In other words, time is a measurable substance.

This measurable substance can directly influence cultural lifestyles, the willingness of people to listen to others, and even the speed of a person's movements or speech. Moreover, if working in a cross cultural environment, one must understand the opposing culture's concept of time in order to understand the proper etiquette in relation to it. For example, if a person makes an appointment with someone, that person is expected to keep their appointment, according to the specific culture's concept of time. And this concept varies widely across cultures, depending upon whether the culture is polychronic or monochronic.

The study of time's role in communication – particularly when it comes to non-verbal communication – is called chronemics. Chronemics evaluates the many ways in which cultures perceive time, structure it, value it and, ultimately, the way individuals of these cultures respond to time frames. A culture's concept of time encapsulates many aspects of a culture and its people, including an individual's punctuality and the extent of his or her patience when it comes to waiting.

The chronemics of various cultures can be divided into two opposing conceptualizations of time: as mentioned above, these are polychonic and monochronic time systems. Polychronic time systems involve multiple activities, done fluidly and simultaneously. Think of the multi-tasker, who folds clothes while watching tv or runs errands while walking the dog. Instead of getting one task done at a time, those who prefer a polychronic time system like to accomplish several things at once.

Polychronicity is more prevalent in African, Latin American, Arab, and South Asian cultures; cultures which are less concerned about precision and minute-by-minute playback. Generally speaking, tasks are of less importance than relationships in polychronic cultures. More important are traditions, community, seasonal cycles and the unchanging pattern of festivities, particularly those which stem from religion.

Some polychronic cultures may even seem to have no concept of time at all. Take the Pirahã tribe, for instance. This Amazonian tribe's attitude toward time is illustrated not only in their behavioral patterns, but in their language. With no past tense, perception of time is based only in the present. That which they cannot see, no longer exists. This may also attribute to the fact that the tribe has no creation myth or designated religion. The Pirahã is a tribe without time, seemingly frozen in time.

Similarly, a number of Native American tribes – including the Hopi tribe, located in Arizona – do not have verb tenses or perceive time in a linear fashion. More often, their religious ideas suggest that time is cyclical. This cyclical view of time is demonstrated in other religions and ancient philosophies as well, including in Buddhism and Hinduism. Consider, for instance, the "wheel of time" and other illustrations of Buddhist tradition.

The perception of time in polychronic cultures may seem informal to the West. In this time system, missing a deadline or running late does not reflect upon a person's "rudeness" or lack of consideration; more to the point, relationships, themselves, are of the ultimate importance. In fact, it's not uncommon for people who live in polychronic cultures to create an impossible schedule for themselves by making many appointments at once. They don't kid themselves that they'll be able to get to all appointments on time; rather, they are not ruled by their timetable and will get to these appointments in their own time.

This concept of time may seem unfathomable to those who belong to a monochronic culture, where a strict division of time is dictated by specific tasks. Precision is key to arranging and managing a person's agenda and, in the world of business, schedules are set in stone. The United States, the United Kingdom, Germany, Turkey, Japan, Canada, Switzerland, Scandinavia, Taiwan, and South Korea are all examples of monochronic cultures. Idioms have even been coined to illustrate how these cultures view time. "To work against the clock," for instance, demonstrates the necessity to rush and meet deadlines. When you have time to spare and no upcoming deadline, you're told to "take your time." When you have time to waste, you're "killing time." In monochronic cultures, time is tangible. Time is money, after all.

This is why monochronic cultures typically value punctuality. Because "time is money," no one wants to waste their own time; or, more to the point, no one wants others to waste it. Tasks, schedules, commitments are taken seriously in monochronic cultures to the point that you may be judged on your punctuality, your productivity and your organizational skills.

Monochronic time systems sprang from the Industrial Revolution, which required that workers become mechanisms of a machine – in a specific place, at a specific time, in order to complete the task at hand which, at that point, frequently involved factory work. This conceptualization of time has since evolved to rule the lives of those in monochronic society, where everything revolves around strict schedules, whether it be transportation, school, work, sports, or even entertainment. If you want to catch your favorite tv show, you must tune in at its specific time slot.

These differences in time perception lead to misunderstandings about certain cultures and the individuals within said cultures. Polychronic people might believe monochronic folks to be untrustworthy, ruled by formalities and less invested in relationships, while monochronists might see polychronists as lazy and lacking a sense of responsibility and discipline. But, looking at these two systems objectively, you'll note pros and cons to both time systems.

While those in a polychronic culture may not be as ambitious when it comes to completing tasks within a set time perimeter, they are enjoying the aspects of life they most value – relationships, traditions, festivities, celebrations. On the other hand, although those in monochronic time systems may not be as invested in taking a minute to "smell the roses," they are completing their tasks effectively and efficiently, pushing the limits, creating and evolving at a faster pace and are working to afford their desired quality of life.

Whether you're of the opinion that "things happen when they happen" or "things happen when you make them happen," your perception of time will likely clash with others' when you're working in a cross cultural environment.

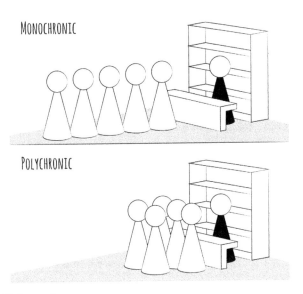

MONOCHRONIC

POLYCHRONIC

Time Orientation

Those who adhere to a monchronic time system, as opposed to a polychronic time system, will differ in many aspects when it comes to the way in which they work and the time frame in which tasks are completed.

Monochronic people complete one task at a time, focusing on that single task, while polychronic people may be doing many things at once, while focusing on the goings-on that surround them. Monochronic people are dedicated to their job and are invested in results; therefore, they take deadlines and timetables seriously. Polychronic people are dedicated to their friends, family, and relationships. Though they, too, are invested in goals and objectives, they do not consider the time frame in which these goals or objectives are met to be important. Likewise, polychronic cultures value community and connectivity, while those in a monochronic culture often find individuality and privacy of greater importance. Additionally, polychronic people are not strict planners. They alter their plans frequently and are high-context, considering themselves as already possessing the necessary information. Monochronic people commit themselves to plans and do not like deviating from them. They are considered low-context, more often requiring information in order to make a decision. Monochronic people commit to practical relationships that often have a short lifespan and consider punctuality essential across the board, no matter the situation or relationship. Polychronic people prefer permanent relationships with indefinite lifespans and consider punctuality to be relative to the situation or relationship.

In monochronic cultures, aspects of time management, negotiation and behavior within an organization differ from polychronic culture. When it comes to deadlines, for instance, a monochronic person will push themselves to meet the deadline, often stressing over completing their task on time. In polychronic cultures, whether the task is completed or not by the proposed "deadline" is irrelevant. There are no consequences, no fall-outs, no firings and no one is concerned.

Similarly, if a businessman in a monochronic culture is involved in negotiation, a deadline is set whereby the deal must be settled. If the acting parties do not agree on a settlement within the confines of the timeframe, then often the deal is dropped altogether. In a polychronic culture, the two parties will negotiate until they settle. If a deadline on negotiations is set at all, it means nothing whatsoever.

As per an individual's behavior within an organization, more often than not, monochronic people are task-oriented and manage projects on their own, with an enforced hierarchy. Polychronic people are interaction-oriented and the "people" are managed, rather than the projects. If a hierarchy is even established, it may be considered somewhat irrelevant.

All of this is due to the fact that time perception is learned, just as values and norms are learned behaviors of a culture. As a child, the perception of time is based upon the values of society and, thereby, is absorbed in a way that orients the child toward a certain psychological time cognitivism. Four time orientations exist. These are past, time-line, present, and future. Communication is influenced specifically by each of these orientations, altering the urgency and content of whatever is being communicated. In general, older countries – like China, India and Britain, for instance – are considered past-oriented, while newer countries – like the US – are predominantly future-oriented. There is also a present-oriented cultural identity – one example is France – in which the people live for today.

Cultural values dictate the way time is perceived. For instance, the "American Dream" directs most Americans to be forward-looking and forward-thinking. This means they are often striving towards milestones and, ultimately, success in order to achieve this dream. And as dreams are always in the future, they are running against the clock, fast-paced and frenzied. On the other hand, those cultures who are past-orientated – India, for instance – have a broader scope of time, viewing minutes and hours as somewhat inconsequential. Life in past-orientated countries is not as rushed or ruled by the clock. This includes whole industries, such as hospitals and transport. A late train in India is not only possible, it's to be expected.

Those with past oriented cognitivity do not rightly grasp elapsed time and often interchange the present with the past and vice versa. Time-line cognitivity is a linear way of looking at time, which allows individuals to focus on details but often hinders multi-tasking. Present-oriented cognitivity is often linked to those with low risk aversion; in other words, thrill-seekers. They're often the one's shouting, "Yolo!" before bungee jumping off a bridge. Future-oriented cognitivity allows individuals to identify the broader picture, set goals and make plans to achieve them.

CONSEQUENCE AT THE WORK PLACE	MONOCHRONISTIC	POLYCHRONISTIC
WHEN A DEADLINE APPROACHES FOR A PROJECT	EMPLOYEE FEELS STRESS, SPEEDS UP	NOTHING HAPPENS
BEHAVIOR IN NEGOTATION	PUT DEADLINE ON NEGOTIATIONS	NEGOTIATE UNTIL AGREEMENT IS FOUND REMARK: MAY BE A HANDICAP FOR MC. PC MAY WAIT UNTIL DEADLINE APPROACHES, AND THEN MC WILL CAVE IN
BEHAVIOR WITHIN AN ORGANIZATION	TASK ORIENTED, YOU MANAGE ,,PROJECTS'', HIERARCHY IS ENFORCED	INTERACTION ORIENTED, YOU MANAGE ,,PEOPLE'', HIERARCHY IS FLATTER, OR MAY NOT EVEN EXIST

As you may have probably guessed, monochronic cultures are often future-oriented, while polychronic cultures are largely past-oriented. These differences in time perspectives contribute to diplomatic conflicts. For example, if America is trying to reach a trade agreement with Zimbabwe, a deadline for negotiations might be set by the Americans, and yet, Zimbabwe might see this deadline as a mere suggestion. Whereas American culture seeks to solve problems quickly, Zimbabwe's culture (and those of other past-oriented polychronic cultures) is less anxious and in no rush. Additionally, the fact that America has an individualistic and low context culture means the negotiation will be entered with an objective and a strategy to reach the objective, likely with projected schedules, timelines and specified dates all prepared. Zimbabwe's collectivist, high-context culture, on the other hand, anticipates a substantial dialogue, in which relationships are built upon broad topics of discussion for an extended period of time before the specifics of the negotiation are discussed. They intend to reach an agreement that is exceptional, so that they can save face. Meeting a deadline does not save them face; rather, the negotiation's outcome does.

Learning about and understanding the differences between cultures in regards to time systems and cultural time orientation is paramount for negotiation, management and communication in foreign cultures.

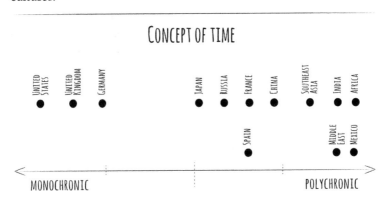

CONCEPT OF TIME

UNITED STATES • UNITED KINGDOM • GERMANY •   JAPAN • RUSSIA • FRANCE • CHINA • SOUTHEAST ASIA • INDIA • AFRICA •

SPAIN •   MIDDLE EAST • MEXICO •

MONOCHRONIC   POLYCHRONIC

Does fate define my career?

You were late to work. You missed a deadline. A colleague with less seniority received a promotion over you. Do your actions, choices and performance influence this chain reaction, or do environmental factors play a greater role in cause and effect?

The degree to which an individual believes they're in control of their life and the events that occur therein is referred to in psychology as the locus of control. This concept of personality studies was developed by Julian B. Rotter in 1954 and, along with self-efficacy, neuroticism and self-esteem, is one of the four dimensions of fundamental self-evaluation. This particular element of appraisal highlights the individual's conceptualization of "locus" (Latin meaning "place") as being either internal or external. An individual with an internal locus of control believes that one is in control of one's life, while someone with an external locus of control believes in chance, fate or destiny; the environment controls one's life, and nothing a person does can determine the outcome.

The difference between an internal locus of control and an external locus of control is illustrated in the Indian proverb, "You can walk around softly everywhere by putting on a pair of shoes, or you can demand that the whole Earth become covered by soft leather." In order to be more comfortable walking, those with an internal locus of control put on a pair of shoes; those with an external locus of control demand that the environment change to suit their needs and desires.

Those with an internal locus tend to be more ambitious and optimistic, as they have a sense of purpose; the part they play influences the outcome. These individuals feel responsible for their own happiness or unhappiness, as well as for their successes and failures. They believe in change and may consider the motto, "where there's a will, there's a way," as their gold standard. If they're waxing poetic, they might say, "I am the master of my fate: I am the captain of my soul," as written by William Ernest Henley in *Invictus*. They exercise this belief by holding not only themselves, but others, as well, accountable for their actions and the results of these actions.

Those with an external locus of control are often more realistic or fatalistic when it comes to events in their lives. As fate plays such a significant role in the web of life around the world, these individuals feel that their destiny is pre-charted and their personal control over their future is limited. Because of this, they accept the events in their lives as something written in the stars. They also tend to believe that success is at least partly influenced by luck or good fortune. The motto for someone with an external locus of control might be "life is what happens to you."

To put this into perspective in a workplace environment, think about the reaction of your colleagues when a goal isn't reached. Some will apologize for their part in it, while others will blame those around them or environmental factors that may have impacted the end result. For those with an internal locus of control, any mistakes personally made which may have contributed to the group's failure would be considered their own individual fault. Those with an external locus of control might call out a select few in the group who they consider at fault or blame underachieving on external factors, like the market or other parties involved.

Cross cultural Factors

Though locus of control is often studied in relation to personality orientation, social psychologists also examine the cultural factors that influence a majority locus of control within any given culture and the cross cultural implications therein. What they've found is that, like anything, though the degree of external and internal locus of control varies amongst individuals in a culture, there is often a general worldview in regards to fate and self-control amongst any given population. For instance, Americans and many European cultures are often more internal on the spectrum than their Japanese or Chinese counterparts. This makes Westerners the directors of their own fate, tying in with their values relating to individuality and ambition. When cultures have a more external locus of control, they are likely to accept things as they are, without questioning the individual's role in the grand scheme of things. This is representative in the below chart: 89% of questioned Americans will agree with the statement, "What happens to me is my own doing," while only 35% of Chinese will agree with this statement.

Moreover, in any given country, the locus of control may vary across the various national cultures as well, particularly if the nation is more ethnically and culturally diverse. For instance, in America, the African American population has a more external locus of control than the white population. And these differences aren't only ethnically determined; a survey between two states – Alabama and Illinois – showed a startling difference in the locus of control of these regions in relation to preparing for natural disasters. The study was done in an attempt to understand why fewer people have died in tornados in Illinois than in Alabama. Four counties were surveyed, and the results indicated that Illinois residents have an internal locus of control, while Alabama residents have an external locus of control. This difference in the belief of an individual's ability to control events in one's life might directly influence the degree and methods by which the two regions prepare for natural disasters. Those in Illinois, with their internal locus of control, would approach both the precautions for natural disasters and reacting to a tornado warning in a more active way than those in Alabama, with their external locus of control. It may then be concluded that regional locus of control plays a pivotal role in the amount of storm-related casualties.

WICH OF THE FOLLOWING TWO STATEMENTS DO YOU MOST AGREE WITH?

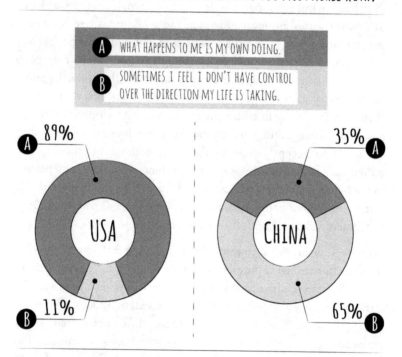

A — WHAT HAPPENS TO ME IS MY OWN DOING.

B — SOMETIMES I FEEL I DON'T HAVE CONTROL OVER THE DIRECTION MY LIFE IS TAKING.

USA: A 89%, B 11%

CHINA: A 35%, B 65%

Cross cultural and gender differences in locus of control lead to issues in conflict resolution, accountability and leadership acceptance. For example, leadership preferences correlate directly with an individual's locus of control. A study found that females more widely report an internal locus of control and prefer democratic leadership styles, while males lean toward an external locus of control and prefer autocratic leadership styles. The study tested undergraduate students from both eastern and Western cultures.[35]

In a cross cultural workplace, an individual's locus of control can be understood through primary or secondary control efforts, particularly when it comes to active or passive behaviors. Primary control is a trait found more often in those from an individualist culture and involves an individual directly intervening in order to control his or her environment or standing within the company. Secondary control is a trait found more often in those from a collectivist culture and involves the individual aligning him or herself with someone more powerful or with a group that has already established power within the company. In this way, the individual is still attempting to control his or her environment or fate to a degree; however, this is considered a more external locus of control, while primary control is considered internal. Most individuals in a collectivist culture prefer secondary control, because their culture values the submission of personal control and the avoidance of conflict.

Studies indicate that life satisfaction and subjective well-being between cultures with an internal locus and those with an external locus differ. Those with an internal locus believe they are in the driver seat and are responsible for their own self-fulfillment. They influence the outcome of events in their own lives, and thereby consider that the outcome and environment may be predictable to some extent. This is why individualist societies, with their internal locus of control, may have a more positive subjective well-being, as they actively pursue their desires and are optimistic that these desires will be reached. Those with an external locus are being thrown into a churning sea without any control over whether they sink or swim. This may result in anxiety, a pessimistic outlook on their ability to affect change when it comes to freedoms and human rights, and an overall lower subjective well-being. However, collectivist societies often offer a stronger support system structure, which serves as a more certain safety net to those being tossed in the churning sea. Though the individualist, with their internal locus, may be more confident in their ability to swim, if they do find their abilities to be lacking, they are more likely to despair. This may partially influence the higher suicide rates in individualist societies when compared to collectivist societies.

Whether the individual is borne from a collectivist or individualist culture, the internal locus of control has been found to more often correlate with academic achievement, lower levels of stress and depression, social maturity and motivation. Coping strategies also differ between those with internal or external locus of control. Those with an external locus often suffer from higher stress levels, because the individual sees a situation or the culmination of events as beyond his or her control. With this inability to cope, chronic stress can affect a person's long-term physical and mental well-being.

DIALOGUE	INTERPRETATION
ANN: DID YOU TAKE THE MEDICINE?	ANN IS CONVINCED THAT THE RIGHT DOCTOR OR RIGHT MEDICINE WILL END KAMAL'S PAIN.
KAMAL: YES, I TOOK SOME LAST NIGHT. THANK YOU FOR BRINGING IT.	
ANN: ARE YOU FEELING ANY BETTER?	ANN INSISTS ON HER VISION OF THE FACTS.
KAMAL: I FELT BETTER FOR A WHILE, BUT NOW THE PAIN IS BACK AGAIN.	
ANN: I'M SORRY. LET ME GET YOU SOME MORE PILLS.	
KAMAL: THANK YOU, BUR IT'S NOT REALLY NECESSARY.	WHILE KAMAL MAY TRY THE MEDICINE, HE REACHES A POINT WHERE HE CONCLUDES THAT THIS PARTICULAR PAIN MUST SIMPLY BE ENDURED. LIKE PLEASURE AND HAPPINESS, PAIN IS PART OF LIFE AND MUST RUN ITS NATURAL COURSE.

A culture's locus of control may be apparent through their media and basic elements of daily life. In Western cultures, the subtleties lie in simple things, like self-help guides, the prevalence of therapists and coaches, and even something as basic as magazine headlines that offer the "top ten ways" to improve some aspect of appearance – all of these available outlets of individual improvement indicate that the individual is in control. More overtly, a culture's values and norms suggest whether or not the culture's locus of control is internal or external. A Westerner's forward-thinking ideology and valuation of independence correlates directly with the internal locus of control which is, in fact, the prevailing psyche in Western cultures. Someone from a more external cultural locus of control, like that of Muslim cultures, is guided by the ideology that life has been created for them, and not the other way around. This is reflected in the culture's strict rules of law and fundamental traditions, which are dictated to them by God who, according to their cultural ideology, directs the course of not only individual lives, but the whole of humanity.

Though Muslim clerics seem to possess an internal locus, in that they control all aspects of their community's views, whether political or otherwise, they are considered the vehicle of God's instruction; their control is viewed as God's control, through man. In this way, the hand of God directs all, rendering an internal locus of control for the individuals in this society unnecessary. When a culture is guided by traditions and rules and does not value self-accountability or individual freedoms, the individuals of said culture are more likely to blame others or the hand of fate for doing them harm. They also may expect others to be responsible for fixing problems before holding themselves accountable.

Through the concept of locus of control, we may now better understand the behavior of the Mossis described at the beginning of this chapter. No Westerner would knowingly drink the poisoned water offered by a village chief, because his internal locus indicates that he is master of his own life. But if fate or God dictate your life's course, then according to the Mossi external locus, you should not fight against it. The fictitious dialogue depicted above illustrates these radically different perceptions. While Ann, the British nurse, intervenes to change the course of Kamal's sickness, Kamal, the Indian patient, may accept his condition and fate without intervening.

Understanding these differences in locus of control in relation to cultural, gender and individual personality can help you understand a colleague's thought processing, making you more effective at accommodating their behavior or dealing with it constructively.

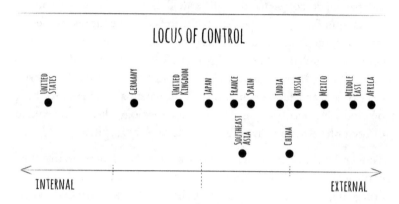

LOCUS OF CONTROL

What we learned in this chapter:

- One cannot quite grasp their mentality and worldview unless he suspends some of his own deepest assumptions about society and human nature.

- Building blocks of culture provide significant data about the differences in values from society to society.

- Building blocks include individualism vs. collectivism, rule-based vs. relationship-based cultures, polychronism vs. monochronism and internal vs. external locus of control.

6. The Trap of Ethnocentricity

These four building blocks of culture – concept of self, personal vs. societal responsibility, concept of time and locus of control – will help you understand cultural differences and adapt your management methods when moving from one to another culture. An overview of these building blocks is illustrated in the chart below. Do you notice something strange? The US is always on the far left side. This is a consequence of ethnocentricity; even great and famous researchers like Geert Hofstede cannot free themselves from their own cultural heritage and produce a chart from a purely objective frame of reference.

Judging other cultures based on the intrinsic values of one's own is called ethnocentrism. Dimensions in your culture may differ from another's, as the values and standards are chosen according to what each distinct culture feels is important. Whether the values relate to behavior, religion, customs or even language, differentiations are made in relation to one's own ideology and cultural identity, resulting in one determining the other's culture to be "wrong" and their own to be "right." Ethnocentrism is psychologically natural and can be either positive or negative, as well as vague or distinct.

Let's consider the US, for example. Americans value individualism and consider it a criteria distinguishing America from other cultures. The "American Dream" hypothetically allows anyone who strives to work hard to afford the lifestyle relative to their efforts. Additionally, time evaluation in the States is future-oriented, while the values of justice and fairness necessitate that the same rules apply to everyone.

We would consider these concepts "typically American," which is why America is on the extreme end of all four building blocks of culture. Because Americans value individualism, equality in front of the law, efficient use of time and being master of your own fate, these ideologies are considered an important categorization in their cross cultural research.

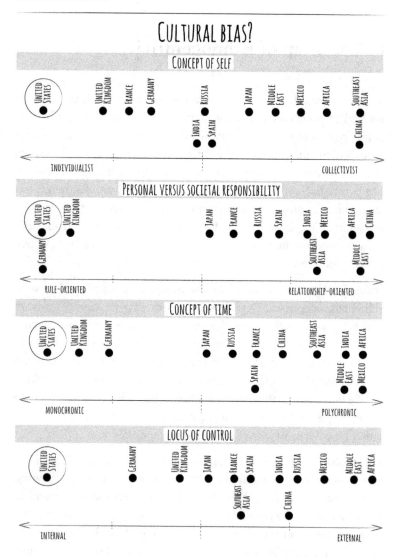

However, if a collectivist society, like China, were to create criteria by which to judge other cultures, their spectrum may not highlight individualistic tendencies; rather collectivist ideology would be at the center. China's global economic might is expanding and their research into cross cultural management will as well. It's safe to say that their new system would categorize other cultures according to their own values, evaluating them and the relative degree to which these cultures compare. This is ethnocentrism at work.

Let me give you a personal example. Shortly after the fall of the communist party in 1991, I travelled to Albania as a journalist, navigating the remote, mountainous region close to the ex-Yugoslavian border. In many villages, I was the first foreigner to march into town since the German soldiers of World War II. Of the many impressions I had of the region, one stands out that I will never forget: the unconditional hospitality of these people. Despite extreme poverty, they prepared lavish meals for this foreign stranger. In one village, they went so far as to kill one of the three sheep to serve me, despite my attempts to discourage them from sacrificing so greatly on my behalf. This is the norm in their culture.

In every home, there is one room with a bed, ready at any given time to accommodate a guest. I've experienced similar hospitality in other areas of the world and have come to the conclusion that hospitality is best wherever there is no telephone. This may be because, with no telephone to communicate, people arrive unannounced. Consequently, hosts need to be ready for surprise visitors at a moment's notice. In such cultures, active hospitality and open doors, receiving unexpected guests at the dinner table, is as developed as passive hospitality. On the other end of the spectrum, many Westerners do not invite themselves into the homes of strangers or even acquaintances. Even when a bed is available, a Westerner may choose to stay at a hotel instead. But in Albania and other less connected areas of the world, hospitality is a deeply entrenched value.

Now imagine a university of cross cultural management being built in Albania, a university studying other countries in the far corners of the world. Albania values hospitality, so the Albanian researchers may conclude that the hospitality-index is essential to the categorization of cultures. In their mind, such generosity is the glue of society; it allows free travel, promotes an open mind and ensures communal ties. But, when traveling abroad, they discover that other cultures do not offer hospitality to the same standard as Albania's. Some restrict unconditional hospitality to persons they know well, while strangers are excluded altogether. In still other countries, hospitality (in the sense of always having open doors and a bed) is offered only to close family members. Even further, in some, you have to *pay* for hospitality at a B&B. According to their research into other world cultures, the Albanians may then conclude that Albania is on the higher end of the scale in relation to the hospitality-index, and that this is a good thing. This is ethnocentrism – evaluating the values of other cultures based upon your own. The point of all this is that ethnocentricity is not exclusive to the culturally ill-informed; even professional researchers are ethnocentric.

Ethnocentrism and the Workplace

Now, let's take this a step further and examine the part ethnocentrism can play in a cross cultural workplace or environment. In international business ventures, one individual may approach communication differently than someone from another culture. In fact, that individual may have a different way of thinking, different traditions, different methods of communication and may simply process everything differently than their cross cultural counterparts. This may not seem like a significant issue, but when the first individual does not understand that these differences are determined by culture and refuses to acknowledge or adapt, he or she may attempt to force his or her own ethnocentric business values and standards upon the other. Not only are you the monkey, but you're also trying to impose your "monkey ways" on others. This can cause rifts in the workplace. The idea that one's own cultural values are superior can make ethnocentrism a toxic trait in a cross cultural environment.

Ethnocentrism is not a trait specific to prejudiced, bigoted or uneducated individuals. We previously learned that Maslow's pyramid offers an ethnocentric view, and still it is taught in management schools around the world. Actually, American experts are the most proficient producers of management literature, and few of them are aware of how culturally biased their theories are…ironic, since they are experts in the subject.

Due to the societal integration of culture, all individuals are informed that their way of life is the most logical and should be the universal way of the world. With such views, all are affected by ethnocentricity. Making any attempt to be more open can be difficult, even when we are aware of our cultural bias. But in order to prevent ethnocentrism from skewing our perspective, particularly in a workplace environment, we must come to accept that our own values are not absolute. Only then can we alter our perspective accordingly and adjust our behaviors to differing cultural values and norms. When ethnocentrism melts away, tolerance and acceptance allow the individual to thrive in a culture that is not their own, adopting the new "rights and wrongs," the new standards and methods practiced in another culture's business environment. Though, inherently you may feel you are going against your gut instinct in doing so, this adjustment to another culture's values demonstrates respect and a willingness to alter your behaviors in order to be successful by another culture's standards.

In some aspects in business, ethnocentrism may work to your advantage – playing to the ethnocentrism of your customer, for instance. If you're promoting a product in a hipster city in America, like Portland or Boulder, for example, branding your product as "local" plays on your customer's pride in the authentic homegrown (and, therefore, "superior") quality of a product. Even further, a business advertising the same product in different cultures will alter their message in order that it pertains to the culture within which it's being integrated. For instance, returning to our example of hospitality, an American hotel chain opening in Albania would adapt its press release to accommodate the values of Albanian culture. Whereas, in America, this hotel's opening might stress the spacious rooms, the clean modernity of the hotel's layout, the professionalism of the staff and the hotel's privacy and security, in Albania, a press release would likely highlight the hotel's homey, family feel, its traditional offerings, and other pertinent elements; it might highlight, for instance, that you don't need a reservation, as hospitality tradition requires that there is always a room available. The message communicated to the public must appeal to the culture's values in order to sell. This is Advertising 101. To sell a product, one must appeal to the ethnocentricity of the masses. And the same goes to thriving in the workplace: you must adapt your sales pitch – or yourself – to the culture to which you're appealing.

Ethnocentrism and Communication

When communicating internationally, cultural variables based on ethnocentricity can create barriers. Variables may include language, nonverbal communication norms, authority ranks, technological and natural environment and social environment. Knowledge of these variables in relation to the cultures with which you are communicating can smooth the process and help you prepare to conquer your own inherent ethnocentricity.

First, let's look at language. A good translation can make or break communication. In fact, linguistic misunderstandings can occur between any two cultures, whether they involve minor differences between languages, larger translation issues, or even culturally-grounded differences between two cultures that speak the same language (American English versus British English, for example).

Being that the minor details are vital to negotiation in business, minor differences between languages can blur the fine print. Larger translation errors are easier to detect and, thus, easier to correct. On the other hand, correcting them does take time which may put pressure on negotiations and may be viewed as unprofessional to those whose language is being used. Further, dialects, accents and cultural differences in language can prove equally problematic in international negotiations between two cultures who speak the same language. These cultural differences include sociolinguistics, which is a language's social patterning that may distinguish class or other national prejudices and augment certain stereotypes. For instance, in Britain, specific accents designate lower and middle classes from the aristocracy. An individual from a wealthier class may sound "posh" to the British, while the accent of someone from a lower class may be considered coarse; either can produce prejudices about the person speaking. While an American may not be able to differentiate the subtle differences, those within the culture hear them clearly and may judge accordingly. Americans have their own prejudices based upon accent, dialect and sociolinguistics as well. An American who lives in the South has a specific social patterning that may reinforce a prejudice related to stereotypes about intelligence and level of education associated with certain regions. All of this is rooted in history; the national prejudices from years and even centuries past lingering to present day.

To make cross cultural communication more complicated, nonverbal communication cues can further produce misunderstanding. Body language and other nonverbal behavior – such as eye contact, wardrobe in the workplace, personal space and behavior of touching – are standard in each culture. Your ethnocentrism will mean you are comfortable in your own culture's social norms in relation to verbal and nonverbal communication and, likely, uncomfortable in another culture's, even going so far as to consider the other's wrong or distasteful. Think of it this way – if you grow up in a family that frequently embraces one another, then embracing another person, whether family or stranger, will feel completely natural to you. On the other hand, if you've been raised by parents who rarely hug, when another person goes in to embrace or connect with you, you may be reluctant, stiff or even refuse the physical contact. In order to overcome these differences, time and familiarity with this behavior of touch make you grow comfortable in a more physical culture; but if you welcome the embrace with open arms (pun intended), you will soon become more accepting and even demonstrative in this form of nonverbal communication, despite its not being the norm in your personal or cultural identity.

Another example of workplace structures affected by ethnocentricity is the power structure. One person's ethnocentric position on authority may differ from that of another's, based on culture. How does this affect business? Well, when communicating across cultures, social ranking and authority can determine whether or not a message is deemed important enough to deliver or receive. The authority of the sender will also dictate the speed in which the message is delivered and the recipient to whom it's delivered. If you're low on the totem pole according to the specific culture's valuation of authority, then your correspondence may be deemed insignificant.

Additionally, if one culture embraces a low "power distance," then decisions are less often based on authority than those in a culture with a greater power distance. If you're French, you're probably used to a strict authoritarian model. But if you move to Sweden, you may feel like a fish out of water, as the more decentralized authoritarian structure promotes a participative management model, breaking down the barriers in your own status quo. If you want to thrive in your new environment, you must abandon or ignore your ethnocentric beliefs on authoritarian structure and be willing to adopt the Swedish model of participation.

A culture's technological environment, as well as its natural environment, will also dictate the character of a culture and the way it communicates. For example, a Westerner's ethnocentric concept of technology is generally positive. Technology is seen as a way to stay connected to people and to one's workplace and social environment. Businesses that implement technology to improve communication and other aspects of modernization are looking towards the future which, based upon Western values, is a good thing. Those of central African cultures, however, may have a skeptical view of technology, as the environment that exists physically is deemed most important. Still other cultures, like those of East Asia, attempt to integrate a balance between the existing environment and technology, as neither is viewed as more important than the other.

Lastly, cultural social environments decide the degree of value placed on class structure, politics, gender expectations, prejudices, nepotism, social mobility and other important aspects that influence the workplace environment. Though, in some Western cultures, *what* you know may be regarded as more important than *who* you know in the hiring process, in other cultures, such as those in Africa or Latin America, it's not uncommon for someone who has familial connections to be hired over someone who is more qualified for the job. These differences in the hiring process depend upon the culture's perception of familial ties. Those with a high concept obligation to family see nepotism as a way to demonstrate their commitment to its members. They may also benefit from trusting the relation to perform adequately. Those with a low concept obligation to family consider fair hiring practices to mean equal opportunity. The "best man for the job" wins, rather than someone with blood ties. In theory, upward social mobility exists for all those who are willing to put in the work, receive an education and obtain the experience needed to prosper in their career. This is why the "American Dream" was once considered something open to any person willing to pull themselves up by their bootstraps.

These social structures may be the most difficult differences to accept in the workplace when contrasted against one's own ethnocentric values. This is because they may hit a moral nerve, particularly when it comes to class structures and caste systems – or, when the shoe is on the other foot, the lack thereof. For example, Westerners – Americans, in particular – highly value equality; thus, when a Westerner witnesses the subjugation of women in Islamic cultures or the existence of castes in a social system, reserving judgement may prove difficult for the Westerner. When a company from one or another of these cultures wishes to work with a company whose cultural values oppose theirs, they must bridge social structures that contradict their own, and the individuals in these companies must also be able and willing to avoid condemning the other for their culture's systemic beliefs. Though the individual may inherently regard these structures are unjust and is not expected to accept them as otherwise, restraining oneself from projecting one's own values and opinions on the issues in question will be pivotal to one's ability to succeed cross culturally in that business relationship.

Breaking Down Barriers of Ethnocentricity

To put this all into perspective, a few basic tactics can be used to break down barriers of inherent ethnocentricity. As we've discussed, the first step is to be *aware* of the cultural differences.

Once you're aware of the differences, you must decide on your reaction toward these differences. You can *accept* them without condemning them, you can *adapt* your behavior or you can *adopt* the values of your host culture. The next section will illustrate how you can use these tactics to react accordingly to cultural differences and to avoid the trap of ethnocentricity.

In the last section of the book, we'll unearth a strategy to taking *action* and learning a culture. Knowing the culture with which you'll be working and putting in the legwork to understand its language, customs, social structures and history will prepare you for success in your cross cultural exchange. Not only should you always incorporate the proper cultural business etiquette into your dealings with another culture, but you should also engage with the current and historical events that have shaped this culture and its customs. This demonstrates your intention to be culturally sensitive in your dealings and your willingness to lay the groundwork for peaceful relations and smooth, direct communication.

Global markets are expanding and domestic economies are becoming increasingly dependent upon the success of the whole. Such interdependency exacerbates the necessity for all cultures to deal cross culturally in a tolerant manner and to understand that ethnocentric prejudices can disturb harmony in global business relationships. Overcoming the ego inherent in ethnocentricity and accepting that there is not a universal right and wrong will enable positive cross cultural relationships, improved productivity and, in the end, successful business ventures.

What we learned in this chapter:

- Ethnocentrism means to evaluate the values of other cultures based upon your own.

- Ethnocentrism is not a trait specific to prejudiced, bigoted or uneducated individuals; all people have an ethnocentric view of the world.

- In order to prevent ethnocentrism from skewing our perspective, particularly in a workplace environment, we must accept that our own values are not absolute, alter our perspective accordingly and adjust our behaviors to differing cultural values and norms.

- When communicating internationally, cultural variables based on ethnocentricity – such as language, nonverbal communication norms, authority ranks, and technological, natural and social environments – can create barriers, so one must be aware of these variables.

PART III: ACCEPT, ADAPT, ADOPT

Now that we've journeyed through the world of cultural differences and educated ourselves on the ways in which these differences are imbedded in culture and the extent to which they are, how do we now successfully manage in a foreign culture? Well, firstly, we must acknowledge that some personalities perform better in a multi-cultural environment than others. Studies often find that those with social initiative, emotional stability, open-mindedness, flexibility and empathy are better at transitioning across cultures than those without these qualities. And the reality is that oftentimes those managers sent to work in cross cultural environments are lacking in one or several of these areas. During my tenure working in international companies, I've recognized that business professionals are often sent abroad, not for their cross cultural competence or adaptability, but for their business acumen and professional success in their home country.

I've been sent all over the world as a manager. When I was working for an insurance company, my skills and knowledge about insurance was essential, but I was never questioned about my multi-cultural competence. While companies do need people abroad who know their business, how do managers whose strengths are not social initiative, open-mindedness or empathy deal with integrating into another culture?

I'm personally convinced that whether or not your personality is more easily adaptable to foreign cultures, avoiding monkey moments is foremost a matter of will power and accessing the right tools as much as it is a matter of personality. The three A's – *accepting, adapting,* and *adopting* – can serve as a foundation upon which to build when managing in a foreign culture. They won't alter your personality, but they will allow you to assess and improve your cross cultural skills. They will also allow you to react to potential cultural conflicts in a methodical way.

Maybe you don't know whether or not your personality is compatible with cross cultural leadership. To assist in self-assessment, let's start with a couple hypothetical scenarios. For the best results, answer each question honestly.

The first scenario involves grief. The processing of grief differs across cultures. How do you grieve a death? And what do you think is the "appropriate" way to grieve? Is it to be stoic and silent? Or is it to be open emotionally?

If you grew up in a Western culture, then your expectations regarding funerals may be as described by cultural anthropologist, Kelly Swazey: "The funerals I've attended have all been very much the same. Relatives and friends arrive in all black and take seats in the church or synagogue pews for a somber ceremony where prayers are said, memories are shared and tears are shed." Generally, this is the way we, in the West, approach grief.

Now imagine that the death is a close relative, and you're in charge of organizing the funeral. The partner of the departed is from the Middle East and will invite many Middle Eastern guests to the funeral. During the funeral, these guests cry out loudly and moan in their grief. Is this an acceptable form of grief, or do you see this behavior as disrespectful toward the relatives of the departed and/or those who mourn silently? As the funeral's organizer, how far will you adapt the mourning ceremony to accommodate different forms of grief?

This scenario can help you assess how accepting you are regarding other's cultural behaviors. Now imagine that the mourning ceremony does not take place in the US, but in the Middle East. You are invited. Will you keep silent during the ceremony, or will you also stand up during the ceremony and express your grief in loud sobs?

If you decide not to adapt and to keep silent, do you realize you're the monkey? The people around you may interpret your behavior as disrespectful toward the dead. Is this interpretation okay with you? And finally, if you were to move to this country, might you adopt the mourning behavior to the point that it becomes completely natural to grieve aloud?

Does this exercise seem easy to you? Then repeat it in relation to the following forms of cultural funerary traditions. Acknowledge whether you'd be able to accept, adapt or adopt these cultural grieving behaviors following the death of one of your close relatives:

- Blindfold the dead person and expose them on a chair next to the main entrance of the house (Benguet in Northwestern Philippines)

- Chop the dead body to pieces and place them on a mountaintop, exposed to the elements and the vultures (Vajrayana Buddhists in Mongolia and Tibet)

- Exhume the dead body every couple of years, spraying it with wine or perfume, and dance with the body to a band playing joyful music (Malagasy people of Madagascar)[36]

Here are a few more questions to assess your ability to accept, adapt and adopt. Ask yourself to what degree you agree with the following statements:

- People are responsible for their own actions.

- The outcome of events is beyond our control.

- Giving vague and tentative answers is dishonest.

- It is best to avoid direct and honest answers in order not to hurt or embarrass someone.

- Intelligent and efficient people use time wisely and are always punctual.

- Being punctual to work or meetings is not as important as spending time with family or close friends.

- The best way to gain information is to ask direct questions.

- Asking direct questions is rude and intrusive.

- Calling people by their first names shows that you are friendly.

- It is disrespectful to call people by their first names unless they expressly give you permission to do so.

- It is rude not to look at a person who is speaking to you.

- Engaging in direct eye contact with persons of higher status is rude.

These questions come in pairs. The stronger you lean towards one or the other of the statements, the more difficult it will be for you to integrate into a culture that leans the other way. Cultural competency will allow you to find both positions acceptable and respectable behaviors. What is the "right" way will no longer depend solely on your conviction or education. Though change is difficult, learning how to properly accept, adapt and adopt will help you successfully manage in a foreign culture.

7. Learning to Accept

The first step to successful management in a foreign culture is accepting the differences between the culture and your own. This may sound simple, but is it? We've all grown up with certain cultural values. They help us distinguish between the good and the bad. We defend the good and condemn the bad. But how can we behave in an integer way in a world where good and bad is not black and white, where right and wrong is ambiguous?

Let's take the simple concept of marriage, for example. Marriage, according to many people's values and beliefs, should be a union between a man and a woman. Currently, this defining factor is commonly debated in Europe and the US, the question being whether or not same-sex marriage should be acknowledged by the government. Although some traditional societies accept same-sex couplings as marriage, same-sex marriage, overall, has not been a major subject of cross cultural discussion. Rather, another definition of marriage has weighed far more consequential in cross cultural debate: polygamy.

Only about a third of humanity defines marriage as the union between one man and one woman. This, rather, is the definition for only a minority of the world's population. A greater proportion accepts that a man can have more than one wife. At the thought of polygamy, most Westerners will find themselves up against a number of conflicts in relation to their values and norms. Everything about polygamy is wrong. Romantic love should be directed at one person, as should physical love. Moreover, in order to find his/her identity, a child should grow up with one father and one mother.

When working professionally in a foreign culture, you likely won't discuss whether or not polygamy is moral with your colleagues. But the example illustrates the potential problems of conscience when in contact with other cultures and their values. And plenty of less profound issues of conscience can put you in direct conflict with your peers in the work place. For instance, should you accept the hiring practice of your directors when they take on family members instead of qualified candidates? Is a gift a bribe or just a traditional gesture? Do you accept that women are treated as inferior to men in your company? Should female staff be allowed to wear a niqap, even when in contact with customers? If every company in the country is circumventing the tax laws, should you accept a competitive disadvantage by being honest, or should you accept and adapt these principles and behaviors? Should you stop selling a product if it's used for purposes that are inconsistent with your cultural values (as European chemical companies did when they refused to manufacture drugs used for executions in the US)? How will you be able to cope with these conflicts, knowing you cannot change the society in which you live, nor can you dismantle your own convictions? There are solutions and strategies to coping, and they begin with the four principles of cultural acceptance: don't judge, accept ambiguity, tolerate actively and explain yourself.

Don't judge

The first step to successful cross cultural management is to recognize other cultures as valid and to accept them as viable alternatives to your own worldview. You accept that people are genuinely different from you, and you accept the inevitability of other value systems and behavioral norms. Accepting means you do not judge; instead, you try to be as "culture-neutral" as possible, seeing differences as neither good nor bad, but rather as a fact of life. It is not up to the monkey to pass judgment on the other animals in the zoo. This may seem obvious, but in practice, it is difficult. We've all been raised with the conviction that our culture is the right one, if not the best in all the world. Ask an American which country is number one, and he/she will answer, "the US," with full conviction. But French, German, Japanese, Russian and Chinese citizens will all claim their nation is supreme…as will citizens in all other countries with strong nationalism. Consider world rankings. When a list of "the best countries to live in" is produced, you often find it appears in this descending order:

- Norway
- Switzerland
- USA
- The Netherlands
- Australia
- Sweden
- Germany

These are the richest countries per capita in the world (excluding small city-nations and oil-producing countries). So, the citizens of these nations should be proud and happy, shouldn't they?

Now, consider the following ranking:

- South Africa
- Ghana
- Greece
- Italy
- Brazil
- United Kingdom

This is a selection of six countries, ranked according to their suicide rate, the lowest being on top. All six countries have substantially lower suicide rates than the six countries mentioned in the first ranking. It might be that, on average, citizens from Ghana are happier than US citizens, and certainly some citizens from Ghana will affirm that their country is the best in the world. But such things are subjective and so is the scale that defines happiness. You cannot judge the happiness of people with dollars, nor can you measure happiness based solely upon suicide rates. So rather than trying to determine some objective way to judge cultural traits, it's better not to judge at all. When working in another culture, one has to learn that "better" or "worse" doesn't exist in relation to cultural differences. Accept the differences, instead, as what they are: simply differences. Don't judge them. Accept that some people eat dogs, like others eat cows. Accept that some people drink wine, while others condemn alcohol as sinful, etc.

We previously discussed the different conceptions of family, love and sexuality. Values and norms related to these aspects of our lives are deeply rooted. They are amongst the first imprints made during our primary socialization, which is why it may be particularly difficult not to judge attitudes that are vastly different from our own regarding these issues.

In his book, *The Culture Code*, Clotaire Rapaille analyzes different approaches to love and sex by Americans, Italians, French and Japanese. Because he is aware that the topic is sensitive, he goes to great lengths to persuade the reader not to be judgmental about the results of his research. "Some of you will find the following pages disturbing," he says and later writes, "The revelation of the following […] may be upsetting to you, but please remember that the codes are value neutral." [37] He reminds his reader repeatedly that the intention in conducting this research is not to pass judgment upon any culture. Why does a scientific author have to go to such lengths to remind his readers to objectively review the results without condemnation? Essentially, because the topics researched are sex, love and seduction, and the values surrounding these topics are ones we are prepared to defend at all costs. In our collective cultural perspective, the ways in which we approach and view love, sex and seduction are the "right" ways. We consider these values natural; thus, there is a natural inclination to see them as universal and judge those whose opinions on these topics differ. When seeking to communicate and manage successfully across cultures, the foremost restriction you must place on yourself is to stop judging others. The results of Rapaille's research[38]:

- For Americans, love is all about finding Mr. or Mrs. Right. This search is the central theme influencing the concepts of marriage, seduction and sexuality. Because of the harshness of reality, love is then closely associated with false expectation, to the point that a jewelry company in America can advertise the value of the diamond as a symbol for eternal love with Mr. Right, and in the same sentence, stress its resale value. As most relationships end, look on the bright side: at least you can profit from the loss of love by reselling the ring.

- In France, love and pleasure are intertwined. Notions of true love and Mr. Right are irrelevant. Instead, the refinement of pleasure is paramount, and romance is highly sophisticated. Love means helping your partner achieve as much pleasure as possible, even if this requires finding someone else to provide some of it. French couples can of course be devoted to each other, but their definition of devotion differs greatly from the American definition. Fidelity, for instance, is not nearly as important to them. That is why the mistress of the French president, François Mitterand, could attend his funeral, and no one in France batted an eye, nor did they understand the American drama about the relationship between Bill Clinton and his intern.

- Italians believe that life is a comedy rather than a tragedy, and one should laugh whenever possible. They expect love to contain strong dimensions of pleasure, beauty and, above all, fun. If love becomes too dramatic or too difficult, it is unsatisfying. And, anyway, the ultimate love lies not within the arms of Mr. or Mrs. Right, but rather in the maternal love of Mama. Men romance women but seek true love from their mothers, while women express love by becoming mothers.

- And, finally, the Japanese. This culture doesn't understand why Westerners marry young ("If he is young, how can he have the experience to make the right decisions?"). But their greatest contempt is reserved for the notion that Westerners marry for love. "Love is a temporary disease," the Japanese told the researcher. "It is foolish to base something as important as the creation of a family on something so temporary."

These are four very different conceptions of some of the most important and intimate things in our lives: love, sexuality and family. All four have their values, and all four's values are grounded in rationale. All four can be considered prominent countries and valuable cultures. So the question is, knowing this, why would we then judge others and place our cultural values above another's? Instead of searching for the elusive answer to this question, simplify your search by accepting that we are different and that being different is a beautiful thing.

Accept Ambiguity

The human mind is, for the most part, set in stone; most believe they are "in the know." As human beings, we don't like being uncertain or confused; we seek answers and explanations, a pattern we can recognize to make sense of what's happening around us. In the face of an elusive solution or a murky, messy problem, most people are ill at ease, and in a multicultural environment, uncertainty is guaranteed. You may not understand people's reactions, and the lines between what is good and what is bad, right from wrong, begin to blur. Our brains desperately try to make sense out of the conflicting environment. They try to return to a scenario in which the world was orderly and understandable. Our brains are trained to do this. If a situation cannot be resolved, then the people involved stressed, which is seldom a good predisposition for successful management.

This is why, in a multicultural environment, one needs to accept ambiguity. Doing so means remaining perpetually in uncertainty or always questioning, despite never knowing the answer or the direction in which to find it. Accepting ambiguity requires relinquishing control – even though a solution isn't guaranteed – to make room for new and emerging connections that may crystalize and clarify the direction. It also means accepting the fact that the same question may have many answers, each with different but potentially positive results.

The concept of ambiguity tolerance has attracted research in various branches of psychology for more than fifty years, and one of the first studies on the subject involved the analysis of ethnic prejudices in California. Ambiguity tolerance has since been conceived as a personality variable, as a part of company culture and as a part of national cultural. The latest was introduced by Geert Hofstede in the early 80's, under the concept of "uncertainty avoidance." In their research paper, Furnham/Ribchester define ambiguity tolerance in the following way: Ambiguity tolerance refers to the way and degree to which an individual or group perceives and processes information about ambiguous situations or stimuli when confronted by an array of unfamiliar, complex, or incongruent clues. Someone with a low tolerance of ambiguity experiences stress, reacts prematurely, and avoids ambiguous stimuli. At the other end of the scale, however, a person with high tolerance for ambiguity perceives such situations and stimuli as desirable, challenging and interesting.[39] Hofstede uses a far shorter definition for the concept of ambiguity tolerance. His chapter on the subject is simply entitled: "What is different is dangerous."[40]

Hofstede recounts the experience of a couple of American grandparents vacationing in a small Italian town. The grandparents were babysitting their grandchildren, whose American parents (temporarily located in Italy) were away on a trip. The children loved to play with the local Italian children on the central piazza. The American children were allowed to run around; they would fall down, get up again and the grandparents felt there was little real danger in doing so. The Italians grandparents were much more conscientious. They would not let their children out of sight, and when one fell, they were quick to pick the child up and brush off the dirt.

Italy has a fairly low ambiguity tolerance compared with the US. The distinctions between clean/dirty and safe/dangerous are among the first concepts a child learns. Italian grandmothers saw dirt and danger in the piazza, where the American grandparents saw none. Moreover, dirt and danger are not limited to matter. Feelings of dirty and dangerous people are also consequential.

Racism is often bred by a parent's ideology. Children learn that people from a particular category are dirty and dangerous. They learn to avoid children from social, ethnic, religious or political out-groups. Ideas, too, can be considered dirty and dangerous. Children learn that some ideas are good and others taboo. In some cultures, sharp distinctions are made between good and evil ideas. There is a concern about Truth with a capital 'T'. Ideas that differ from this Truth are dangerous and polluting. Little room is left for doubt or relativism.[41] The stronger the system of rules and norms the lower the ambiguity tolerance.

Cultures with a high ambiguity tolerance also have their classifications regarding dirt and danger, but these classifications are less precise and more likely to operate flexibly regarding unknown situations, people, and ideas. In these societies, rules are more elastic, the world is viewed as basically benevolent and to experience novel situations is encouraged.

For example, let's look at the differences in ambiguity tolerance between English and German culture in relation to queuing. In British tradition, queuing is accepted in a polite fashion. German visitors are always astonished to see the stoic and orderly queuing in front of shops, offices or cashiers. Now, the Germans are also known to be orderly; but what really astonishes them is that, in the UK, queuing occurs without defined rules: there are no signs telling people to queue. The high ambiguity tolerance culture of the UK works on principles, leaving space for personal freedom and decision-making, while the German culture of low ambiguity tolerance works on rules.

Cultures have a tendency toward either ambiguity or certainty. According to the culture in which a person grows up, he/she may be able to adapt more or less easily to the need for ambiguity tolerance in cross cultural management. For instance, an individual raised in the diversity of New York may inherently be more tolerant toward different cultures than someone who spent his whole life in the Bavarian Alps. But those who come from remote places or cultures of low ambiguity tolerance can still improve their cross cultural competence. Everyone has the ability to adapt and advance their skillset. Here are some pointers to do so:

- **Stay neutral and suspend judgment.** As mentioned above, any judgment must be weighed with caution in a multicultural environment. Delay expressing positive or negative opinions about topical discussions or explorations.

- **Avoid assumptions.** Open the mind and be curious instead of resistant to what's happening around you. Ask questions that start with "why" and inquire about cultural differences. Look deeper by saying, "Tell me more about that."

- **Take your time.** A world that's asking for order is demanding speed as well, but take your time. Slow things down and take your time to examine, to ask more questions and to reflect upon the answers.

- **Relax consciously.** When raised in a culture with low ambiguity tolerance, you may feel stressed when rules are not clearly dictated, allowing for conflicting positions or more than one truth. Find personal ways to reduce inner stress in such situations, such as deep breathing methods or meditation.

Increasing your personal ambiguity tolerance may be more advantageous than simply improving management skills and adaptability. Tolerance for ambiguity will enable you to deal with uncertain situations in a sensible and calm way in all business and personal relationships. For Bruce Barringer, high ambiguity tolerance is a key characteristic of all successful business owners. "Business owners with a high tolerance for ambiguity can normally handle new and uncertain situations with relative ease, while business owners with a low tolerance for ambiguity would handle the same situations with more angst and unease." [42] Entrepreneur, Jeff Sandefer, writes in *Forbes Magazine*, "An entrepreneur's journey is a hero's journey, but it's a much more difficult and tortured journey than most of us would like to believe. And it's a tolerance for ambiguity that makes all the difference."[43]

Active Tolerance

Tolerance is an ambiguous concept for many, particularly those in a Western success- and career-oriented culture, where tolerance may often be regarded as weakness or lack of principle. Some consider tolerance an inability to stand up for one's own opinion or convictions. To this point, I'd like to introduce a different definition of tolerance, which I call "active tolerance." In essence, active tolerance allows one to firmly defend one's own point of view, while still demonstrating all the respect and consideration for diverging opinions.

My father worked in development aid for a Christian organization, and, in his missionary travels to Africa, he was conflicted when confronted with polygamy. His norms where not only cultural; they were spiritual. The union between man and woman, in his eyes, was something sacred. It was about the will of God. Cultural conflict often becomes significantly more powerful, when the values and norms in question are tied to religious beliefs. To accept divergent behavior becomes a matter of obeying or disobeying God. Suddenly the monkey moment is not skin-deep; it's deeply attached to sin, virtue and eternal life.

Traditionally, Christian missionaries in Africa forced polygamous men to separate from all but their first wife. When arriving to Africa in the seventies, my father was convinced that this principle was righteous. But after some time, he discovered the tragic consequences in its execution. The discarded wives ended up both impoverished and shunned. They became the village outcasts, belonging to no man, no family and with no possibility for future prospects. Neither was the single wife who remained in the marriage happy; she now had to assume all the family chores alone, with the additional charge of the children from the other wives.

While my father was deeply moved by this, on the other hand, he was still convinced that many negative consequences result from polygamy. In the old times, the male mortality rate was far higher than that of women, producing a gender imbalance; therefore, the obligation of the brother to marry the wives of a deceased male sibling ensured some form of social security for the women. That was in the past. But in today's world, polygamy in Africa has overwhelmingly negative consequences, being that male mortality has aligned with that of women. There are now not enough women, which means younger girls are being married off to older men. In some cases, girls are promised for marriage even before their births. To this day, my father remains staunchly against forced marriage and polygamy. But this begs the question: with such staunchly opposing views on such an important issue, how can you work together with people from polygamous cultures? My father was convinced that forcing men to turn out their existing wives was morally wrong, but so was polygamy, itself. How could he work in this society without implicitly accepting polygamy? Should he be tolerant toward it? Should he accept polygamy as simply a differing cultural value?

Cultural tolerance is a dangerous concept for two reasons. One danger is that to accept behaviors and norms which are immoral on a human level is to accept injustice. The second danger is that, in becoming too tolerant, you can lose your own values and cultural identity. This is why active tolerance is a preferable concept to completely objective tolerance. It allows you to retain your values and identity without accepting universally unjust attitudes, while still seeking to understand these attitudes and why they exist. Active tolerance is embedded in the first strategy for cultural integration: *acceptance*.

Active tolerance, in its essence, is about respect. It's about acknowledging different viewpoints and different life experiences as being just as valid as your own, while still maintaining your own diverging values. *Accepting* doesn't necessarily mean to share a point of view or to agree on a certain topic. For my father, active tolerance meant to accept that polygamy has been part of the local culture, that it served a useful purpose in the past and that people who engaged in polygamy did so in good faith. He accepted that polygamy may be acceptable to all involved parties, even though this reality may be difficult for a Westerner to understand. He learned to distinguish between forced marriages and fully consensual polygamy. But still, while respecting the opposing point of view, he remained firmly convinced of his own.

Active tolerance, performed correctly, requires that you actively make an effort to understand different viewpoints. Not a single person comes from the same place. No one has the same life experiences. We are all individuals and, if we don't share our experiences, we cannot learn from one another. But we don't necessarily have to agree. Active tolerance means to respect and understand the reasons someone behaves or identifies with the world differently, while remaining constant in your own point of view if your perspective has not been changed by theirs.

The US and Europe share a common history and cultural heritage. More commonalities can be found in our cultural values than differences. Nevertheless, there are some striking differences. An obvious one is the differing view on capital punishment. Many Americans support the death penalty, while most Europeans condemn it. On both sides of the Atlantic, the discussion is emotional, and there's not much room for compromise. Either you kill a condemned human being, or you don't. I was partially raised within European culture and have always been a firm opponent of capital punishment. When living in Madrid, I integrated into the English-speaking expatriate community. One day, I attended the Sunday morning service of the Southern Baptist Church of Madrid. During the sermon, the pastor discussed capital punishment in accordance with God's law. Citing from the Bible, he explained how capital punishment is an essential norm for a functioning society, and that it is, indeed, God's explicit will. My opinion and emotion got the better of me, and in the middle of the Sunday morning sermon, I raised my hand. When the pastor looked at me, I shouted towards the pulpit, "I must strongly oppose!"

At that time, I knew nothing about American values and culture, but I found myself in a situation where a man publically expressed an opinion with which I deeply disagreed. My conviction was adamantly opposed to the death penalty.

A couple of years later, I moved to southern conservative Richmond, Virginia. I lived in a neighborhood where everyone was in favor capital punishment. These neighbors befriended us, our kids played together, and during our long discussions on the porch in the evening, the question of the morality of capital punishment cropped up. As we spoke, I started to understand the rationale behind the opposing point of view; I discovered that my American friends wanted exactly the same as I did: a safe environment in which to raise our children. We only disagreed on the means by which to make this environment safe. I am still a fervent opponent of capital punishment, but whenever I voice my opinion, I do it with tolerance and respect for those who do not share it. I apply active tolerance. Nowadays, I'd never raise my hand during a Sunday morning service, because it's the wrong place and time to offer my opinion; doing so demonstrated a lack of respect toward the attendants and the pastor.

My father has now retired. He still condemns polygamy and its negative effects on present-day Africa. And still, he serves the continent. He built a shelter for girls fleeing forced marriages, but he also convinced the church council that no man should be made to turn out his wives. One of my father's best friends was the village chieftain of Binde – a man who married twelve women. His friendships and actions demonstrate his active tolerance. I learned from my father to fight against diverging opinion but to always be deeply respectful to the persons who hold them. This is active tolerance, the essence of accepting elements of a foreign culture – the first step for cultural integration. Apply active tolerance, if you your conscience won't allow you to adapt or adopt certain principles. If the cultural gap is too wide, don't accept the opposing point of view, but do accept that the person who has the divergent opinion does so with the same integrity, conviction and positive intent as you do.

At this point, I must also add that there are limits to cultural tolerance. Many crimes have been committed under the legitimization of some cultural traditions: female circumcision, beating of children, sex slavery, burying living wives with their deceased husbands. The list is endless. This begs the question: Where do we draw the line?

In 2009, an image of a girl being flogged in public in a remote area of Pakistan went viral. The harsh punishment was dealt, because the girl went outdoors with a man who was not her father. Should we tolerate such norms, for the sake of religious and cultural respect? Randy Cohen, in his column, "The Ethicist," for the *New York Times* provides a direct answer: "We should not. Tolerance ends where harms begins." An action does not receive a free pass just because it is embedded in an enduring cultural tradition. [44] Whenever the physical or psychological integrity of a person is harmed, then cultural tolerance, whether it be active or passive, should end. As is often true in multicultural discussion, this line is again not highly defined.

Let's look at another question of tolerance: Is male circumcision an acceptable physical harm? I've worked in a top position at a plastic surgery company whose main business is to harm bodies in order that women might better comply with the cultural norms of beauty. Our sense of beauty is strongly influenced by culture. The ideal for feminine beauty in Latin America is big breasts and a large posterior, while Europeans prefer smaller breasts, which is why small breast implants are termed "French style" in the US. Additionally, some African cultures actually prefer flat chests. So if beauty is a cultural concept, doesn't society psychologically harm those who do not conform to the ideal? When the pressure to conform is so strong that many decide to take medical risks and tolerate physical pain to comply with these norms, then you can only deduce that these standards are harmful. And, yet, we often not only tolerate, but accept societal beauty standards in our own culture.

In the end, there is no universal line. When living in another culture, everyone must draw the line for themselves. We must each draw our personal line of tolerance that will not be crossed under any circumstances. For me, whenever the physical or psychological integrity of a person is affected in a sustained or irreversible way, my cultural tolerance comes to an abrupt end. Wikipedia highlights this idea. The biggest human knowledge repository, under the term of "tolerance," lists all the philosophers who've written on the subject and then references the declaration of the "right of men." This right – the right of being alive and being allowed to live unharmed by others – should be the red line of cultural tolerance no one crosses.

Explain Yourself

If you choose to accept with active tolerance, you don't necessarily have to adapt your behavior. You can stay a monkey – a nice and friendly monkey, who doesn't judge or condemn, but remains unquestionably different. In the eyes of locals, you may behave oddly and, even considering your best intentions, your deviant behavior may still be perceived as offensive. You can't expect the culture you visit to be more culturally tolerant than you are. You must acknowledge that you are the visitor and, therefore, if someone must adapt, it should be you, not the other way around. If you choose to be actively tolerant but continue in your own cultural behavior, it is up to you to explain yourself clearly, when you feel this monkey moment of misunderstanding. Instead of ignoring it, speak openly about it and explain why your views and behaviors differ.

Take, for example, Swiss behavior versus the German behavior. Swiss people are substantially less formal than their German neighbors. This is noticeable in the usage of the informal, "du," instead of the more formal, "sie." Both words correspond to the English, "you," but one is used among friends in combination with the first name, while the other is reserved for formal relations. In Swiss companies, most people switch quickly over to the informal, "du," even when speaking to superiors. In this way, the German head of a large Swiss financial group experienced his monkey moment, when he continued using the formal, "sie," with his direct reports in Switzerland. This may be akin to an American manager insisting to be called by his last name, while everyone in the company uses the first name, as is common in the US. Being that he never lived abroad, the German didn't realize he'd created a cultural gap between himself and his team. In the eyes of the employees, his image was one of arrogance and inapproachability. After a couple of years, the executive team participated in a bicycle race around Switzerland. The annual "Tortour" brings cycle enthusiasts together who, for 48 hours, race nonstop around Switzerland. Some Swiss executives form a cycling team, so the German CEO proposed to participate at the Tortour as a kind of team-building exercise. The team participated and actually did quite well, but rather than being remembered for their success, the team is remembered, even after a couple of years, for using the formal, "sie." Everyone on the course heard the teammates use it amongst themselves, and its usage became a topic of discussion. The formality drew similarities to a team football captain insisting on being called "Mr. Beckham" or "Mr. Brady" by his own teammates. This negatively affected both the CEO's image, and the image of the company.

One day, the CEO realized his monkey moment. After four years working daily with his senior executive team, he decided to switch to the informal, "du"; and he did so in a way that reinstated many lost sympathies. He took the time to explain his behavior and the rationale behind it. At an executive meeting, he said, "I've been raised in a very traditional German family. And it is not that I want to be formal, but it is just very hard to be informal, as it sounds inappropriate to me. In my mind, informal language equates to a lack respect, but I also understand that you feel differently about it in Switzerland, and so I propose that we start call each other by our first names." In explaining his behavior, he won over his team. In reality, if he would have explained his behavior from the start, his direct reports would likely have understood and would have been far more tolerant of his slips into formal language. This goes to show that when you feel you've had a monkey moment, explaining yourself to the people around you can only improve your stead.

More importantly, be personal in your approach. Always explain to your monkey behavior to your colleagues in person, face to face. Monkey moments are confusing to all parties involved, and the confusion is not easily resolved via email; in fact, misunderstanding will likely be compounded if you approach its resolution in this way. In an everyday discussion, only 7% of communication is verbal and yet, astonishingly, verbal communication is what most managers concentrate on. In a cross cultural environment, this can be fatal. 58% of communication is in body language and another 35% is in tone of the voice. If you choose to resolve a misunderstanding through email, you'll use only verbal communication and will therefore lose 93% of the interpersonal interpretation of what you're communicating. And what makes matters worse is you won't be able to read the reception from your colleagues, so you won't know whether or not your email bridged the cultural gap or broadened it. Therefore, if you feel a monkey moment or if you decide to accept a behavior but not to adapt, then take the time to explain yourself verbally, personally and face to face.

What we learned in this chapter:

- Accepting requires that you don't judge the local culture, you accept ambiguity, you actively tolerate and you explain your monkey behaviors.

- In order to pass no judgement, you must be as "culture-neutral" as possible, seeing differences as neither good nor bad, but rather as a fact of life.

- Accepting ambiguity requires relinquishing control – even though a solution isn't guaranteed – to make room for new and emerging connections. It also means accepting the fact that the same question may have many answers.

- Active tolerance allows one to firmly defend one's own point of view, while still demonstrating all the respect and consideration for diverging opinions.

- Instead of ignoring monkey moments, speak openly about them and explain why your views and behaviors differ.

8. Learning to Adapt

Accepting behavior which seems unfamiliar, illogical or even threatening to one's own worldview without judgment or condemnation is the inevitable first step to blending in with another culture. Successful leadership begins with being accepted as an individual, and it requires that you accept others in return. But sooner or later, accepting the other's culture won't be enough. Like the German manager in Switzerland, you must further alter your behavior in order to be accepted. This alteration in behavior is called adaption.

When you adapt, you change your behavior, but your values don't change – a change in values will take more time and major internal transformations – but you may begin to consider that the other's values are valid enough to accept and adapt to them. When immersed in a new culture, many aspects of your life will require adaption. Some may be obvious, others subtle and most will come at little personal cost to you. You will swiftly learn how to greet in Japan and how to dress formally in Germany. As long as the new behavior is in accordance or at least in no direct contradiction with your own culture's norms and values, then processing unfamiliar behavior is fast, easy and painless. You may not even notice you've adapted to another culture.

But sometimes adapting will mean discomfort. When you act in a new and unfamiliar way, the contradiction between your new behavior and your old values may not come fast or easy. The change in behavior may create emotional stress, as with the Japanese woman who had to learn to greet with kisses in Spain. Doing so did cost her, as greeting a stranger so familiarly and intimately not only contradicted her norms and values but produced physical discomfort, all of which she had to overcome in order to be accepted. To adapt, the monkey must come out of his cage. He is still a monkey, but he starts to take on some human behaviors. He'd like to jump and swing around on tree limbs, but he accepts that, if he wants to "fit in" with the humans, he'll have to walk slowly on two feet; he'll have to adapt.

When inconsistencies exist between your cultural behaviors and norms and the other's, stress results. We commonly term these changes in behavior and the resulting feelings of anxiety as "coming out of your comfort zone." Just imagine having to eat fried scorpions over a business lunch. How would you react?

Some people handle this stress better than others and adjust themselves accordingly. A person's capacity to handle stress will define how far and how fast he or she will adapt to any new culture. Whether you can step out of your comfort zone or not, sooner or later, in order to survive in different cultures or in a changing world, you must adapt. Consider the following advice to ease and speed this process.

Seeking the "Why"

Human beings find it difficult to accept what they don't understand. When we refuse to accept, adapting to seemingly irrational or random behavior becomes virtually impossible. Understanding *why* someone behaves in a specific way, makes adapting a lot easier. As a monkey, you probably wouldn't recognize the rationale behind peanut-throwing. Sure, it's clear to humans why they throw peanuts, but consider the monkey's perspective. His handler feeds him on a regular basis and yet, although he's no longer hungry, these humans gather around his home, dressed in t-shirts, shorts and baseball caps, and continuously lob peanuts his way. To the monkey, this makes no sense at all. "What a strange, illogical behavior," he thinks. "I have leaves to eat and plenty of leftovers from my handler's feeding this morning. Don't these odd human creatures see this? What's the logic in throwing me more food than I can eat in a lifetime?"

To understand humans, the monkey must ask *why* humans insist on throwing peanuts at him. Once the monkey takes a minute to sit down and ponder the reasoning behind these creatures and their behavior, he may arrive at the conclusion that the spectator isn't necessarily throwing peanuts to *feed* him; they're throwing peanuts to *observe* him. A sleeping monkey is boring to humans; a monkey jumping around, gathering and eating peanuts is far more interesting. The entire exchange is actually more rewarding for the humans than for the monkey, as they appreciate any form of communication or interaction with animals. So the pondering monkey arrives at the conclusion that there is, indeed, a rationale behind the peanut-throwing, and he realizes what is unfamiliar is not necessarily irrational.

In order to survive, we are conditioned to act rationally or, at least, to act in a way that is considered rational in a certain place and period of time. Physicist, D. Hillis, explains it like this: "We like to organize events into chains of cause and effects that explain the consequences of our actions. [...] This makes sense from an evolutionary standpoint. The ultimate job of our nervous system is to make actionable decisions, and predicting the consequences of those decisions is important to our survival."[45] Human beings have been rationalizing since the dawn of civilization. They created society and etiquette, they built cities, they waged war. They had to learn how to do all these things. All of this is not possible without some form of rationale or logic. So how does cultural rationale come into existence?

It all starts with observing the world around you. Imagine growing up somewhere in the African savannah, far away from modern civilization. Every morning, you see the sun rise on one side of the village and set on the other. The land around you is entirely flat, apart from some sparse mountains and hills. You observe this impressive, endless, flat surface and, based on this observation, you assume the world is flat. This assumption isn't unfounded; it's a hypothesis – and then a belief – justified by your own observation and rationale. Whether you've concluded the world is a disk or a square or any other shape with a flat surface, the point is you firmly believe that the earth is flat and a void exists at the end of it.

A 1980 South African comedy, entitled *The Gods Must Be Crazy*, illustrated this scenario. The film begins with a small plane flying over one of these endless South African plains. The pilot is drinking a Coke, and after emptying the bottle, he throws it out the window. Later, a bushman finds this strange, shiny object. Completely unaware of modern civilization, he wonders what it is and how it's used. According to the bushman's rationale, the gods must have sent it, since it fell from the sky. The bushman brings the Coke bottle to his tribe, and they use the empty bottle for various daily tasks – in place of a grinding stone, for instance. Quickly the shiny object becomes the source of discord in this small traditional community. The bottle is considered a prized possession, and everyone wants to own it, but there's only one in existence (or so they believe). After strong disputes over the bottle's ownership, the elders of the tribe decide that, to return peace, they must give this bottle, this gift of the gods, back to its owner. They designate a bushman to walk to the end of the earth and throw the bottle over the rim into the void. From the perspective of those of us who live in the modern world and know that Coke bottles are innocuous and the world is round, the desirability of the Coke bottle and the elders' decision to rid of it off the edge of the earth is completely nonsensical. Even the village's gods act in a way that's incongruous with a God relatable to most of the Western world. Most modern Westerners would agree that God does not throw empty Coke bottles from the sky. If an American crossed the continent on foot, carrying an empty bottle with the objective to throw it over the edge of the earth, he would be considered irrational, certainly not reasonable, and likely mad. But did the bushmen in the movie behave unreasonably? According to their beliefs, no, not at all. Their world is flat, so it makes absolute sense that one might walk to the edge of it and discard a bottle into the void. If your behavior is in accordance with your beliefs, then you act logically based upon your culture's rationale.

Let's apply this concept to an office environment. Many Westerners working with Indian colleagues or employees find their behaviors to be tedious, ambiguous and indecisive. The Western culture favors clear, straight forward dialogue. Direct questions require direct answers without any ambiguity to distort a dialogue's meaning. Being that Western managers champion simple and direct business interactions, they may not understand the rationale behind the indirect behavior of Indian colleagues or employees. The incongruities in communication and the Indian need for managerial approval results in friction between Westerners and their Indian business associates.

I've personally experienced this friction, and it's only when I met Mr. Waseem Hussain that I understood the rationale behind the behavior. Being born from Indian parents but having spent his entire life in Switzerland, Mr. Hussain grew up bicultural, with insights into the European and Indian mentalities. He is the perfect zookeeper to help monkeys understand Indian culture, and his simple explanation behind this behavior follows: "Why can't Indians give a clear answer to a clear issue? Well, the majority of Indians believe in many Gods. If there are many Gods, then there are logically also many truths." Moreover, Mr. Hussain references the Indian concept of harmony to explain their refusal to answer directly. When you ask an Indian employee if a job can be completed "by 5 o'clock tomorrow," typically he or she will respond, "Yes, no problem"; however, the Indian "Yes" rarely corresponds with its Western counterpart. More often than not, the job won't be finished on time. By agreeing to a set deadline without any real intention to complete the work by that deadline, on the surface, the Indian considers himself in harmony with his Western counterpart. If he does not agree, he's in disharmony, which makes him uncomfortable.

Consider Western culture and its own singular rationale regarding these issues. Most Western managers grow up in a Christian environment, believing in a single Christian God and, being as such, they've been conditioned to believe in single universal truths. However, universal truths rarely exist in a cross cultural business environment, and in order to successfully manage, you'll need to be capable of accepting ambiguities and understand that there is always a rationale behind beliefs and behaviors.

What we may consider rational behavior is not universal or absolute. Reason is always relative to your own worldview and environment. Even if the behavior of another culture appears alien to you, all cultures act rational and reasonable in relation to their beliefs, values and norms. Therefore, understanding becomes essential to effective management across culture. Do not assume there is no rationale behind behavior or that the behavior is silly; there *is* rationale, and it is your job as a manager to uncover it and adapt accordingly. Most importantly, never judge or condemn a behavior you do not understand; rather, ask yourself why the person behaves like this by adopting, for a moment, their cultural worldview.

Research has identified four managerial styles to coping with stress in relation to making complex business decisions. [46] The optimal form of managerial decision-making – the form most taught in management school – involves the careful collection of facts and the consideration of alternatives. The application of this style is also the method by which managers most pride themselves, but in reality three additional strategies exist. One involves complacency and spontaneity: ignoring a thorough decision-making process and simply taking the first available course of action. Another involves passing the decision off to someone more qualified and knowledgeable about the subject matter and all aspects of the issue; for instance, a supervisor, a specialist or a consultant. The last decision-making style is to panic by making hasty, ill-conceived decisions. This style is not recommended.

Your form of managerial decision-making is of course predominately defined by your personality, and you can find variations of these four strategies in all cultures. But interestingly, research has highlighted that the distribution of the style varies according to the culture. In Japan and other East-Asian countries, the text-book strategy – evaluating alternatives based on a careful collection of facts – is less predominant than in Western countries, like Australia or the US. Does that mean East-Asian managers are less effective or less rational? Certainly not. They act on a different set of cultural values and norms, and their preferred decision process may simply be the dominant pattern in their collectivist culture. For instance, Japanese managers more openly base decisions on intuition and emotion. How the decision may be received and how it will affect the societal fabric is of primary concern in their decision-making process. When the society's value is not the survival of the individual, but the welfare of the whole group, then this is logical. People act rationally within their cultural values and norms.

The rationality of your decision is based on your life experience, and your life experience is significantly influenced by the cultural environment in which you've grown up. Generally, managers use simple models to make their decisions. No extensive analyzation is required in everyday decision-making; previous experience and personal rule of thumb enables faster and more efficient progress. But, of course, these decisions and their makers are also culturally biased, and so it can be concluded that your own decision-making isn't all that rational. Researchers identified three mechanisms by which the decision-making process is biased: availability, representativeness and anchoring. Let's take a look at each.

Availability

Availability is the extent to which an occurrence or an event is brought to the forefront of a manager's mind, influencing his or her judgement on frequency and probability. An emotional event or one that is easily imagined is more regularly recalled than vague or uninteresting events, thereby making it more prevalent in one's mind. For example, in a US experiment, participants were asked whether more deaths were caused by vehicular accidents or stomach cancer each year. Most believed vehicular accidents had a higher fatality rate than stomach cancer, when in actuality, stomach cancer causes twice as many deaths annually. The frequency and vivid nature of motor vehicle deaths in media accounts has created a bias in US culture that influences the perception in frequency of these two events. For the same reason, Thai people are likely to have much higher estimates of the worldwide death rate from being trampled by water buffalo than are people living in the United States. In this way, cultural differences can lead to different perception and judgement.

Representativeness

A manager's assessment of the likelihood that an event will occur depends upon how well the event fits within their mental model. The higher the similarity, the higher the expected frequency of the event. For instance, the mental model of a loving relationship assumes a lifelong partnership; divorce is not part of the equation. Consequently, many people do not sign a pre-nuptial agreement, because they are convinced the high divorce rate will not apply to them, but the fact is that, in some Western cities, marriage ending in divorce is more likely than lifelong love. Representativeness is so powerful that it overrules the logic of probability. As we already know, mental models are strongly influenced by culture, so decisions based on fact and probability are actually culturally influenced as well.

This principle can have a wide range of implications in the process of making business decisions and in the greater business world. For example, let's take a look at Allianz, a major worldwide insurance company. Present in eleven African countries, upon reviewing its strategy in Africa, the business was profitable but fairly small. The future of the company could lie anywhere between aggressive growth through acquisition and selling off the business entirely. In March 2014, a growth strategy was presented to and rejected by the board of the insurance company, on the grounds that corruption is too prevalent in Africa and may pose serious reputational risk for the insurance group. This, alone, is not surprising. But interestingly, confirmed by the Transparence International list which rates national corruption around the globe, the same insurance group was active throughout Eastern Europe in many countries with far worse corruption than their African counterparts. Due to the fact that Europe's mental model portrays all of Africa as extremely corrupt, profitability and a successful business venture was dismissed based on representativeness – or the wrong assumption of probabilities.

Anchoring

Managers often make decisions by starting from some initial point and then slowly adjusting until they reach a final decision. The initial point is called the anchor and is also culturally influenced. Numerous examples of bias result from anchoring. For instance, some school systems separate the children at an early age into various performance groups. A child from a low performance group will often be regarded as a poor performer, even if his results are actually better than some of the children in the high performance group, simply because the members of the latter group were once categorized as superior.

In cross cultural negotiation, anchoring can strongly influence the outcome of negotiations. Take this simple example: When a tourist comes to the souks and markets of northern Africa to buy a carpet, he is an easy target for exploitation, because his anchoring for carpets is so high; based upon his own social fabric, he expects to pay higher prices for quality goods and is unaware that carpets are normally sold so cheaply in northern Africa. Therefore, this tourist is easily taken advantage of.

Another example of anchoring in price negotiation can be seen in the real estate prices in Vancouver. When the Hong Kong Chinese emigrated to Vancouver, though not rich, they were known to pay high housing prices, simply because Hong Kong has extremely high real estate rates. As their initial anchor was high, they were exploited and ended up settling on higher rents and paying more than the locals.

These are only three ways in which culture can influence our decision-making. Research is continuously being done to evaluate why and how we make our "rational" decisions, and as it pertains to business and culture, studies have revealed that:

- to a far higher degree than their Chinese counterparts, US managers assume that big events must be the result of big causes ("Kennedy can't have been killed by a lone gunman; it must be a conspiracy").

- Mexican managers are more confident in the veracity of their decisions than their American counterparts and are more likely to escalate their commitment – throw good money after bad, as the Americans would say.

- Chinese managers produce far less thorough risk assessments than their American counterparts, as they find fewer reasons that a decision could potentially go wrong.

While it is impossible to summarize here all the implications of cultural bias in decision-making, one important aspect to keep in mind is that managers make decisions based on a simplified mental model. Managers who come from another cultural background will perceive the world differently and develop different mental decision models; therefore, subjective realities will vary across the board. But, again, this does not mean they act irrationally, though according to your own subjective cultural reality and perception, it may appear they do. They make decisions rationally according to their cultural framework.

With this information at hand, as a manager in another culture, you should always assume those around you act rationally according to their own culture. Never judge or condemn someone's actions or decisions, because they seem illogical or irrational to you before becoming familiar with the cultural perception and reality surrounding you. Doing so will make it much easier to accept behavior which at first seemed strange or even offensive to you.

Creating Analogies

A German business consultant had a mandate to reorganize a French company. She started to travel frequently to Paris but found it extremely difficult to make any progress with her project. Despite the company being centralized and highly hierarchical, she often had problems when it came to identifying the decision makers. Many people tried to interfere with the project or claimed to be the decision makers, despite not appearing directly related to the project in any hierarchical function. The longer the project lasted, the less support they gave her, until it reached the point where she was unable to access the information or even make an appointment with management. Trips to Paris were no longer an excitement, but a chore. She was on the verge of leaving the project, when she decided instead to look for someone who could help her understand the basic functioning of a stereotypical French company.

At a friend's wedding party, she met a French manager who'd spent the last fifteen years in Germany. In an instant, he explained how to deal with the company in a way that made everything crystal clear: "Forget your German vision of a company functioning like clockwork. French companies are royal courts. The CEO is the king and, around him, there are dozens of noblemen, servants, knights, all trying to win the king's attention and to build their own little fiefdom. In this world, you have to act like a small earl. Be humble in the right moment. Be bold in the right moment. Be courteous when required. Be rude when needed. Build your political relationship and network, until you have the ear and favor of the king or one of his important ministers."

French companies are not monarchies, but France is a country with strong monarchies dating back a thousand years, followed by a strong, centralized presidential state, so it follows that this history has influenced French thinking and, therefore, also the inner workings of French companies. It is not for nothing that President François Mitterand was called the "last French King." The German business consultant adapted her behavior to this new vision and, though it was still a difficult and painful experience, at least she could now better understand the company's dynamic. The analogy, "French companies are like royal courts," created a new frame of interpretation for the daily experiences, which had at first seemed irrational from the perspective of a manager whose experiences were grounded in a well-oiled German company.

HIGH POWER DISTANCE	LOW POWER DISTANCE
CHILDREN ARE REQUIRED TO BE OBEDIENT AND RESPECTFUL TO PARENTS, TEACHERS AND ELDERLY PEOPLE	CHILDREN ARE ALLOWED TO CONTRADICT PARENTS. THERE IS MORE TWO-WAY DISCUSSION IN CLASSROOMS
EMPLOYEES DO NOT CHALLENGE THEIR SUPERIORS DIRECTLY	SUPERIORS MAY CONSULT WITH SUBORDINATES BEFORE MAKING A DECISION
EMPLOYEES ARE RELUCTANT TO DISCUSS PROBLEMS OR CONCERNS WITH THEIR SUPERIORS	EMPLOYEES BRING CONCERN AND GRIEVANCES TO THE ATTENTION OF MANAGEMENT
THE IDEAL BOSS IS A FATHERLY AUTOCRAT	THE IDEAL BOSS INSPIRES THE WORKERS TO STRIVE VOLUNTARILY TOWARD A COMMON GOAL
THERE ARE LARGE DIFFERENCES IN SALARY AND SKILLS	SALARY DIFFERENCES ARE SMALLER AND WORKERS MAY RESENT EXCESSIVE PERKS ON THE PART OF EXECUTIVES
IT IS ACCEPTED THAT A FEW ARE DESTINED TO RULE AND MANY ARE DESTINED TO FOLLOW	SUPERIORS MUST EARN THEIR POSITION AND HOLD IT FOR LIMITED TIME

Analogies are powerful images which assist your mind in quickly adapting the mental model required for a certain situation and environment. We all base our daily decision on our past experience, on our trainings and our education. This has created in our brain a mental model allowing us to make decisions without knowing every single detail of reality. Mental models are images, representations or schemes of how we perceive and understand the world around us. We form mental models of just about everything – cars, airplanes, corporations, ballet, opera, markets and their evolution, competition, operations, customer loyalty, consumer marketing, innovation, operational excellence, knowledge development and management, and so on.

Like all models, mental models are abstractions of reality. The model is less complex than the real world. No matter how well constructed, all models are wrong in some context or time. Unfortunately, mental models are also difficult to change. And that is where analogies come in. Analogies trick our brains into mixing the mental models of two different areas such as "companies" and "royal courts." Suddenly, we see these things in a new light, and we come to new conclusions and possibly make different decisions based upon this new perspective.

Analogies translate an unknown social construct into something you can comprehend. If the analogy is good, then many of the decisions you make according to this corrected mental model will be rational in relation to the culture's social constructs. Of course, an analogy is never perfect, but often a good analogy will always be better than the culturally distorted view you've brought from abroad.

Geert Hofstede developed further dimensions than those detailed in the previous chapters, including "power distance" and "uncertainty avoidance," which are specifically geared towards behavior in the workplace.

Power distance is defined as the extent to which the less powerful members of institutions and organizations expect and accept that power is distributed unequally. In a culture with high power distance, the employees will never challenge their superior directly. The ideal boss is a fatherly autocrat. Often the countries for which high power distance is the model are vertically segregated, and the division between the rich and the poor is generally accepted. On the opposite end of the spectrum, cultures with low power distance seek a more egalitarian distribution of power. Superiors are expected to consult with their employees and to de-emphasize their hierarchical status.

Uncertainty avoidance measures to what degree people in a society accept chaos and unpredictability. A high uncertainty avoidance ranking indicates the country has a low tolerance for uncertainty and ambiguity, thereby producing a rule-oriented society that institutes laws, rules, regulations and controls in order to reduce uncertainty. A low uncertainty avoidance ranking indicates the country is less concerned about ambiguity and uncertainty and has more tolerance for a variety of opinions, resulting in a society that is less rule-oriented, more readily accepts change and takes more and greater risks.

Hofstede put these two dimensions on the two axes of a matrix and created a great set of helpful analogies.

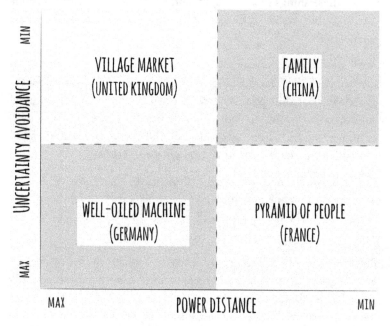

A typical German company works like a "well-oiled machine" or a clock. All wheels work in cohesion (i.e. rules regulate the company) and all wheels are equally important for the proper functioning of the watch (i.e. low power distance). A German company usually has decentralized decision-making and a narrow span of control, with top management working as a team. The company is managed on all levels by a detailed set or rules, put into practice through a number of forms and handbooks. German companies are highly efficient but are usually not very flexible. Creativity is not highly valued, while quality and conformity are significantly important.

A typical French company can be compared to a "pyramid of people" or, as previously mentioned, a royal court. The king sits on top, while below the dukes, the earls, the viscounts, the barons and, many levels below, the peasants. And similar to a real royal court, French companies have their fair share of intrigue, due to the combination of high power distance and high uncertainty avoidance. Decision-making is centralized and the company is usually coordinated from the top with little downward delegation. A complex network of informal relationships bridges the hierarchical levels. Authority and power are valued most. You'll often find these types of companies in Southern Europe and Latin America.

A typical Chinese company can be compared to the functioning of a family with a patriarch at its head. The company is operated by a complex combination that couples high power distance with low uncertainty avoidance, typical for hierarchical societies. In Chinese companies, relationships within the company and loyalty to the company are strong. Employees tend to work their whole life for the same employer. On the other hand, an entrepreneurial spirit and a willingness to bend rules and take risks is more recently being embraced, making China a future economic super power.

Lastly, a typical English company is a village market, utilizing rather flat hierarchies combined with risk-taking, resulting in the archetypal Anglo-Saxon entrepreneurial spirit.

The four analogies – the pyramid, the well-oiled machine, the family, and the village market – are not perfect; nevertheless, they summarize in one word a specific mental model for business management within these cultures.

Cultures are complex, and it may be completely impractical to learn a huge new set of behavioral rules, altering your own cultural identity in this situation or that. Analogies provide you a rough idea of just how a system works, translated into a familiar and relatable concept. As mentioned, analogies are never perfect, but they are a useful tool to help you understand and behave correctly in a new environment, which might otherwise appear completely chaotic and incomprehensible. They offer a simple starting point from which to intuitively make the right decisions. With time, these relatively simple models will be replaced by the growing experience you gain while managing and living in a foreign culture. So, when discussing your new culture with expats, pick their brains for an analogy or pick up on one through discussion. For those who've lived as an expat for any length of time in another culture, the nuances of that culture will have been absorbed and will likely recur in discussion. Harness these nuances and build upon them. Create an analogy that provides a clear mental model from which you can anchor your decisions.

As a child, the author and professor, Clotaire Rapaille, was exposed to several cultures, and as a professor, he dedicated his research to discovering why people around the world are so different. His insight became so relevant for global companies that he found himself in the position of personal advisor for ten high-ranking CEO's and is currently kept on retainer by half of the Fortune 100 companies. In his bestselling book, *The Culture Code,* he uses simple analogies to understand other cultures in a sophisticated, efficient and concise way.

He was mandated by Chrysler to help develop the retro-car, the PT Cruiser. The concept of the car was shaped through in-depth focus groups, analyzing the deeper "code" of what a car represents in the US. American children learn during primary socialization the importance of the family car. Later, they want a car that will trigger memories of Sunday drives, the freedom of getting behind the wheel for the first time, the excitement of youthful passion. The first sexual experience for more than 80% of Americans takes place in the backseat of a car. The car is analogous in America with *identity*. The PT Cruiser was the perfect answer to this strong emotional relationship between Americans and their vehicles.

Just as the production planning for the PT Cruiser began, Chrysler was taken over by the German car manufacturer Daimler-Benz (Mercedes). Germans have a very different relationship with their vehicles. They aren't allowed to drive before the age of 18, so few would associate their first sexual experience with a car. Germans pride themselves on quality of engineering, and so the first thought that springs to mind when thinking of cars would be quality. Cars in Germany represent *engineering*.

These cultural differences nearly killed the PT Cruiser project. While the individualistic retro-design of the car touched upon all the emotional strings of Americans, it was, at best, average from an engineering point of view. German executives responded negatively to the modest technological quality of the car. Believing that the PT Cruiser would be a marketing disaster, they relegated production to a minor plant in Mexico. And yet, the car became an instant success in the US and could have sold a lot more in the first year if the plant would have been better equipped to keep up with demand.[47]

Other examples of analogies across cultures include those involving managing and negotiating. In Africa, one might say, "here, you manage families and not individuals," a typical analogy in a collectivist culture. In Russia, one might compare negotiations to "playing poker," while negotiating with Germans may be compared to "playing chess." Moreover, the language of negotiating often uses sports jargon, including "fairplay" in negotiating a contract; some might even suggest negotiating is like war, with only minimal rules. Everyone wants to "win" a negotiation, but the means and the tactics will differ substantially across cultures, and creating analogies will help you come out on top by framing the other culture's behavior in a way that allows you to more often make the right decisions.

One of the most interesting analogies involves negotiating in China. For many Westerner, dealing with the Chinese is an enigma. One moment you feel confident in mutual trust and cooperation, the next, you feel you've been tricked into something you hadn't anticipated, only to be supported again the next day. The seemingly random and unpredictable pattern was given deeper meaning, once a good friend had explained to me the rice field analogy. The Chinese grow up with rice. From early childhood to old age, a Chinese person will eat rice every day. When driving through the countryside, he'll see the terraces of rice fields, all flooded with a common irrigation system. Cultivating rice requires a lot more cooperation than cultivating crops in Europe or the US. The water has to flow through the fields, from one terrace down to the next. Working your own little piece of land without consideration for the rest of the village will not produce results. So an equilibrium between cooperation and holding your own must remain. Think about it: you're working in a rice field, connected to the same water system as your business partner's field. You'll need to cooperate with your business partner in order to achieve success, but you will also need to be clever to combat those who attempt to take advantage, or in order to seek your own advantage. Just walking away and splitting from a cheating business partner, like you might do in the Western world, is simply not an option. So, if you negotiate with Chinese partners, the analogy of the rice fields might allow insight into Chinese mentality.

Using Stereotypes Wisely

Analogies are simple explanations for complex issues. They are like roadmaps, simplifying reality to give you direction. If you've ever tried to find your way in a city with the satellite view of Google Earth, then you know the difference. With so many details, you cannot find your way. If you switch to the map view, suddenly you have a lot less information, but it's the most pertinent information, the information you need, in order to get to wherever you're going. Analogies work like road maps...but be careful; they are very simplified views. Stereotypes work in a similar fashion. They, too, offer you a simplified view regarding the behavior of people from other cultures. But they can also be dangerous and create a toxic and intolerant perspective; they may be correct in one situation, completely wrong in another, and are quite often unfair, prejudicial, disrespectful and discriminatory.

Stereotypes are thoughts and beliefs about a certain group's behaviors and ideology. They usually involve characteristics that are different from one's own culture and, in our minds, envelope an entire group. Italians are jovial. Americans are superficial. Swiss are punctual. British have a stiff upper lip. Russians love vodka. French are good lovers and drink wine. Spaniards are proud people and take siestas. Indians speak funny English and have brains wired for software-development. Japanese are always polite and never show their feeling. The list is endless.

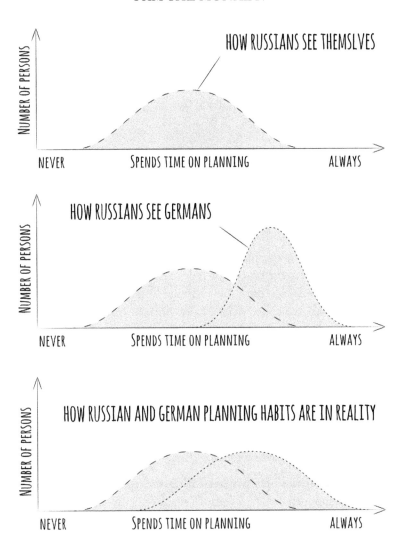

The word stereotype was actually first used in a different context, derived from the Greek words, "stereos," meaning firm and solid, and "typos," meaning impression; hence, the literal translation "solid impression." The term was applied to the printing trade in 1798 by Firmin Didot to describe a printing plate that duplicated any typography. The duplicate printing plate, or the stereotype, was used for printing instead of the original. In 1922, "stereotype" was first applied in the modern psychological sense by the American journalist, Walter Lippmann. In analogy to the printing process, a stereotype is supposed to be a "solid impression" regarding the characteristics of a certain group of people. Research shows that stereotypes are often cemented in people's minds, and therefore, Lippmann was correct in applying this term to the way we think of other groups and cultures.

Stereotypes are not all evil; sometimes they can be helpful to navigating new cultures. Let's take Ralf, for example. This German manager runs a company which is expanding into Russia, and as head of business development, he is intimately involved in this venture. One morning the Russian project manager phones him up. He's assisting in the opening of the new office in St. Petersburg. He informs Ralf that the planning is well under way, and everything should go according be completed on time. Ralf follows up with some questions regarding the planning and, to his astonishment, only receives vague answers. Every time he presses for further details, the Russian manager answers with ambiguity; he says that, at this point, only the rough planning is done but that everything is under control. The conversation leaves Ralf uneasy, and his confidence in a timely opening is shaken. He expresses his worries to his boss, who answers with a smile: "Don't worry. Russians are not good at planning. If you plan too much, they say, you will never be able to show your talents of improvisation. But you'll see, the offices will be finished on time."

Ralf's boss answers his worries with a stereotype, but one that is actually supported by scientific research. Russians place less emphasis on detailed planning and are less prospective than, for instance, Germans or Austrians. Research has shown that they prefer not to invest time in potential future problems, but rather to solve them as they occur.[48] In this example, a stereotype provided an easy answer to Ralf's stress and defused a potential conflict in international business relations. The stereotype helped Ralf understand the rationality behind the behavior of his Russian counterpart.

On the opposite end, the Russian might have expressed to his boss his own worries about Ralf's lack of confidence in him. His boss might have then explained the stereotypical German mindset. "German businessmen are proud of their planning skills, which are often very detailed and far-reaching. They try to anticipate potential issues and to develop alternatives before the issues occur. They do this not only to reduce risk, but also to use time as efficiently as possible." This would be a generally true stereotype; to Germans, time is a costly resource and shouldn't be wasted, thus Germans invest energy and place emphasis on detailed planning. In this way, stereotypes can be useful for mutual understanding.

We have used stereotypes regularly in this book. For instance, we have often mentioned "Western culture," and we all associate some values, beliefs and norms with this culture. But what exactly is Western culture? Western culture is often identified with the common set of values and norms one might find in Europe and countries heavily influenced by European populations, such as those of North America or Australia. Of course, these values vary widely, and there are substantial differences from country to country. But strong commonalities are also plain, due to the common heritage which reaches back to the Greek and Roman Empires and a continuous and strong influence by Judeo-Christian religions. Since the period of Enlightenment in the 18th century, European culture has become increasingly secular, rationalist and oriented towards scientific and social progress. Overall, Europeans share common values regarding democracy, political pluralism and the separation of church and state.

Though we never defined Western culture, somehow we all understood its ideology. We must therefore have imbedded in our brains a stereotype of how someone from the West might behave, as opposed to, for instance, someone from an Eastern culture. While we recognize that not all Europeans, Americans or Australians are equal and there are substantial difference between countries and, moreover, between regions and, even further, between every individual personality, we still know that generic broad common behaviors exist.

Stereotypes are not all-encompassing; not every Russian likes to improvise, nor is every German an avid planner. There are certainly some Russians who are excellent planners and may even be far better and spend more time on detailed planning than the average German. The figure above shows how the Russians see their own inclination for planning; some Russians like planning and some don't. They acknowledge that most value improvisation more than planning, which is why the curve is slightly to the left of the middle. Then there are the Germans. From a Russian's perspective, most Germans are fanatic planners. So we see an evenly distributed curve for the Russians self-evaluation, while all the Germans fall under the same stereotype. The reality is actually more like the lowest chart. It's true that, on average, the German company culture favors and produces managers who emphasize planning, but this does not apply to all Germans. Therefore, stereotypes are only useful when arriving at a general understanding about the preferences of a culture, as they may provide some generic odds regarding individuals in the specified group. But, in other cases, the stereotype may color your opinion of an individual in an unflattering and untrue way.

Applying stereotypes wisely involves making a basic assumption on the behavior, values or norms of a person according to his or her culture, but then opening your mind to the individuality of all people. For example, when sitting in a plane, I would be more inclined to talk with the person next to me if he held an American passport as opposed to a Swiss one. This is because I know the Swiss generally don't like small talk, while many Americans find it courteous. But of course, I would also keep in mind the fact that some Americans don't like to chat on the plane, while some Swiss might enjoy it. If you test the waters and find that the individual fits the stereotype, then use your observation to proceed at your own discretion.

Heiri Müller, a famous Swiss TV anchorman, took the train from Zurich to Chur. The passenger in front of him recognized the famous anchorman but did not say a word until the train arrived at its destination. Then he stood up, held out his hand and said, "Mr. Müller, it has been a pleasure to travel with you." This Swiss passenger fits the Swiss stereotype perfectly.

Finally, let's take a look again at unfair stereotypes. As mentioned before, the dog-eating stereotype in Korea nearly led to a US boycott of the World Soccer Games when, in all actuality, the practice of eating dogs has been banned by law and is only applicable to a tiny minority of Koreans. Switzerland hosted the European Soccer Championship together with Austria in 2008. In Switzerland, it is not uncommon for farmers in the mountains to eat cats; the practice hasn't been outlawed and some still do it to this day. And yet, there was no backlash when Switzerland hosted the European Soccer Championship. This illustrates how stereotypes seldom provide a complete and true image of a culture and its practices. Use stereotypes constructively as your starting point but proceed with caution. In the instance of the Russian project manager, accept that Russians don't generally make detailed plans and be prepared for work-arounds, but also be prepared to find Russians who will exceed your culturally-biased expectations.

Changing Perspective
(or putting yourself in someone else's shoes)

When investigating personality traits for good management, empathy always emerges as one of the principal attributes to facilitating cross cultural relations. Empathy relates to one's capacity to share and understand feelings and emotions and is often characterized as the ability to "put yourself in someone else's shoes."

Empathy is often used interchangeably with its more commonly used cousin, sympathy. However, these are not one in the same; there are innate differences between sympathy and empathy. Sympathy is to care about and feel for someone else's trouble, grief or misfortune. It is to acknowledge another's emotional hardships and provide comfort and assurance.

Empathy goes a step further. Empathy is formed from the ancient Greek word, "empatheia." The prefix, "en," translates to "in," while the root, "pathos," means "feeling" or "passion." The word literally means to be "in feeling."

So when you're empathizing with another person, you're getting into the feelings of said person. Empathy is not only about being commensurate with the hardship of someone else. Empathy is to assume their feelings upon yourself and allow yourself to feel what they feel. Being as such, when it comes to cross cultural management, empathy is the more important of the two.

A small example will clarify the difference: Imagine you are a fourth grade teacher in New York. You have a new student starting in your class, and the child is visibly frightened. He just moved with his parents from New Zealand to the US. You show the student sympathy by demonstrating that you understanding his situation and by trying to comfort him as best you can. But to show empathy, you must imagine what it would be like to be a pre-adolescent in a new place, yourself. You may not be able to replicate the feeling exactly, but surely you can imagine what it must feel like, based on similar experiences of discomfort in a strange, unknown place. When you empathize, your understanding of the child's situation will be far deeper and, therefore, you'll also be able to better provide the child confidence through your words, your presence and in your treatment of him. By putting yourself in the shoes of this fourth grader, you tried to see the world through his eyes. This is empathy.

Empathy allows people from different cultural backgrounds to relate to one another by placing themselves in the other person's position. Once you take a moment to consider a person's background, culture, experiences and personality, then imagining their mentality and actions becomes easier. You are then able to deal with any conflicts that arise with that person, because your empathy has allowed for understanding. In return, you expect that person to do the same by putting themselves in your shoes. From an emotional standpoint, empathy draws from the golden rule: "treat others as you would like to be treated."

Empathy is a trait of your personality and cannot be easily acquired or altered. Some people are by nature more empathic than others. But changing perspective is also a voluntary act. The ability to shift perspective and see the world from the standpoint of your host's culture is necessary for successful cross cultural adaption. Chapter one illustrated this shift with the "monkey experiment." The radical change of perspective pushed you to try and view the world through the eyes of a monkey.

Changing perspective allows us to slip into another person's skin, in order to understand how that person thinks and feels. To some, empathy is natural, and they can slip into another's skin more easily than others. Most people who grew up in a multicultural environment have the innate ability to change perspective fluidly, because, for them, more than one world exists. Switching from one reality to the other is familiar and instinctive. For others, shifting perspective may be much more difficult, but it can be accomplished voluntarily by simply asking yourself how you'd feel if a foreigner exhibited a similar behavior to you in your home country. By simply asking yourself to tap into another's situation, you are able to produce this shift in perspective. And when you do, you'll see how obvious most major cultural blunders are.

Take, for example, our favorite Walmart CEO once again. He refused to learn German and declared English as the company language in the Germany. If you are a US citizen working for BMW in New York, how would you react if the new US-CEO of BMW declared German as the company language and consistently refused to learn and speak English? Or how would a UK worker in the Land Rover factory in Sulihill feel if the new owners of the car manufacturer, the Indian company Tata, declared Hindi as the company language?

Consider, also, the issue Americans took with Korea's traditional habit of eating dogs. Now imagine if India would have refused to participate at the Olympics in Atlanta on the grounds that Americans eat steak and hamburgers, produced from holy cows.

The Japanese learn from childhood, onward, that there should be no physical contact with foreigners. Touching the face is taboo and is considered to be very intimate. Now imagine how a Japanese person feels when he is hugged by a Russian or kissed by a Spanish woman. The act would be akin to a Westerner's private parts being touched as a greeting. Wouldn't this feel awkward and uncomfortable for you?

In his blog on *Psychology Today*, psychologist, J. E. Sherman, recounts how an individual – and, in the end, a hero – was able to put himself in the shoes of the Soviet president and may have saved the world from nuclear war.

> "At the height of the Cold War the Soviets had installed missiles in Cuba, 225 miles off the coast of Florida. Under this threat President Kennedy thought his best option was an airstrike to bomb the missiles which would have undoubtedly led to an escalating nuclear war. Kennedy didn't see another way out. We couldn't let the Soviets just get away with it. Tommy Thompson, a senior foreign service officer who had lived with the Soviet Premier Khrushchev advised against it. Thompson, a competent shoe-shifter put himself in Khrushchev's shoes. He recognized that Khrushchev wasn't expecting the US to find out about the missiles so early and hadn't foreseen the potential for direct confrontation. He would be looking for a way to save face, to claim that he had saved Cuba from attack. He convinced Kennedy to make the softer offer that if Khrushchev pulled out, the US wouldn't retaliate. Khrushchev went for it, and we were all spared Armageddon."[49]

To become more like Tommy Thompson, you must learn to look at things from the other person's point of view. Everyone can improve upon their shoe-shifting abilities by first making it a conscious process. When you are in a situation of cultural conflict, ask yourself the following question: "How would I react if the exact same situation happened to me in my home country?" This requires some imagination, but you'll quickly source out some empathy and insight by imagining what your potential thoughts, actions and emotions would be if the shoe was on the other foot. This change in perspective will enable you to be more tolerant toward other points of view, and it will ease your ability to adapt to other cultures.

The second way to make this a conscious process is to listen actively. Active listening is considered one of the most powerful psychological tools to improving mutual understanding. You've probably already heard of this essential tool, or you may already practice it daily in your business relations.

Generally, when people talk to each other, they don't listen attentively. Most often, we are distracted – half listening, half thinking about something else. Moreover, when people are engaged in conflict, they are even more likely to be too busy formulating a response to what is being said than listening. They assume they've heard what their opponent is saying many times before, so rather than paying attention, they focus on how they can win the argument.

Active listening is a structured form of listening and responding which focuses one's attention on the speaker. The listener must take care to attend to the speaker fully, and then repeat, in his or her own words, what the speaker has said. You don't have to agree with the speaker. You must simply state what you believe the speaker has expressed. Repeating, in your own words, the speaker's point of view, forces you to switch perspective. You shift shoes. The speaker will then identify whether or not you fully understood him. If there is a misunderstanding, the speaker can then explain himself more thoroughly. Being able to engage in this way obviously offers many benefits when it comes not only to cross cultural understanding, but understanding, in general.

Repeating what you've heard will prevent misunderstandings. In reformulating another's thoughts in your own words, you inevitably apply your own cultural framework to what you've heard. At this point, cultural differences will rise to the surface. If your interpretation leads to a different understanding of the speaker's thoughts, then the speaker will notice the misunderstanding at this moment and can clarify what they meant. It's like you put on the other's shoes, and he now points out you're wearing them the wrong way.

Next to shoe-shifting, another important benefit of active listening is that it tends to open people up, to get them to speak more. When people are in conflict, they often contradict one another, denying their opponent's situational perspective. This tends to make each person defensive, and they will either lash out or withdraw and say nothing more. However, if each person feels as though their opponent wants to listen and is attuned to their concerns, they are more likely to explain in detail what they feel and why. If both parties in a conflict can better explain their issues and understand their opponent's concerns, the chances of being able to develop a solution to their mutual problem are much greater.

The ability to shift perspective and listen actively is not only important for cross cultural management, it's important for being human. Training this ability will improve your relationships, will improve your insights, and will make you a better leader, in general. As psychologist, Alfred Adler, noted: "It is the individual who is not interested in his fellow men who has the greatest difficulties in life and provides the greatest injury to others."

The importance of changing perspective for cultural understanding was demonstrate in a very bold and courageous move by the Saudi journalist, Nadine Al-Budair. In her fight against sectarian violence, she wrote an article in the Kuwaiti daily newspaper, *Al-Rai*, about terrorism, but inverting locations and religions. She wondered how Muslims would have acted if Christians had blown themselves up in their midst or tried to force their faith on them: "Imagine a Western youth coming here and carrying out a suicide mission in one of our public squares in the name of the Cross. Imagine that two skyscrapers had collapsed in some Arab capital, and that an extremist Christian group, donning millennium-old garb, had emerged to take responsibility for the event, while stressing its determination to revive Christian teachings or some Christian rulings, according to its understanding, to live like in the time [of Jesus] and his disciples, and to implement certain edicts of Christian scholars." [50] The article resonated worldwide. Change of perspective is a very powerful tool for cross cultural understanding. Just imagine...

What we learned in this chapter:

- Adapting requires that you seek the "why," create analogies to better understand local culture, use stereotypes wisely and change your perspective.

- Never judge or condemn a behavior you do not understand; rather, ask yourself why the person behaves like this by adopting, for a moment, their cultural worldview.

- Analogies create a new, simplified frame of interpretation for daily experiences, which at first may seem irrational.

- Like analogies, stereotypes present a simplified view regarding the behavior of people from other cultures, but they can be dangerous and must be applied wisely.

- Empathy – or putting yourself in another's shoes – is essential to understanding.

9. Learning to Adopt

There is nothing to be written about learning to adopt. Adoption of a culture requires a lot of time, but eventually it will come naturally. Remember the example of the fried scorpion dish in Southern China? If you live long enough among your Chinese friends, then one day, you will also appreciate the crunchy taste of fried scorpions. Don't bother about finding methods or strategies to get there. Concentrate on *awareness*, *accepting* and *adapting*, and the last step will come with time. With willpower, you may change your behavior. You may also voluntarily adapt to the norms of your host country. But you can't change your deep rooted values by simply deciding to do so. Your values will need time and openness to change, along with your willingness to journey through a new culture. Just let it happen. You'll discover a new self, a new freedom to move within various cultures and new freedom from your own culture, as well.

PART IV: ACTION

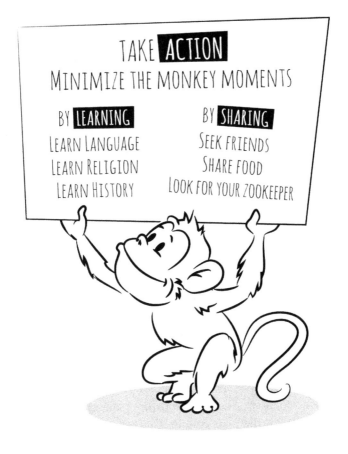

How to Learn about a Foreign Culture

You may be an expatriate in another country or an international manager working in one's on country, together with another culture; whatever the case, you must prepare yourself for integration. Effective managers don't enter business negotiations unprepared or without objectives and a strategy to achieving them. While business is meticulously planned, often with aid from a fleet of assistants, preparing scenarios and presentations to engage clients or potential business partners, potential cross cultural monkey moments are often overlooked. Although pre-departure cross cultural skills training is important for adjustment, many organizations simply do not provide this to their managers and expatriates. Most learning of culturally appropriate behaviors actually happens in the host country. The "trainers" will be your colleagues at work and your newfound friends. The venue will be your workplace, your neighborhood shops and restaurants, your apartment and local streets, basically your entire host country. And the hands-on training will be the daily interactions with the host culture. Cultural swimming lessons for expats often start in the host country's deep-end.

But one can and should prepare for these moments, and learning how to prepare is not only possible, it's necessary to successfully integrating into another culture. We call this phase, "action." Action involves consciously and willingly doing what you can to better adapt to another culture at a faster pace. In doing so, you will encounter fewer monkey moments.

We've discussed the first step of cross cultural integration – arriving at awareness of cultural differences – which reduces cultural monkey moments through three possible strategies: accepting, adapting and adopting. These steps are generic and work in any culture. They are a multi-tool by which, once you've learned each tool's utilities, your performance will be enhanced in any multicultural environment. But you can do more than generally prepare. Once you know the country to which you'll be sent, you can start preparing yourself for the specific cultural norms and values you'll encounter there. But instead of force-feeding you, the reader, skills to adapt to Chinese or Japanese or Brazilian cultures, we will describe the methodology of learning the scope of a new culture efficiently so that it may be applicable to all cases.

These detailed steps can be undertaken by employees and senior managers, alike. If you're a senior manager sending expatriates abroad, you can use the proposed steps to make an integration plan for your employees. Cultural integration should be one of the primary objectives for expatriating employees, as working with locals will highly factor into the success of your business venture. Cultural integration should not be treated as less important than other project objectives.

The conscious process of integrating into another culture is akin to learning a language. First, seek cultural knowledge in textbooks, history books and vocabulary. Soaking up this knowledge can be approached similarly to any college 101 course. But unlike college, you will also need to immerse yourself. Consider language training – you cannot expect to learn a language fluently while remaining in your classroom without any contact with native speakers. You must be immersed, in order to master pronunciation, broaden vocabulary, and understand all the nuances of a language.

Learning the scope of a culture is essentially the same. There is a purely theoretical learning process, with books and copious notes, and then there is immersion, which we'll call "sharing." Theoretical learning can be done in your home, while immersion will only be possible in sharing time, food and activities with those from the foreign culture.

Learning a culture is particularly difficult for people who grew up in Western cultures. In his landmark book, *The Clash of Civilization*, Samuel P. Huntington wrote, "It is my hypothesis that the fundamental source of conflict in this new world will not be primarily ideological or primarily economic. The great divisions among humankind and the dominating source of conflict will be cultural. [...] The clash of civilizations will dominate global politics. The fault lines between civilizations will be the battle lines of the future." He regards two civilizations as particular dangerous: Western civilization and the Muslim world. After he published his article and later his book in the nineties, many of his predictions were realized, in particular the numerous conflicts along the fault lines of these two opposing civilizations. For simplicity, we'll define civilization as a set of cultures that share similar history and values.

Western and Muslim cultures share two potentially dangerous characteristics: a superiority complex in relation to other civilizations and a willingness to enforce their civilization's "superior" values and norms universally. Both civilizations have a long history invading other cultures and violently imposing their ways of life. All civilizations wage wars, but the common reason for warring was often access to resources, rather than to convert other nations to another lifestyle. Undoubtedly, religion plays a role in this type of aggression. If belonging to a civilization is based on race, such as with Chinese or Slavic civilizations, for example, then these countries cannot easily expand. On the other hand, if belonging to a civilization is based on behavior, norms and values, then conquered people can be converted to a different lifestyle. Today's Africa offers a good example of these two types of civilizations. European colonialism in the 20th century was an economic exploitation and a cultural invasion. Europeans built schools, universities and churches. The West exported its values and norms, due to the conviction of the political actors of the time that their values were superior to others. The latest form of cultural exportation can be seen in failed attempts to implement working democracies in northern Africa in the past decade. Apart from Tunisia, the experiment concluded with failed states and civil war, such as those in Libya and Syria, among others. I am a strong supporter of democracy, but I'm also convinced that such forms of self-government require a cultural shift (for instance, a shift in the prevalence of national culture over ethnic culture), and these shifts take time and cannot be imposed by external force.

This was the West's approach to integrating into Africa. Now, let's look at China. China is acting differently on the African continent. Without the world noticing, China has become Africa's biggest trading partner, exchanging about $160 billion worth of goods a year. More than a million Chinese, most of them laborers and traders, have moved to the continent in the first decade of the 21st century.[51] But contrary to Western colonialism, the Chinese make virtually no attempts to promote Chinese culture there. You won't find Chinese cultural centers, schools, think tanks or missionaries in Africa. China does not seek to alter African society or political systems, for better or for worse. China is not in Africa to expand its civilization or its culture to this new continent. The reasons are purely economic.

This is why people of Western culture have such a difficult time integrating into foreign cultures. For members of a civilization which considers itself superior with an inherent willingness to spread its norms and values to other people, true integration will only be achieved when the members begin to view the host culture as equal, despite the greater economic, military and scientific accomplishment in the West. We're all proud of our own cultures, and that's a good thing. But to manage successfully within another culture, an objective perspective on cultural values and norms is necessary, especially if you were borne from Western culture.

Learn to admire achievements of other cultures

Economically, Western culture has been remarkably successful. But has the West always been economically superior? For centuries, Muslim cultures were even more economically sound and powerful and were scientifically more advanced than European ones. And indeed, the rise of the Japanese economy in the 1980's, producing global brands like Toyota and Sony, resulted in the American fear of competition in the global market, so much so that it was one of the initiators for cross cultural research. The rise of China's economic power in the last thirty years also proves that Western culture does not hold a monopoly over economic success. Actually, the richest man of all time was neither Bill Gates nor Warren Buffet. He was an emperor virtually unknown to most of us, named Mansa Musa. As the reigning emperor of the Mali empire, Musa commanded a fortune worth $400 billion, a value of more than four times the wealth of the world's current richest person. Musa was born in 1280 and lived until 1337 as a devout Muslim, constructing numerous educational centers and mosques across Africa.[52]

Another achievement of Western culture must also be put in perspective: democracy. Before condemning cultures whose political systems differ, we should note that the current form of democracy in the West was borne through the brutality of war in both America and in Europe, as well as two world wars.

Considering the history of your own culture's achievements, while recognizing the achievements of other cultures will allow you to put things into context in order to gain objectivity. All cultures in this world are part of human heritage and are equally valuable to our evolution as a human race.

Look at your own culture through another's lens

As mentioned before, measured in dollars and cents, the West is remarkably successful. But when measuring the rates of suicide around the world, many Western countries are much worse off than their third world counterparts. Measured in one's own terms, one's own culture will always come out on top. But this is an ethnocentric viewpoint. Instead, in order to see yourself through another culture's lens, you must judge your own culture by the standards of your host culture. For instance, many African cultures highly value the wisdom of elders. For them, a key element for societal health is represented through the degree to which society respects and cares for elderly people. To most African cultures, nursing homes would never exist in a healthy society, because family should personally care for their elders. Being as such, they are often shocked about how Western society treats elderly people. When viewing your culture through another's lens, consider aspects of hospitality, wealth sharing, family, honor, helping one another, etc. in relation to the standards of your host country's culture. This will provide you with a calibrated picture of your own culture from their standpoint.

Being proud of differences and knowing who we are is a good thing. But while it's of course important to take pride in one's own cultural heritage, it's also important not to assume your superiority. If you want to successfully manage people with various cultural backgrounds, your cultural ego must not get in the way of integration. Try to be proud of being different, instead of being superior.

While adapting to another culture may be particularly difficult for Westerners, it is in no way impossible. After all, you can start by sitting at a table and reading from text books, an action of which most anyone who's gone to school is familiar.

10. The Learning

Culture is a hugely complex social construction of specific behavior, values and norms. Culture defines how we think, how we speak, how we clothe ourselves. It influences the chosen political system, the laws, the educational system. It defines the inner workings of a family, even down to what happens in the bedroom. Learning a foreign culture can therefore be a difficult task. And when it comes to business transitions, you may not have more than a couple of weeks – at best a couple of months – to prepare yourself for this new responsibility in a foreign country. Concentrating on the most relevant and defining factors of a culture is, therefore, important. Among the thousands of elements that form a culture, three areas are far more important than others, and these are language, history and religion.

Language

When you're globalizing a brand, it's always a good idea to check whether your name, logo or tagline translates across cultures. Your tagline might mean something completely different in the regions where you're expanding than it does in your home country. Any marketing specialist knows the importance of language for business success and examples of failure abound[53]:

- Coca-Cola's brand name, when first marketed in China, was sometimes translated as "Bite The Wax Tadpole."
- Coors translated its slogan, "Turn It Loose," into Spanish, where it is a colloquial term for having diarrhea.
- Electrolux at one time marketed its vacuum cleaners in the U.S. with the tag line: "Nothing sucks like an Electrolux."
- Ford blundered when marketing the Pinto in Brazil, because the term in Brazilian Portuguese means "tiny male genitals."
- KFC made Chinese consumers a bit apprehensive when "finger licking good" was translated as "eat your fingers off."
- Mercedes-Benz entered the Chinese market under the brand name "Bensi," which means, "rush to die."
- Parker Pen, when expanding into Mexico, mistranslated "It won't leak in your pocket and embarrass you" into "It won't leak in your pocket and make you pregnant."
- Pepsi's slogan, "Pepsi Brings You Back to Life," was debuted in China as "Pepsi Brings You Back from the Grave."

While these examples are rather funny, the purpose of learning a language goes far beyond finding a culturally adaptable slogan to help your business sell products. Learning a language is an intrinsic part of learning a culture. Xiao Geng, a Chinese linguistic researcher, said, "It is a common fact that in our foreign language teaching, we are not only taught language itself but also we are taught culture of that nation. Language stores all the social lives and experience of a nation, and reflects all the characteristics of a nation's culture. When a child learns a language of a nation, at the same time, he is learning the culture of the nation. If a person is not familiar with the culture of a nation, he can't learn the language of the nation well. Language is inextricably bound up with culture. Culture values are both reflected by and carried through the language."[54]

The link between foreign language learning and culture learning was established by linguists and anthropologists a long time ago. In *Part I: Awareness*, we saw how family structure is reflected in the language. In most Western languages, titles of family members do not distinguish between the brother of the father and the brother of the mother; both are called "uncle." On the other hand, our single word, "cousin," translates into four different words in Yanomani. Similarly, a collectivist culture's choice of language often differs from that of an individualist culture. The Chinese, for example, like to say, "More people produce greater strength," while Westerners might say, "God helps those who help themselves." This is because individualist cultures emphasize the efforts of individuals, while collectivist cultures emphasize those of the group.

Language, in many aspects, is the verbal expression of culture. Language provides us with the categories we use when expressing our thoughts, and many linguists argue that language is the defining element of what and how we think. Therefore, learning a culture's language has three basic purposes:

- **To understand each other.** Above all, language is a means to communicate. In a business environment, learning language for this purpose may no longer be required, due to the fact that international companies have adopted English as the official business language. Most of today's managers, especially the younger generation, speak fluent English. Therefore, to understand each other may paradoxically be the least important reason to learn a language in regards to managing successfully.

- **To learn the culture.** As mentioned above, culture and language are interwoven. In learning the language, you learn how people think. You learn their values and their norms. When my father met the tribe of the Mossi in the 70's, the spelling of their language was not even agreed upon, so my father wrote the dictionaries, himself. As he wrote, at first he was astonished about the importance of greetings, as dozens of different greetings exist for different occasions. You may greet a group of people on a field differently if all are at work or if some are resting under a tree. The location of your meeting impacts the greeting, whether you meet someone in the market, at work or under a tree. Not only is the greeting standardized, but so is the answer to it. For example, once greeted, you are expected to ask after the other person's health. "Yibeoog ya Laafi?" you might ask in the morning, or "Zaabr ya Laafi?" in the evening. The response to either question will be "Laafi bala." And so, all greetings are formalized.

You will also learn to say goodbye with typical indirect African politeness. Instead of a single word – goodbye – , you will ask, "Where is the way?" and your host will answer, "There is a way"; in doing so, you may leave the house. When my father became fluent and understood conversations, he moved onto the Mossi's sayings and expressions. He sat down and learned hundreds of traditional sayings and their significance, such as, "When the crocodile is sick, then the buffalo can drink." This is a statement of optimism, meaning everything in life has a positive side. And amongst the Mossi, there is even a saying about the difficulty of their own greeting customs: "Saan puusem yaa ziibo," meaning, "The greetings are a heavy burden for foreigners." This is why, in learning a language, you are, in fact, learning a culture.[55]

- **To show respect:** Demonstrating respect is the most important reason to learn a language. When the CEO of Walmart declared English as the company language in Germany, his actions were considered an affront, one that partially led to billions of dollars lost and a humiliating withdrawal by the huge conglomerate from the German market. If you are a US citizen working for BMW in New York, how would you react if the new US-CEO of BMW refused to learn English and, instead, declared German as the company language? Or how would a UK worker in the Land Rover factory in Solihull (UK) feel if the new owners of the car manufacturer, the Indian company, Tata, declared Hindi as the company language?

Instead, do as the British CEO of Daewoo did. In 2003, the struggling Korean automaker launched a series of television commercials to boost sales in its home market. The two main competitors, Hyundai Motor and Kia Motors, were homegrown Korean companies, while Daewoon was owned mostly by the US company, General Motors. Polls revealed that the average Korean consumer viewed GM as an outsider with questionable commitment to the Korean market. Nick Reilly, the company's British-born CEO, decided the commercials should address the Korean market on a personal level. In fact, he chose to appear, himself, in the Korean television commercial, which made national news in Korea and reverberated throughout the global automotive industry. He was not the first automotive CEO to appear on TV, but the effort he made in connecting with and respecting his Korean audience, through speaking in its language, is what hit home with viewers. In speaking Korean, Reilly demonstrated the company's commitment to Korea. A high-ranking manager from the English-speaking world demonstrating true competency in a foreign language was a tremendous show of respect for the Korean people.[56]

As the primary objective of learning a foreign language – to communicate – is no longer the most important, due to the prevalence of English, many English-speakers bypass the time and effort of learning a language and simply rely on their English competency. Indeed, English is the lingua franca of today's world, and, historically, it is by no means the first one. Aramaic was spoken throughout the Middle East in pre-Christian times, the common language between three ancient powers: Assyria, Persia and Babylonia. Greek was the prominent language during the Hellenistic empire, spread further by Alexander the Great, while Latin was the common European language during Roman times. For most speakers, Latin was not their first language, but rather was mainly used to communicate with occupiers or between people speaking uncommon languages. Christianity also favored Latin for many centuries. Later, Spanish and then French became the lingua franca in many parts of the world, supplanting the indigenous languages by force or by necessity. Distinct languages in Africa are numbered in the thousands (more than 2,000 distinct languages, to be exact) and account for a third of all languages in the world; but due to colonialism, the official languages in many countries are either French, English or Portuguese. The twentieth century saw the rise of an English lingua franca. English is of course spoken in the original United Kingdom, in the core emigration countries USA, Canada and Australia, and in many previous colonies such as Nigeria or Ghana. But more importantly, in the twentieth century, English was adopted as the world's unofficial business language.

THE WORLD'S MOST COMMONLY SPOKEN LANGUAGES

MANDARIN CHINESE	MORE THAN 1 BILLION
HINDI/URDU	500 MILLION
ENGLISH	450 MILLION
SPANISH	393 MILLION
RUSSIAN	275 MILLION
ARABIC	245 MILLION
BENGALI	211 MILLION
PORTUGUESE	191 MILLION
MALAY-INDONESIAN	160 MILLION
FRENCH	129 MILLION

Until the fall of the Iron Curtain, half of the world's school children learned Russian as a second language. The Fall of the Berlin Wall realized the final victory of English, and today English is the second language taught in the schools of nearly all countries of the world. While France tried desperately to promote the influence of the French language, la "Francophonie," these attempts were in vain. Even in diplomacy, the traditional area of French-speaking, the language of Moliere has been supplanted by English and relegated to a mere ceremonial role. From the 12th to the 15th century French was actually the most important language in Britain, which makes this revolution of language even more astonishing. The royal coat of arms of the United Kingdom still features in French the motto of the British Monarch "Dieu et mon droit."

Today English is prevalent across the world. This is why you may ask rightly whether or not there's even a point in learning another foreign language. English is the most dominant lingua franca in world's history, so if you've already mastered this universal language, why bother learning French or German or Russian or any other language?

Edward Trimnell wrote a whole book to answer this question. In his book, entitled, *Why You Need A Foreign Language & How To Learn One*, he makes the case for learning foreign languages, by explaining that "global English" is often only a version of the language – "English Light," so to speak. This "English Light" may be sufficient enough to help one find baggage claim at Narita Airport in Tokyo, but it is not going to be enough to land a deal with a potential Japanese client. If you want the ability to share more complex, nuanced ideas with non-English speakers, then you will almost certainly need language skills to do so. [57]

Another reason to hone language skills is that the days may be numbered on English's reign as the lingua franca. The rise of China and regional economic-blocs, such as Mercosur, will promote new business languages. Chinese is, in fact, the hottest new language to learn in Argentina and Chile, as China has become the most important trading partner for these countries. Actually, Chinese is already the second language in Canada, due to Asian immigration. Mandarin is now more common than the country's official second language, French.

The prevalence of English has also seen resistance by some countries who promote linguistic nationalism. France has pushed the use of French for years, with little success, and Germany has also recently made an effort to promote German. In some international organizations, diplomats have threatened to boycott meetings if their language is not officially translated.

Another indicator that English might soon lose influence is the Internet. English web content dropped from over 90% in the late nineties to less than 40% a couple years ago. Global companies present their websites in dozens of foreign languages. Trimnell explains this transition simply: "Buy from the world in your language, sell to them in theirs…"[58] Whether for understanding, for learning the culture or for demonstrating respect, learning the language of your host culture is the most essential step to managing in a foreign country.

Religion

When Huntington in his landmark book, *Clash of Civilizations*, identified the civilizations in question, his major criterion was religion: Christianity along the frontier of Western civilization, Islamic civilization, the Sinic-, Hindu-, Orthodox- and Buddhist-influenced civilizations. Interestingly, when GLOBE research clustered its 59 countries according to cultural dimensions, none of them being religious, their results were similar. The predominant religion fundamentally affects, shapes and defines the values, norms and behaviors in its society.[59]

Few values and norms are more deeply rooted in our personality than those originating from religion. Religion influences outlook, communication, behavior and lifestyle. More than eight in ten people identify with a religious group, and 5.8 billion people out of the world's population of 8 billion consider themselves religiously affiliated, according to a 2010 demographic study conducted by Pew Research. From an anthropological point of view, religion is only a subset of culture, but the influence of a society's predominant religion on the overall culture of said society should not be underestimated.

Travel to virtually any city in the world and, while visiting, consider the tremendous influence of the predominant religion. From closed shops on Friday, Saturday or Sunday to churches, cemeteries, holy tombs, holy rivers, holy sources and much more, religion influences the landscape of a city. Even virulent atheist governments, like that of the Soviet Union, have never been able to eradicate religion in the minds of the people. Ornate orthodox churches continue to line the streets of Moscow, and many Russians remain steadfast in their faith. In Albania, the dictator, Envers Hoxa, tried to eradicate any religious influence through force. He destroyed churches, forbade all religious rituals, even banned tombstones in the form of crosses. As a journalist, I travelled to Albania shortly after the regime's fall. In the mountains near Yugoslavia, I stumbled upon a church. The building had been transformed into a "house of culture" by the ruling party. The tombstones had all been overturned, but the crosses were still recognizable. And most astonishingly, the inner walls of the church were scribbled full of professions of faith.

Culture and religion are so intimately entwined that they're impossible to separate them. Even the ruthless force of a dictator cannot dampen the spirit of the deeply religious. As with diet and sexuality, religion is acquired during primary socialization and therefore is deeply imbedded in our minds, whether or not we consider ourselves believers. Even secular societies in Europe still celebrate Christian traditions, like Christmas, Easter or religious wedding ceremonies. In most societies, religion plays a strong normative function during primary socialization and influences all three key elements of a culture: behaviors, norms and values. Religion is so powerful, every area of human culture is impacted by it, including government, education, literature, music, law, art and history.

In 1990, a couple of American and Canadian researchers set out to analyze how culture and religion interact. Their objective was to uncover whether religion or culture was more important in influencing drinking behavior among college students. In terms of culture's influence regarding drinking patterns and problems, studies have shown that countries differ. It was assumed that different values, public policies, politics and economic systems of countries lead to variations in alcohol consumption and alcohol-related issues within any particular country. For instance, American students tend to drink more overall and to have more alcohol-related problems than their Canadian counterparts, perhaps due to the later legal drinking age.

Researchers analyzed the drinking behaviors of non-abstinent Catholics, moderately abstinent Protestants and abstinent Jews. The results were what one would expect. When there was no conflict of values (i.e. for non-abstinent Catholics) the drinking habits aligned with those of the country's culture. On the other hand, when conflicts did arise, the drinking habits aligned with the religious norms. For instance, no differences in drinking habits were found between Canadian and American Jews, because both primarily followed the religion's strict abstinence law.[60]

Religious norms regarding alcohol have imbedded themselves into the national culture of many countries. Islamic countries, for example, require that outsiders adapt to the norm of abstaining from alcohol when visiting. Simply accepting the cultural norms without adapting or adopting may cause serious legal troubles for visitors or even imprisonment. Christianity has also influenced cultural drinking habits. If you visit a Catholic country, you might find that drinking wine or beer with lunch is normal, while in Protestant countries, it isn't. You may also see differences in alcohol consumption within the different states of Germany or Switzerland, as well as in America's traditional Bible Belt, where Protestant religious beliefs have even influenced law-making. Approximately 39 counties in the state of Kentucky are "dry," which means sale and possession of alcohol is prohibited, a consequence of the historically dominant Protestant religion. You won't find such laws in Rome or even Italy, the central capital of the Catholic Church.

Thus, dominant religions profoundly impact the lifestyles of all country nationals – believers or non-believers. To understand culture, therefore, you must understand the basic rules and ideology of the dominant religion.

Religious imprints on culture will even directly influence business rationale; accounting, for instance. "Religion is more than a belief; it constitutes a way of life, involving unique practices and perspectives in accounting," writes Meredith Young in her thesis regarding cultural influence on accounting.[61]

Accounting has been practiced for thousands of years in many societies and in different forms – from clay tables in Mesopotamia, to papyrus in Egypt, to the knots system of the Incas. Let's look at the early Church of England, for instance.

The Church viewed the world as a division of the sacred and the profane, meaning that every action and activity was defined either as holy or sinful. Money and a focus on handling money were considered profane activities. This belief was based on the verse in Matthew 6:24, which states, "No one can serve two masters. Either you will hate the one and love the other, or you will be devoted to the one and despise the other. You cannot serve both God and money." Therefore, the Church of England saw accounting as a profane practice and harmful to the Church. Few modern Christians would maintain this point of view, but the division between holy and profane has remained. Accounting is still regarded as profane and should not be mixed up with religious principles or laws.

On the other hand, Islam does not share this ideological division between the sacred and the profane. Worldly acts are related to and prepare a person for higher religious acts. Muslims believe everything should be done according to the religious acts Allah has dictated in the Quran, and this includes accounting.

The Quran discusses keeping account of transactions in Albaqarah, Verse 282, stating: "O you who believe! When you contract a debt for a fixed period, write it down. Let scribe write it down in justice between you. Let not the scribe refuse to write as Allah has taught him, so let him write..." Accountability is highly regarded within Islamic culture. Muslims believe they will have to account to Allah everything done in their lives on the Day of Judgment. They believe a book is waiting for them, recording their good deeds and, accordingly, they will receive rewards or punishment. In order for their book of good deeds to be pristine, Muslims must abide by every aspect of Islamic law. Regulations regarding practices when recording financial transactions are in place, which require that Muslim accountants be bound by these laws. They must obey them, for they will one day be held accountable for their actions.

The specific accounting and financial practices of Islamic culture are unique. Among other practices, the charging of interest is forbidden, a tax is imposed for redistribution to poor people (zakat), and full disclosure in financial statements is stressed in order to maintain social accountability. The Islamic Financial Accounting Standard Board (IFASB) has published its own standards by which all Islamic-based companies can comply. As Western accounting practices become international standard, the differences between Western and Islamic accounting pose a problem. Some differences even conflict with the very tenets of Islam.

When discussing culture and religion, an important distinction should be made: on one hand, personal faith can influence individual behavior, while on the other hand, some religious practices influence cultural behavior. A Muslim may pray five times a day in the direction of Mecca, a Christian may go to church every Sunday, a Jew may wear a Kipa, those who practice Shintoism may visit shrines. These are not necessarily cultural behaviors; rather, they are religious behaviors, practiced out of personal conviction. To distinguish between cultural and personal behaviors, observe the norms, values and behaviors of non-believers or liberal believers. The Christian holidays, Christmas and Easter, became part of Western culture. Believers and non-believers share many rituals during these holidays, such as decorating the tree, giving each other gifts or going to church on the holiday. On the other hand, attending weekly Sunday morning mass is not necessarily an element of Western culture. Most people who attend church in Europe do it out of personal conviction.

Some southern states in the US may be different; church-going may be culturally expected, and attendance may even be necessary to thriving professionally or politically. In Mississippi, for instance, attending mass is still an essential social happening, and therefore, may be considered a cultural element. The distinction between a behavior conditioned by religion and one conditioned by culture is not easy to see at first glance. For many, the learning of culture and the learning of religious practices go hand-in-hand, but when adapting to a foreign culture, the distinction is important. You may disregard behaviors tied to a personal belief, but you will have to accept, adapt or adopt to religious norms, values or behaviors which have become part of the cultural heritage. This is why studying the dominant religions of a culture is an important preparatory measure when living and managing within foreign nations.

Heineken during the 1994 World Cup is an example of when business mixes adversely with religious cultural norms. With more linguistic and religious knowledge, Heineken may have avoided an embarrassing recall of their beer bottles. The company had printed all the participating countries' flags on its bottle, among them the flag of Saudi Arabia, which depicts a holy verse. In response to Islam being associated with an alcoholic beverage, Muslims from all over the world were hostile. The brewer was forced to recall all bottles and discontinue its promotion.

History

Educating yourself in your host country's history will demonstrate your respect and interest in the country. Learning the history of the foreign culture in which you are working is paramount to thriving in it. To understand the rationale behind a specific behavior – the "why" –, you will often trace the answer to the culture's distant past.

For example, toasting is a habit common in many countries. So, say you're from a culture where, when drinking beer with your friends, you might clink your glasses together for a toast. You're relocated to Budapest, and you go out for a beer with your colleagues after your first day on the job. As is tradition in your own culture, you lift your glass, say something like, "Let's drink on the success of our cooperation," and hold out your glass expectantly, only to find that no one clinks with you. Everyone is staring at you like you're the monkey.

If you would have done a little research into cultural customs, you would have found that Hungarian people do not clink glasses of beer. You may simply accept this newly learned behavior, or you may follow up this monkey moment by educating yourself. Why does a European country defy the average cultural norms of the continent and refuse to clink glasses with beer? What you would find in this case is that your behavior would have been perfectly normal with wine. Hungary has been a powerful nation in Europe for centuries, offering a rich cultural and architectural heritage of which the nation is proud. During the Hungarian Revolution of 1848 against the Habsburg-ruled Austrian Empire, the killing of Hungarian generals was celebrated with beer by Austrian executioners, which is why, to this date, Hungarians do not clink with beer. Knowledge of a country's history will help you understand your host culture's present-day customs.

Travel blogger, Helen, a French national, recounts the following experience, relating to cross cultural differences: "When I first moved to California, it was the first time I consciously heard people joking about WWII and Nazis. Before, I associated WWII with collective shame and guilt. It wasn't something you made fun of. I'm not saying this was true for everyone, but it was my perception at the time. So when I moved to California, I began to understand that history influences our perception not only of history, but also of the present and of the people we meet."[62]

To learn a culture, you first must learn the language, the religion and the history. History is the third of these essential elements. The importance of history on the culture of a nation is that present environments of every nation are the direct result of the nation's history. Marcu Garvey, journalist and activist, said: "A people without the knowledge of their past history, origin and culture is like a tree without roots." History defines who we are. History provides us identity, and this is unquestionably one of the reasons all modern nations encourage the teaching of history in some form. Historical data includes evidence about how families, groups, institutions and whole countries were formed and about how they have evolved while retaining cohesion.

History and culture are closely linked. One obvious way history impacts culture is through politics. Historical events directly influence the politics of all countries. A perfect example of this would be the Soviet Union, whose great historical mark was the October Revolution of 1918. Soviet culture consequently developed in a way that would have been radically different had the October Revolution not instituted a totalitarian communist government. In fact, the Soviet regime deliberately set out to mold and shape the national culture in order that it support the ideals and values of Soviet communism. This deliberate shaping of culture can still be found today in the architecture, political views, popular attitudes, art, literature, and historical records of Russia and other post-soviet republics.

Through world history, we have some notions about the development of global cultures. We know how American culture became today's melting pot through voluntary immigration, largely from Europe, and forced immigration, largely from Africa. We know how dozens of major wars have shaped the landscape of Europe. We know how English became the common language in the US and Australia, while Latin Americans speak Portuguese or Spanish. We know that powerful dynasties have ruled Russia, China and Japan, shaping them into the societies they are today. This general knowledge may be useful for small talk, but insufficient when it comes to understanding your host culture.

Foremost, learning the history of your host culture, like learning the language, is a sign of respect and genuine interest, but you'll need more than general knowledge for this respect and interest to be apparent. Every country is proud of its past, because history largely defines national identity. I moved to America in early 2000. Being a global citizen, I was generally interested in world history and politics, and I knew bits and pieces about the American Civil War, primarily that its objective was the abolition of slavery, with opposition being between the North and the South. For me, the American Civil War was as remote as the 100 Years War between France and England or the defeat of the Spanish Armada by England's famous captain, Francis Drake. For most Europeans, the litany of wars before the first and second world wars belong to the distant past, so I saw no necessity when preparing for my stay in America to dig further into US history than the recent past and general culture. Well, it was necessary.

I happened to be relocated to Richmond, Virginia, the capital of the southern secessionists. In Richmond, the Civil War is still alive in the minds and hearts of the people. I learned quickly that cracking jokes about it, like, "The civil war was when the North attacked America," carried for Virginians a deeper truth. The people are still not fans of Abraham Lincoln, the president who's generally venerated as the greatest leader America has ever seen. As recently as 2003, some residents of Richmond protested against the placement of a statue of President Lincoln in the city center.

Sometimes religion and history coalesce. The 2008 Olympic opening ceremony in Peking, China kicked off with a quote from Confucius—an adage noting that it's a great pleasure to have friends come to visit from afar. Later, three thousand performers, dressed as Confucius' disciples, paraded through the Bird's Nest Stadium. Confucius is a key representative of the Chinese mind. Reaching back nearly 1,500 years in history, Confucius (552-479BC) is arguably the most influential person in Chinese history, and his teachings continue to resonate and deeply influence modern Chinese society. If you take the time to examine Chinese history, you will understand why China believes its country belongs alongside the world's major powers. You'll also understand why most Chinese value a strong, unified and proudly nationalistic central government, led by "virtuous" individuals who value the people's interests. You'll understand why Chinese people are not inclined, either historically or culturally, to endorse a Western, liberal, democratic political system. Taking the time to study the history of your host country will improve your understanding of its people, which will allow you to better build trust and respect among your employees. When it comes to business, historical awareness can sometimes make or break your company's success. Maybe if UPS had been history savants, they wouldn't have tried to introduce their brown uniform in Germany. Germans haven't been forced to wear brown shirts since 1945.

Just learning the history on its own may not be enough. History is subjective to interpretation, and any historical event may be interpreted in opposing ways by different cultures. If you're setting out to understand your host culture, then you need to learn the history from their perspective. Historical writing is often biased, and culture is one of many potential lenses through which to look at history. The culture to which a historian belongs will give him a certain framework by which to interpret historical facts. Or, more bluntly, history-writing is often dictated or colored by political or national interest. We may condemn its subjectivity, but we may not ignore it. Understanding a culture means to understand their view of history, whether or not we personally agree with the interpretation. For historians – and all of us, for that matter – cultural bias is difficult to recognize. Growing up in our own culture with our own historical interpretations, we expect our perspective and our norms and values to be the right ones. Stereotypes and cultural preconceptions have proven extraordinarily resistant to facts. Only foreigners might be able to detect distortions in historical "facts" regarding another nation's interpretation. Foreigners may perceive biases and gaps which have eluded the indigenous historian, who is perhaps educated in a particularly nationalist tradition.

One of the most interesting examples of national bias manifests in the difference between North American and Russian history and historians. North Americans are proud of their liberal traditions, which have provided enterprising people a chance to prosper with little impediment; therefore, most are appalled at the severe restrictions on individual freedoms existing under communist regimes. Russians, on the other hand, were taught to see history in Marxist terms. They were taught about how the capitalist class in America exploits the American working class, as well as the hired labor of overseas countries. On the other hand, Russians are proud of their more egalitarian system, in which they believe wealth has been more evenly distributed among the working class. Each presents the other's society as more oppressive than it actually is.[63]

Or take this example of history being taught in Japan, which emphasizes the long and glorious reign of the Japanese empire and deemphasizes tragic events of recent history. Mariko Oi, a Japanese teacher who studied abroad, recounts: "Japanese people often fail to understand why neighboring countries harbor a grudge over events that happened in the 1930s and 40s. The reason, in many cases, is that they barely learned any 20th century history. I myself only got a full picture when I left Japan and went to school in Australia." In her

Japanese textbook, only 19 of the book's 357 pages dealt with events between 1931 and 1945. A single page was dedicated to the 1931 Mukden incident, when Japanese soldiers blew up a railway in Manchuria in China, while another page accounted for all the events leading up to the Sino-Japanese war in 1937, including a single line (in a footnote) about the massacre that took place when Japanese forces invaded Nanjing, known the world over as the Nanjing Massacre or the Rape of Nanjing.

While Japanese schoolchildren may be exposed to just a single notation about this massacre, the Chinese are taught in detail not only about the Rape of Nanjing but about numerous other Japanese war crimes, though these accounts of the war are sometimes criticized for being overly anti-Japanese. The same can be said about Korea, where the education system's emphasis on modern history has resulted in vastly different perceptions of the same events in countries an hour's flying time apart.[64]

And while American textbooks heroically highlight the Manhattan Project, which led to the dropping of the first atom bomb, again, a single sentence is dedicated to the atom bombings of Hiroshima and Nagasaki in Japanese textbooks. The point of this is that if you want to learn about your host culture, you must learn how your host culture views history, and what is not being said is nearly as important as what is.

Let's return to my own monkey moment example when I reduced the American Civil War to a fight over slavery. Historians have debated whether it should be described as a dispute over slavery, over states' rights, over differing economic interests, or perhaps a combination of all three. Some American textbook publishers have chosen to "mystify" the South's secession, largely because they don't want to offend school districts and thereby lose sales. Some of the most widely used history textbooks today even insinuate that the South's motivation for secession was simply to protect states' rights — not to preserve slavery. And this "mystification" can come with significant societal implications. Americans still disagree about "what this cruel war was over"; in fact, a recent national poll found that while 54 percent of Americans identify slavery as the cause, 41 percent do not. Documents, which tie the Civil War unequivocally to the dispute over slavery – including the declarations of the eleven Confederate states, marking their departure from the union, along with speeches like the one Henry Benning gave to the Virginia Convention, which highlighted slavery as the main reason for secession – rarely get much, if any, play in mainstream historical textbooks.[65] In all cultures, history is biased, even differing within separate regions or groups of a single country.

When graduate student, Elizabeth Herman, visited her former high school, Newton South, a few years ago, she was surprised to find that its new history textbooks already include sections detailing 9/11. She began to wonder how textbooks in other countries describe the events of the attack, and this curiosity eventually led to her thesis project at Tufts University, where she graduated in 2010. Now a Fulbright scholar, Herman is continuing her research on how the events of 9/11 are taught around the world. So far, she's analyzed textbooks from thirteen countries, and what she's found is that the attacks of 9/11 on New York are perceived differently around the world:

- American textbooks use volatile language and emphasize the tragedy of the event.
- Chinese, Indian and Brazilian textbooks focus on the audacity of the United States and its actions post-9/11, in particular the illegality of the war, specifically the Iraq War.
- In Pakistan, the textbooks completely omit the identity of the assailants, calling them "unidentified terrorists," while Turkey also omits their extremist Islamic faith.
- China's textbooks mostly speak about 9/11 as a sign of diminishing American hegemony, which is not at all what you see in American textbooks. American textbooks highlight the attack of 9/11 and the aftermath of America come together as a country and supporting one another.

In an interview, Herman indicated how to handle these differences in perception, which for many Americans may not be understandable. A key element in *Learning to Accept* and *Learning to Adapt* is to seek the rationale by asking why some interpretations are different than others. Herman said: "If you hand a student thirteen different ways of looking at 9/11 from thirteen different countries and ask them, [...] Why do you think it's different? Why do you think that Pakistan tells this story one way and Brazil speaks about it a different way? I think that that's the only way that we can actually reach a new understanding of this event."[66]

Of course, you may disagree with some of these interpretations, but arguing with colleagues about their worldview won't help you better manage in a foreign culture. You don't have to adopt their point of view, but you may have to accept it. Seeking the "why" will make it easier to accept. Every country's history has its dark and shameful periods, every country has a subjective selection of historical events and every country has a subjective historical view. Accepting this will help you learn and understand your host country's culture.

What we learned in this chapter:

- Language, in many aspects, is the verbal expression of culture and allows us to communicate, to learn the culture and to show respect.

- Culture is encapsulated by norms and values, and few are more deeply rooted in our personality than those originating from religion.

- In order to understand the rationale behind a specific behavior – the "why" –, you will often trace the answer to the culture's distant past.

11. Sharing

Consciously learning a culture may be a tough and unpleasant process and will certainly require a lot of energy, discipline and time. Many evenings and hours must be invested in learning the language, while reading through religion and history books may not be your favorite activity. But not all learning of culture requires scholastic efforts. This chapter will talk about the easiest and most pleasant part of learning a culture: learning through sharing.

This is the experiential part of learning. Learning a culture cannot be done only sitting at your desk; like anything, learning needs immersion, which in the case of culture means sharing time and food with local friends. An old Russian proverb says it well: "Instead of having 100 rubles, it's better to have 100 friends." This is the best approach to learning culture. Investing in making local friends may even save you money on language trainings…so you might actually end up having the 100 friends *and* the 100 rubles. Even if you're not an expatriate living in a foreign country but an international manager who travels extensively, making friends is still possible if you frequently visit a country. Not only will engaging with the locals tremendously improve your cultural savviness and make the management of international projects so much easier, but you'll be forging life-long friendships in the process. All successful international managers I know share a lot of their leisure time with friends from all over the world.

Making Friends

In making friends and sharing time with them, you will learn a lot about the visible and invisible part of a country's cultural baobab. Sharing time allows you to learn about local cuisine, shopping, festivals and rituals, dress codes, forms of address and greetings, gestures and body language, attitudes towards smoking, alcohol and drugs, gift-giving and neighborliness, daily schedules and so much more. Learning culture is far easier through sharing than it is reading textbooks like this one. While leisure activities make a better sharing experience than business ones, in practice sharing time with local people is an encounter between two cultures and must be treated as such.

For example, when I arrived to Spain as a young CEO, my wife and myself quickly wanted to bond with local people. Spanish people are fairly easy to connect with, at least when compared to my native Swiss culture, which is rather reserved. A couple times, we invited friends to our home for dinner. We cooked, arranged the table and waited for our guests. They didn't come. First, we thought we must have mixed up the date, but when it happened again with another friend, and again a third time, we decided to do what we should have been done to begin with (and what should be done during any cultural conflict), we asked one of our invitees why he didn't come. The answer baffled us: "Well, you didn't call the day before, so we thought the dinner was canceled." As typical Swiss, we plan far in advance. In Switzerland, you can fix a dinner with friends six months ahead. Without confirmation, your guest will knock at the door precisely on time. The Spanish do not work like this, and we had to learn it.

Don't stick to your own flock

Most people tend to share time with those who are similar to themselves; those who hold the same interest, the same values, the same background, the same language and, of course, the same culture. Actually, most people find forging friendships with those from different cultural backgrounds difficult to initiate and even more difficult to maintain. This applies to international managers and expatriates, alike. There's nothing wrong with this; it's just how most of us are built. We prefer the known to the unknown, the familiar to the unfamiliar, the comfortable to the uncomfortable. Once you are aware that it's natural, at first, to feel discomfort, you can develop strategies to finding and maintaining friendships across cultural divides, which is essential for quickly learning a culture.

Expatriates can be roughly categorized into three different types: the *diplomats*, the *internationals* and the *localizers*. The first category are those who travel from country to country but still share time outside of business only with their own country nationals. Diplomats, themselves, often fall into this category, because many nations don't want their diplomats to become entangled in local political and economic spheres. For this reason, diplomats are also moved every couple of years to another country. A big part of the diplomat's job is to care for their own nationals, so this makes perfect sense.

The second category – the *internationals* – are all the expatriates who flock to themselves. They move among the international community, meet the parents at the English, German or French private schools, and attend service at the international Protestant or Catholic Church. The international community in all big cities is a vivid, interesting and welcoming mix of people. There is just one issue: it's the wrong place to learn the local culture through the lens of the locals. While fellow expats may be able to tell you about cultural barriers, they may already have tainted views of the culture, particularly if they've lived in it long enough to have troubles stack up. It's best to take expat cynicism with a grain of salt.

The third category – the *localizers* – are those expatriates who actively seek out local friends and try to integrate into the local culture. The people of this category will, of course, learn the local culture the fastest.

You may ask yourself why any of this matters. Well, the importance of sharing culture is two-fold. First, it allows you to better understand the culture you are managing in and to better understand your employees and your direct reports. And second, as we've highlighted many times, sharing a genuine interest in the people and culture you're immersed in demonstrates respect. Again, think about how you would react if your foreign boss had no local friends.

I observed the difference sharing can make first-hand with the CEO of a major Swiss company. The company belonged to a German group, and the first CEO had no interest in integrating into the local business community. As his main purpose was to build his career in Germany, the employees felt his disinterest, and the company never developed the common culture needed to compete successfully. When a new CEO, also a German, joined the company after a couple of years, the environment and feeling changed dramatically. He showed a genuine interest in the culture and made a number of local friends – in business and personally – in Zurich. Because of this extra step, engagement between mid-level and senior management in the company improved significantly.

As a leader, you must set an example for your employees. If you're not interested in their lives, then they won't follow you. Although money may drive them to do their jobs, they won't work with the same enthusiasm as a talented leader might evoke in his team. As a boss, you want your employees to regard you as "one of them," so you need to seek friends beyond your four office walls. Of course, friendships must be natural and not forced. But if your lifestyle permits, try stretching yourself and add more diverse and multicultural friendships to the existing mix. If you don't engage with local culture, then you'll likely go on living your monkey moments. As you may not even recognize these moments, due to your lack of experience with the locals, accepting cultural differences will be hard for you, let alone adapting or adopting.

A second pitfall for local integration is the lack of opportunity. When being dropped into a new job in a foreign country – or even worse, if you are an international project manager flying from site to site – then engaging with locals regularly may be difficult. You simply don't have time for socializing. More often than not, you'll barely have time to spend time with your family, even less for seeking new friends. Additionally, as an international manager, your income will most likely be way above average, your kids will go to an international school and you'll spend more hours on the golf course than you will having beer with ordinary people.

Learning a culture does not come effortlessly, but you can make some small appeals to common interests. For instance, on my fencing dress, I have the insignias of fencing clubs from Spain and the US. Chatting about sports is an excellent way to get to know people. If you're not a sports fan, another way is to attend cultural events. Ever visit a Greek food festival in Spain or a French movie festival in the US? Cultural festivals are great fun, and you learn about these community cultures. If you belong to a religion, then congregations are another way to dive into local culture (if you avoid the numerous international churches, mainly filled with expatriates).

Simply put, create opportunities to meet people then take the initiative to build bridges of friendship. The local is probably even more shy or uncertain of the strange monkey that you are. As the monkey, it's upon you to approach and make friends.

Understand the local concept of friendship

In order to make friends, you'll also need to understand the local concept of friendship. Many foreigners find it difficult to make friends with locals. There are many reasons for this; sometimes the primary reason lies in the simple fact that being with people you understand is emotionally easier. Other times the concept of friendship may vary so much from country to country that this bonding seems ambiguous. Switzerland, for instance, may be one of the toughest places on earth to make friends, and many expatriates give up, preferring to stay among themselves. One Swiss saying: "True friends are the ones with whom you shared a sandbox." In other words, you can only be friends with people you grew up with. On the other hand, Swiss people often complain about foreigners (in particular, Americans) for being superficial. This view of another's definition of friendship as being "superficial" is because the concept of friendships varies across cultures. Moreover, some discussion topics that may be acceptable in one country will be taboo in another.

Human interaction is in large part about communication and about the way in which we speak to each other and the topics of which we choose to discuss. In most cultures, discussing work-related topics is perfectly fine, although the form in which one does may vary across cultures, as we've seen before. But when and how are you allowed to talk about private topics? When will your choice of subject be perceived as too intrusive or to intimate?

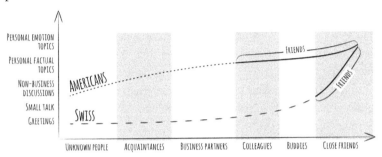

Greetings are the most basic level of personal communication. All cultures have some form of greeting, and it's socially acceptable or even required to greet unknown people. After the greeting, you may engage in small talk, and later in non-work-related discussions. If the contact with the person continues, you'll start to share factual personal information, such as your work, where you live, what your leisure activities are, and more. The most intimate communication begins when you start talking about your true feelings, about what you fear in life, what makes you happy, if you are sad and why. All cultures have expectations about when and how you use different intensities of non-work-related communication.

For instance, let's take a look at Swiss norms. Remember the Swiss TV anchorman's experience in the chapter on stereotypes? He took the train from Zurich to Chur. The passenger in front of him did not say a word until the train arrived at its destination. Then he stood up, held out his hand and said, "Mr. Müller, it has been a pleasure to travel with you." Swiss people do not talk to people they don't know. They may strike up the nerve to greet someone politely, but they don't talk. Africans will chat intensely with whomever is sitting next to them or in the queue before them, while Swiss people won't even engage in small talk at the supermarket queue. Try doing it, and you'll be at the receiving end of a glare. When talking about personal details, Swiss are traditionally secretive and reluctant. Even with work colleagues, they'll avoid talking about private matters, whether the matters are deep or even such mundane details as where they live, what car they drive or where they come from. Personal topics, be they facts or emotions, are reserved for "friends," not for acquaintances or strangers.

What an Australian expatriate wrote about Swedish people may very well also apply to Swiss people: "I can tell that they really want to learn, but they were never taught how to do small talk. When people find out I'm Australian, they try to make small talk with me, but they really struggle. They speak good English; it's just that they don't know what to say."[67]

Americans, on the other hand, are different. Small talk is acceptable and even appreciated pretty much anywhere, whether it's the queue at a supermarket or the neighboring seat on an airplane. Topics amongst friends, acquaintances and strangers are also broader. At a party, Americans will quickly start to talk about their job, their car, their kids. They do this extensively in the workplace, as well.

Knowing these cultural differences in communication and friendship, imagine a Swiss and an American working together. The Swiss will try to stick to work-related topics or generalities, like the weather, while the American will bombard him with personal questions and impart personal details a Swiss would never consider sharing with anyone but close friends.

In the chart above, this difference in communication behavior is explained, as are the different concepts of friendship. You may now understand why it's so difficult to make friends in Switzerland. The bank, HSBC, publishes a survey on the expat quality of life in various foreign countries on a regular basis. Over 21,000 expatriates from 39 countries participated in the 2015 survey. In the area of "making friends," Switzerland nearly ranked last in the category, second only to Sweden. The analysis provided an explanation as to why this may be the case, and it has to do with cultures' varying concepts of friendship. In the US, friendship may mean having a beer in the evening or going to the movies – engaging in friendly and fun activities together. For a Swiss, the concept of "friendship" is far more intimate and permanent. Rather than casual hangouts, Swiss friendship involves being there for someone – your friend – when he/she is in need, sharing the difficult moments and supporting each other. Friendship is not a lighthearted affair; it is considered a life-long commitment, similar to a loving relationship.

The survey also stresses the importance of not being discouraged when seeking friends in countries where the concept of friendship may differ from your own. The authors write about the Swedish and friendship: "Swedes are polite, but they don't do small talk. And while they may appear reserved, they're usually just respecting your privacy. Once you've made local friends, you'll find them loyal and warm, but the way to their hearts can sometimes feel as long, dark and cold as the Nordic winters."

If you are in a foreign country, one more reserved than your own, don't give up. Try to make friends, but be attentive about how it works, because it may be different from how it works at home. Still, be always aware that stereotypes and generalizations are not all-inclusive. You may find Swiss people who are open, and Americans who are reserved. Over and above all cultural differences, all humans crave human-to-human contact. You must investigate how approaching this contact best suits your host culture. If you want to find friends, if you try hard enough, and if you are willing to accept, adapt and adopt, you'll be friendless nowhere in the world.

Going through the loops of cultural adaption

Despite the best intentions, there may come a time where you are just fed up with everything in your daily life, and you conclude that the people in your new location are strange and impossible to live with. You hide inside the house, connecting through satellite TV, the internet and phone calls to your "more civilized" home country. You stay cocooned in your safe world and do not venture out. To go outside might make you upset about all the differences between your host and home countries: Why does everything take longer here?

Why can't I park in front of the store like back home? Everything is so expensive here compared to home. Why can't I meet anyone? You suddenly feel anger and resentment toward the new culture. During this stage, not only will it be nearly impossible to make new friends, but you will potentially lose the contacts you've already made.

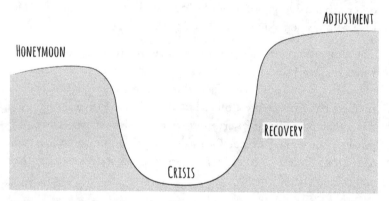

Unfortunately, for many expatriates and international managers, this stage sounds all too familiar. Indeed, the ups and downs of cultural adjustment were summarized in 1955 by the Norwegian sociologist, Sverre Lysgaard. According to his hypothesis, the cultural adjustment follows an inverted bell-curve: "Adjustment as a process over time seems to follow a U-shaped curve: adjustment is felt to be easy and successful to begin with; then follows a 'crisis' in which one feels less well adjusted, somewhat lonely and unhappy; finally one begins to feel better adjusted again, becoming more integrated into the foreign community." Although Lysgaard never produced a diagram to illustrate his theory, several have been developed over the years. They all look something like the one in the chart above.

This model is widely used in cross cultural training sessions, but there is one major issue: it doesn't stand up to scientific scrutiny. To be fair, Lysgaard never intended the U-curve to be taken as gospel, but rather as a hypothesis that called for further research. Subsequent studies have found that only 10% of the population cycles consecutively through these four stages of adjustment. For the rest, it's more complicated. You may go through the stages in a different order, at different times or perhaps not at all. Some expatriates, for example, never enjoy a honeymoon stage — they're unhappy with their host culture from the very first day. Most studies, in fact, indicate that the first few months of expatriation are the most stressful.

The path to adjusting depends on many factors: your personal feelings and expectations about the move, the extent of difference between the two cultures, the amount of social support available, your own personality, etc. The bottom line is there's no timetable for integration. It's a messy, unpredictable process with a timeline all its own. We all adapt at our own pace, in our own way. Inevitably, there will be periods of frustration and depression. There's no way around it, so it's best to apply some African fatalism when frustration and depression do occur: Let it happen, and drink strong tea.

Maria, a Canadian expat wife and culture blogger, said it like this: "Even when I was completely in love with my host country, there were tough times. It was a lot like raising children, in fact: I love my kids more than life itself, but there are plenty of days when I'm convinced I'll never get the hang of this parenting thing. And then the sun comes out again, and life is good." She also drew a diagram of her own experienced cultural adjustment and, rather than a U-curve, it looks like an intricate knot:[68]

Like most things in life, you'll experience pleasurable moments during the learning of a culture and difficult moments, as well. This is normal. Instead of letting the difficult moments stall progress, continue seeking friendships and learning about the culture. The emotional rollercoaster is a normal process, one that will be over once you feel at home, which may take up to a couple of years.

A lot has been written about culture shock. It's been compared to landing in New York with a map of Paris. You'll be unable to find your way, because your map (i.e. your cultural code) is useless in any other territory. Of course, realizing you have the completely wrong map will result in shock and will require adaption. But shock results in one extremely important realization: you *know* that New York is different, and so, you've anticipated the need to adjust your internal, cultural map to meet the needs and the reality of New York.

But actually, culture shock may not be the toughest element of expatriating or international travel; rather, the toughest moment emotionally may be when you return to your home country. It's called reverse culture shock.

Imagine you are returning home to Paris, and once you've landed, although everything looks familiar, you discover that you can't find your way in your home city, because your internal map has changed. Your feet search for the grid of downtown Manhattan, while your mind tries to return to the past; you can't find your way in messy Paris anymore. That's when reverse culture shock will hit you hard. Invariably, I hear this all the time from many expatriates friends I have: the real culture shock is when you come home. Learning and adapting/adopting another culture will change you forever. Your norms, your values and your behavior will adapt to your new world. Upon returning home, though your country probably hasn't changed much, you have. The one place in the world where you thought you belonged no longer feels like home. Prepare yourself for this. Treat your home country like a new country and apply the same techniques you learned abroad to integrate back into the community you were once a part of.

Sharing Food

"Your first relationship as a human being is about food," says Richard Wilk, anthropology professor at the University of Indiana and head of its Food Studies program. "The first social experience we have is being put to the breast or bottle. The social act of eating, is part of how we become human, as much as speaking and taking care of ourselves. Learning to eat is learning to become human."

In all cultures, sharing food is a huge social factor and is often ritualized. Sharing a meal is the best way to make friends, and it can also serve as a test regarding the progress of your integration. What we eat and, in particular, what we like to eat is written in our cultural code at an early stage of our socialization. As children, we learn early on all norms and behaviors related to the body orifices. As this is a matter of survival, these norms are usually strictly enforced by parents. At a later age, your body will be repulsed by anything you learned not to eat – insects, for instance, if you grew up in a Western culture. The food you dislike/like is strongly and permanently influenced by your culture. Immigrants, refugees, expatriates, all those who end up living in another country will drop food preferences from their cultural habits last. Clothing habits, daily routine, even the language spoken at home with the kids can be changed easier than the desire to eat one's own traditional food. Whenever you visit a country festival – be it a French festival in the US or a Greek one in Japan – food will likely be the centerpiece of the festival.

Food culture is not only about what you eat, but also how you eat (with hands, with sticks, with silverware), how you arrange the plates, where you eat (at a table, on the floor), with whom you eat (gender separation, children apart), and so much more. In other words, it's not simply *what* you eat that's interesting, but also how, when, with whom and why. A study among Americans, Japanese and Italians indicated that culture even influences how you present your food. American and Italian participants preferred plates that were casually presented, while Japanese participants preferred plates that were formally arranged. This difference may be due to the individualistic attitudes of Westerners, as opposed to the more collectivist mindset of Easterners. Another significant difference involved how much food was preferred on the plate; American and Japanese participants preferred relatively empty plates which may symbolize their cultural ideal of open space. On the other hand, Italian participants preferred full plates.[69]

Food also has strong ties to history and religion. Every single culture and religion uses food as the cornerstone of their celebrations and holidays. The celebratory nature of food is universal. Every season, every harvest and every holiday has its own food.

Food is like a small representation of the large world in which we've grown up, bringing all elements together on a plate. Compared with other deep imprints of culture, one huge advantage is there's no taboo on food. All cultures love to talk about food. Try talking about sexuality, the importance of honor or the concept of time with foreign acquaintances. Doing so is a minefield. But you'll always be able to talk about different foods, the way they're prepared and what they celebrate. Dinner is not only the perfect place to start a discussion about food, it's also the perfect place to talk and laugh about cultural differences.

Dominique Bouchet, Professor of International Marketing in Denmark, compared the food culture of France and Denmark, finding that significant differences exist between the two, which may come as no surprise. For the French, eating is a social experience, and the French language has an extensive vocabulary for topics related to tastes, eating and food. For the Danish, the nutritional aspect of food is far more important than the social or pleasure aspects. You won't see a Danish shopper smelling and touching fresh ingredients in the supermarket for hours before a daily lunch. What we eat is also a strong defining factor of who we are. Bouchet writes: "Fresh oysters and red meat are seldom appreciated in Denmark, whereas in France exactly red meat is perceived as being more alive, and thereby more powerful and appetizing. The animalistic aspect is seen as something positive in France and Spain, whereas the associations in Denmark and Germany are more in the direction of death and morbidity. The reaction is one of disgust, and therefore it is desirable to kill each and every trace of what is disgusting in a process of frying, boiling, or pasteurizing."[70]

The importance of food as a mirror of our cultural differences and the importance of sharing food can't be underestimated for any cultural integration. Whether you're in a country for a short period of time or for the long-haul, sharing food with your employees and your business partners will tremendously enhance your cultural savviness.

Despite all your personal efforts, sometimes you will need outside help to learn a culture. For this, we return to the zoo.

Look for your Zookeeper

In the first chapter of this book, we took a look at our caged monkey. The monkey wondered what the strange animals – the ones we call "humans" – were doing, staring at him all day long. They made noises he didn't understand. Their fur was oddly colored. Their behavior was inexplicable. Only one of these strange humans behaved in a way that made some sense to him: the zookeeper. The zookeeper did not insist upon throwing peanuts when none of the tribe's apes were hungry. When they were hungry, the zookeeper brought real food. He knew how to move and approach them. The monkey was, therefore, not confused by or afraid of the zookeeper.

When working in a foreign culture, you'll need to find yourself a personal zookeeper who knows how and when to feed you the cultural food that can clarify differences. The zookeeper understands the animal and the humans. He is the bridge builder for the monkey and the rest of the zoo.

An employee of my father came to visit us one day. I was still a child but when visitors came, I often sat with my father under the shade, hidden from the African sun. The visitor on this particular day was André, one of my father's most trusted collaborators. The discussion progressed the normal African way – engaging in a lengthy and friendly discussion about everything under the sun, while drinking water. André had already stood to leave, when at last, the reason for his visit became clear: he needed help transporting some bags of sorghum for a wedding. Both sat down again. My father couldn't help with the transport, so he took time to explain at length the reasons why. My father had too many things going on to take a whole day off to transport the bags on bad roads to the north. After a while, André left. From this day forward, something in the relationship with André had broken. André avoided him. My father felt helpless. He'd taken his time to explain that he'd gladly have done the transport, but making free time was impossible during the few days before the wedding.

When the relationship with André didn't improve, he decided to talk to his zookeeper. My father's zookeeper was Freeman Kabore. Freeman was born to a noble family in Ouagadougou but spent some years studying in Europe. He knew both cultures – African and European. So my father went to see him, and Zookeeper Freeman taught my father something about the Mossi culture. When someone comes to you with an important request, out of politeness, you should not refuse immediately. For people of the Mossi culture, the right answer would have been to say, "I will consider your request. Please come back to see me tomorrow, and I will give you the answer." This shows your friend that you are giving the request some thought, demonstrating the proper respect toward him/her. No matter what your justification is when denying the request, this formality applies.

Zookeepers are important. In business life, the best zookeeper is your assistant. Most executive are accustomed to working closely with their assistants. When arriving to Spain, my assistant gave me daily advice on how to adapt to local culture. The company was in a difficult situation and some tough decision had to be made. I started to question myself, when the third female employee who wanted to speak to me broke down in tears in my office. I discussed this issue with my assistant, and she simply said, "Here in Madrid that's how it works. Don't worry, keep a set of Kleenex in your desk, and when the employee starts to cry, just give her the Kleenex and go on talking rationally." And that is exactly what I did. My assistant helped me put this into context. Spanish culture is more tolerant toward tears in the workplace than my native Swiss culture. My zookeeper also told me how and when to congratulate for births and birthdays, how to greet important business customers, how to dress and how not to, under any circumstance, make copies at the copy machine myself. In Spain, the boss is expected to be the boss. On Geert Hofsted's power distance index, Spain is in the middle, a couple of ranks below Italy. Switzerland, on the other hand, prefers flat hierarchies. My assistant helped me translate the abstract cultural dimension of power distance into concrete changes in my behavior.

Finding a zookeeper is not always easy. It often involves active and passive criticism. This doesn't work without some form of friendship, or at least some trust. But when working abroad, you'll be automatically attracted by such persons for the simple reason that you'll feel understood. People with an international background somehow magically succeed in identifying themselves and flocking together.

The best zookeepers will be the TCK – a short acronym that's well-known among expatriates. It stands for Third Culture Kid. The term was conceived by the researchers, John and Ruth Useem, in the 1950s and was used to describe the children of American citizens working and living abroad.

You know you're a TCK when...

→ "Where are you from?" has more than one reasonable answer

→ You flew before you could walk

→ You go into culture shock upon returning to your "home" country

→ You get homesick reading National Geographic

→ You haggle with the checkout clerk for a lower price

→ Your minor is a foreign language you already speak

→ When asked a question in a certain language, you've absentmindedly respond in a different one

→ You've gotten out of school because of monsoons, bomb threats, and/or popular demonstrations

→ You speak with authority on the subject of airline travel

→ You know how to pack

→ You have the urge to move to a new country every couple of years

→ The thought of sending your kids to public school scares you, while the thought of letting them fly alone doesn't at all

→ You have friends from 29 different countries

→ You sort your friends by continent

→ You realize what a small world it is, after all

These children grow up in more than one culture. At home with their parents, they'll speak English and live like any other American child; but outside of their home, they'll be embedded in a foreign culture. Depending on where they've been expatriated, this could mean going out with German friends on a Friday night or it could mean attending school with French classmates. The American president, Barack Obama, is a well-known TCK. He was born in Hawaii, had a Kenyan father and an American mother and spent a good portion of his youth in Indonesia. I, myself, am a TCK; I grew up in three cultures and learned to alter my behavior, my body language and even my sense of humor accordingly. At home, we were the proper Swiss family. At my French school, I learned French history and geography and spent my free time with French friends. And in the neighborhood, in the market, on the street, I integrated into the local African culture, that of the Mossi tribe.

Growing up in multiple cultures, TCKs develop distinct standards of perspective, interpersonal behavior, work-related norms, codes of lifestyle and communication. They form a new cultural group that does not fall into their home or host culture but rather shares a complex culture only with all other TCKs.

TCKs possess a couple distinct characteristics that allow them to be the perfect zookeepers. They have a natural understanding about the possibility of multiple perspectives: they've been exposed to more than one way to look at a situation or experience. The increased exposure to a variety of perceptions and lifestyles allow TCKs to monitor their emotions and register societal norms and cues more adeptly, so as to be more sensitive to other cultures and ways of life. If you act like a monkey in a foreign culture, TCKs will try to understand you, instead of becoming angry with you.

TCKs are the best zookeepers you can find. If you work in another culture, keep your eyes peeled for them. If you secure their trust, they will be invaluable to your integration process.

What we learned in this chapter:

- You will learn a lot about the visible and invisible part of a country's cultural baobab by making friends and sharing time with them.

- In all cultures, sharing food is a huge social factor and is often ritualized, so having a meal with locals is a great way to learn a culture.

- Find a zookeeper who will help you bridge the gap between your own values and those of the local culture.

Epilogue: Do we really need all this?

Some voices say the world is quickly moving towards a global culture. Cultural differences will decrease over time. Global brands are on the rise and so is global marketing. Our tastes in food, music and clothing are becoming more and more similar. The internet connects the most remote spots on earth and will realize the concept of a global network.

So, is a book like this still necessary or is cross cultural management just an anachronistic skill which will disappear as the world becomes more culturally homogenous?

A couple of years ago, I was invited to speak at an international export marketing conference in Tehran. For my previous speeches on this topic, my presentation involved the rise and importance of global brands. Somehow, the fact that this conference would take place in a country not usually associated with export and global brands made me rethink my views on the topic. When I finally stood at the pulpit, I made a very different speech from those that I'd previously made. I started the presentation with a piece of music, called "Alperose," from the singer/songwriter, Polo Hofer. For most of you, this musician will be unknown, and indeed, at the pulpit, I was confronted with uncomprehensive stares by hundreds of Iranian marketing managers. Polo Hofer and his most famous song is quite a brand in Switzerland. Actually, more Swiss would recognize the song, "Alperose," than today's global hits from Rihanna, Adele and even long-time artists, like Madonna. Because the conference was about global marketing, it seemed pertinent to me to point out that as companies, in focusing on broader markets, we often forget local brands.

Consider your own private spending. How much do you spend on local brands? You'd be astonished to find that it's by far the larger portion of your income. You visit local restaurants, rent your flat from a local or nationwide real estate company, the broker for your insurance is local, so is the lawyer, the sports studio, the cinema, and much more. There isn't a global company for mobile communication, electricity, water, internet or any other facility you pay on a regular base. Your hairdresser, your doctor, your hospital probably don't belong to a global brand. Local business is far more important than high profile discussions on global brand and global economy would indicate.

Let me provide two more examples from industry usually associated with global brands. When talking about global insurance companies, five come to mind: AXA, Allianz, AIG, Zurich and Generali. All are among the top three in their home markets (France, Germany, US, Switzerland and Italy). But despite the global reach of each of these brands, none has been able to beat out competition and become number one in any market outside their home market...until they buy a local player. The point is we often talk about the attractiveness of global brands, but we forget about the prevalence and power of local brands.

A couple years ago, I had a discussion with the CEO of BMW Switzerland. They'd just introduced a new corporate design which would extend into the design of their international shops. He told me proudly, "We just implemented this new design all over the world. You can go into a BMW shop in Shanghai, and it will look exactly like the one here in Zurich." I listened attentively, then asked him how many BMW customers will walk into both the shop in Zurich and the one in Shanghai. He looked at me, somehow puzzled. "Probably none," he answered. Well, then for whom did BMW globally refit their shops? Obviously not for the customers, but rather in order to satisfy some centralized marketing department who strongly believes in the value of global brands.

I believe in global brands too, but I also believe in cultural differences. I believe in being truly close to your customers, and I believe the economy will need managers who know how to manage in different cultures for years to come. It's true that global values are on the rise, but a deep cultural change towards a more uniform world will take much longer than an international manager's normal career arch. In managing abroad, you'll be required to produce results within a couple of months or maybe 2-3 years, so cultural savviness will continue to be a central requirement for international management.

Actually, when it comes to cultural uniformity, recent research shows that the internet does not universalize culture or alter people's way of thinking. People with different cultural backgrounds use the internet differently. In general, people use new tools at their disposal to do the same things they did before the tools existed. [71] So, hierarchical cultures will use the internet in a hierarchical way, communicating downwards. Individualistic cultures will use the internet differently than collectivist cultures. The speed and availability of information may indeed create a global network, but the cultural differences of this network will remain.

Cultural differences and the difficulties they create in the way of successful management should not be understated. We're all human beings, we can communicate fairly well and modern technology has made communication even easier, further allowing for instant translations on your smartphone. But in a competitive world, small differences can impact business in a huge way. If you're vacationing on the Tunisian coast, cultural sensitivity is not a major necessity; but if you're managing a project or the buildup of a company in Tunisia, without cultural sensitivity, your business will fail.

This books provides an easy method by which to minimize cultural problems encountered on your assignment abroad. Before educating yourself on any specific culture, cement your cross cultural foundation by reading *I am the Monkey*. This book brings together general issues faced when managing across culture by providing a framework to understanding the differences and the contexts in which they are founded, thereby allowing you to accept, adapt and adopt. Though this book can serve as a foundation, it shouldn't be the last you read when planning to move and work in another culture. You should also invest in a book to inform you about the specific norms, values and behaviors of your prospective host country. You can find well-written and informative books about any country in the world. Unfortunately, they often concentrate on the tip of the iceberg, the visible behavior of a culture. They'll indicate to the reader how to speak, eat, act, greet and dress, but often will not address the deeper elements of society. Nevertheless, with the framework presented in this book, you'll be able to piece the information together on your own by simply following the steps to avoiding monkey moments:

Awareness

Make yourself aware of the cultural differences through online sources, books, videos, music, whatever you can find. Purchase a book on your prospective host's culture. Doing so will deepen your awareness of the specific cultural differences you may encounter during your stay.

Accept, Adapt, Adopt

Choose your strategy when confronted with specific cultural differences. You can start out by being actively tolerant, accepting the differences without judgment and accepting ambiguity. Continue with your cultural adjustment by adapting your behavior. Adapting is easier when you see why people behave in a certain way. Creating images and analogies to guide you through your daily decisions can help with adaption. Finally, after having stayed some time in the foreign culture, you'll notice you've changed. Adopting will come naturally; you don't have to do anything. Just let it happen, and before you know it, you'll have adopted some of your host culture's norms and values.

Action: Prepare and Share

To speed your cultural adjustment, prepare yourself. Long before entering a country, you can start learning the language and learning about their history and religion. Once you arrive, make local friends. Be proactive about it by breaking bread with them. Remember, sharing culture is often complemented by sharing food.

Culture is about humanity, about who we are. Contact with each of humankind's members, sharing time with them, interacting with all the world's people is, in the end, what makes our lives worth living.

Acknowledgments

I would like to thank Sylvia and Bill Miller. Without them, this book would not have been written. It started the day Sylvia knocked at the door on my family's new home in Richmond, VA. A couple of years down the road, the friendship between our families led to an invitation to lecture on cross cultural management at the Executive MBA of Virginia Commonwealth University. This invitation is the reason why I translated my lecture into English and, ultimately, it led to the writing of this book.

Through Bill, I met Van Wood, professor of international marketing at Virginia Commonwealth University. I presented him the book in a very early stage, and after scribbling down his advice during lunch at the historical Jefferson Hotel in Richmond, I consulted these notes regularly in an attempt to avoid writing a textbook, and rather a guide with practical relevance.

Together with Thomas Gutzwiller, I drove thousands of kilometers on bumpy roads through the heart of Africa. Thomas is the professor and director of the Executive School of Management at the University of St. Gallen and one of the most renowned academics in Switzerland. We had countless discussions either on the front seat of our Toyota Land Cruiser or sitting at night in our camping chairs under the pitch black African sky. After having read the first thirty pages of my notes, he asked me this essential question: "For whom are you writing it?" And thanks to this question, the book became much more focused.

I would like to thank Andriy Achyn for the illustrations. He has a masterful way of depicting complex information in a simple and direct design – and he is particularly good at drawing monkeys.

English is not my native language. In essence, this book has been written by Jessica Holom. She took my poor, painful writings and made them nice, readable and eloquent. She has such a tremendous gift for the English language. Her participation goes way beyond the simple grammatical corrections. She gave this book its character and personality.

I can't thank enough my co-author, Joanne Cackett. Not only did she provide the book's structural essentials, she was also my first reader and, without her encouragement, I certainly would have stopped after the first few pages. Her bright mind, her warm heart and her invaluable international experience were essential contributors to this book.

I would like to thank all my friends who've supported me, and foremost, of course, my family – my wife, Cornelia, and our children, Naomi and Joel – who journeyed alongside me through the usual ups and downs of writing and through the journey of life.

Finally, I would like to give a special thanks to my parents. They brought me to Africa as a child, and this experience, along with their education, opened my mind. Without them, I would never have been able to discover to such an extent the incredible cultural richness of the World.

Notes

1 H. J. Ehrlich, The Wiley book of business quotations, New York: John Wiley, 2002

2 H. B. Gregersen et al., Developing leaders for the global frontier, Sloan Management Review, 40(1) p. 21ff

3 cnn.com, Dog lovers threaten World Cup boycott, August 5, 2001 Posted: 7:31 AM EDT (1131 GMT)

4 C. Trasher and V. LoBue, Do infants find snakes aversive? Infants' physiological responses to "fear-relevant" stimuli, Journal of Experimental Child Psychology, 16 October 2015

5 R. Inglehart and C. Welzel, Changing Mass Priorities: The Link Between Modernization and Democracy. Perspectives on Politics June 2010 (vol 8, No. 2) p. 554

6 Guy Deutscher, Through the Language Glass: Why The World Looks Different In Other Languages, Picador USA, 2011

7 J. B. Deregowski, Perception of that two-pronged trident by two- and three-dimensional perceivers, Journal of Experimental Psychology, Vol 82(1, Pt.1), Oct 1969, p. 9-13

8 W. R. Jankowiak, Sh. L. Volsche and J. R. Garcia, Is the Romantic–Sexual Kiss a Near Human Universal? American Anthropologist, Volume 117, 2015, p. 535–539

9 W. Kolosowa, Durch die Blume gesagt, Spiegel Online, April 7, 2014

10 M. Harris, Our Kind, Who We Are, Where We Came From, Where We Are Going, New York: Vintage Books 1989, p. 195

11 A. Maslow, Motivation and personality, New York, NY: Harper, 1954, p. 91ff

12 G. Hofstede, Culture's Consequences, Sage Publications, 2nd Edition, 2001, S. 32

13 N. Sengupta and M. S. Bhattacharya International Human Resource Management, rev. Ed. 2007, p. 222ff

14 R. J. House et al., Culture, Leadership and Organizations. The GLOBE Study of 62 Societies, Sage Publications, 2004, p. xviii

[15] S. Powell and G. Hofstede: challenges of cultural diversity, Human Resource Management International Digest, Vol. 14 No. 3, 2006, p. 12-15

[16] S. J. Heine, D. R. Lehman and K. Peng, What went wrong with cross cultural comparisons of subjective Likert Scales?: The Reference-Group Effect, 2002, Journal of Personality and Social Psychology

[17] J. Hooker, Working Across Cultures, Stanford University Press, 2003, p. 146

[18] Adapted from J. Hooker, Working Across Cultures, Stanford University Press, 2003, p. 130

[19] F. Trompenaars and C. Hampden-Turner, Riding the waves of culture, Nicholas Brealey Publishing, 3rd edition, 2012, p. 87ff

[20] Adapted from C. Storti, Figuring Foreigners Out, Intercultural Press, 1999, p. 23

[21] H. Triandis, Cross cultural Studies of Individualism and Collectivism. Nebraska Symposium on Motivation, 1989 p. 42

[22] G. Hofstede, Culture's Consequences, Sage Publications, 2nd Edition, 2001, p. 209

[23] F. Trompenaars and C. Hampden-Turner, Riding the waves of culture, Nicholas Brealey Publishing, 3rd edition, 2012, p. 73

[24] F. Trompenaars and C. Hampden-Turner, Riding the waves of culture, Nicholas Brealey Publishing, 3rd edition, 2012, p. 66ff

[25] F. Trompenaars and C. Hampden-Turner, Riding the waves of culture, Nicholas Brealey Publishing, 3rd edition, 2012, p. 73ff

[26] For Instance: R. Ball, Individualism, Collectivism, and Economic Development, Annals of the American Academy of Political and Social Science, Vol. 573, Culture and Development: International Perspectives (Jan., 2001), p. 57-84

[27] F. Trompenaars and C. Hampden-Turner, Riding the waves of culture, Nicholas Brealey Publishing, 3rd edition, 2012, p. 81

[28] A. Maslow, Motivation and personality, New York, NY: Harper, 1954, p. 91ff

[29] G. Hofstede, Culture's Consequences, Sage Publications, 2nd Edition, 2001, S. 32

30 N. Sengupta and M. S. Bhattacharya International Human Resource Management, rev. Ed. 2007, p. 222ff

31 J. N. Hooker, Cultural Differences in Business Communication, Carnegie Mellon University Research Showcase @ CMU 12-2008, P. 9

32 J. N. Hooker, Cultural Differences in Business Communication, Carnegie Mellon University Research Showcase @ CMU 12-2008, P. 7

33 F. Trompenaars and C. Hampden-Turner, Riding the waves of culture, Nicholas Brealey Publishing, 3rd edition, 2012, p. 42

34 I. Alon, Chinese Culture, Organizational Behavior, and International Business Management, 2003, p 246

35 M. A. Hamedoglu et al., The Effect of Locus of Control and Culture on Leader Preferences, International Online Journal of Educational Science, 2012, p. 319ff

36 List compiled by K. Torgovnick May, http://ideas.ted.com/11-fascinating-funeral-traditions-from-around-the-globe/

37 C. Rapaille, The Culture Code, Crown Business, NY, 2006, p. 34

38 C. Rapaille, The Culture Code, Crown Business, NY, 2006, p. 35ff

39 A. Furnham and T. Ribchester, Tolerance of Ambiguity: A Review of the Concept, its Measurement and Application, in Current Psychology, Fall 1995, Volume 14, N. 3 p. 179ff

40 G. Hofstede et al., Cultures and Organizations, McGraw-Hill, 2010, p. 187.

41 G. Hofstede et al., Cultures and Organizations, McGraw-Hill, 2010, 2010, p. 200f

42 B. R. Barringer, Key Characteristic of Successful Business Owners, FTPress, online, January 5, 2009

43 J. Sandefer, The One Key Trait for Successful Entrepreneurs: A Tolerance for Ambiguity, Forbes/Entrepreneurs, online, May 17, 2012

44 The Ethicist, The New York Times, April 14, 2009

45 W. D. Hillis, Cause and Effect, in This idea must die, edited by J. Brockman, Harper Perennial, 2015 p. 77

[46] D. C. Thomas and M. F. Peterson, Cross cultural-Management: Essential Concepts, Sage Publications, 3rd Edition, 2014, p. 93

[47] C. Rapaille, The Culture Code, Crown Business, NY, 2006, p. 26f

[48] V. Lyskov-Strewe and S. Schroll-Machl, Russland. In: A. Thomas et al., Hrsg. Handbuch Interkulturelle Kommunikation und Kooperation, Band 2: Länder, Kulturen und interkulturelle Berufstätigkeit. Göttingen: Vandenhoeck & Ruprecht, 2003. S. 103ff

[49] J. E. Sherman, Empathic Intelligence: To put yourself in their shoes, unlace yours Psychology Today, May 21, 2009

[50] Nadine Al-Boudir, Saudi Writer Asks How Muslims Would Act If Christian Terrorists Blew Themselves Up In Their Midst, The Middle East Media Research Institute, Special Dispatch 6326, February 25, 2016

[51] China in Africa, One among many, China has become big in Africa. Now for the backlash, The Economist, Jan 17th 2015

[52] Time Magazine, July 30, 2015, The 10 Richest People of All Time

[53] G. James, 20 Epic Fails in Global Branding, Inc.com, Oct 29, 2014

[54] X. Geng, Cultural Differences Influence on Language, Qingdao University of Science and Technology Qingdao 266003, China

[55] J. Kinda, Moore Langue Vivante, Université de Ouagadougou, 2003, p. 17ff

[56] E. Trimnell, Why you need a foreign language & how to learn one, Beechmont Crest Pub2nd Edition, 2005, p. 71

[57] E. Trimnell, Why you need a foreign language & how to learn one, Beechmont Crest Pub2nd Edition, 2005

[58] E. Trimnell, Why you need a foreign language & how to learn one, Beechmont Crest Pub2nd Edition, 2005, p70

[59] R. J. House et al., Culture, Leadership and Organizations. The GLOBE Study of 62 Societies, Sage Publications, 2004, p. xviii

[60] Ruth C. Engs et al., Influence of religion and culture on drinking behaviours: a test of hypotheses between Canada and the USA, British Journal of Addiction, 1990, 85, p. 1475ff

61 M. Young, Cultural Influences on Accounting and Its Practices, Liberty University, Spring 2013

62 http://cultureshocktoolbox.com/2013/12/history-influences-culture-shock/

63 C. Behan McCullagh, Bias in Historical Description, Interpretation, and Explanation, History and Theory, Vol. 39, No. 1, February 2000, pp. 39ff

64 M. Oi , What Japanese history lessons leave out, BBC News, Tokyo, 14 March 2013, Magazine

65 Alia Wong, History Class and the Fictions About Race in America, The Atlantic, October 21, 2015

66 Boston NPR News Station, Interview with Elizabeth Hermann, http://www.wbur.org/2011/09/08/911-taught-differently, 2011

67 Sweden 'worst country' for making friends, in The Local, Swedish News in English, published 23 Sep 2015

68 M. Boyardee, U-curve? May be not, I was an expat wife, Blog, August 2012

69 F. Zampollo, B. Wansink, K. Kniffin, M. Shimizu, and A. Omori, Looks Good Enough to Eat: How Food Plating Preferences Differ Across Cultures and Continents, Cross-Cultural Research, 2012, p. 31ff

70 D. Bouchet, Differences in Food Culture - Traditions & Trends. Exemplified with the cultural differences between France-Denmark-Sweden, in Claus Heggun (Ed.): Quality and Risk Management. Proceedings of the 25th International Dairy Congress (21-24. September 1998, Aarhus Denmark), The Danish National Committee of the IDF, Aarhus 1999. pp. 210ff

71 S. Powell and G. Hofstede, Challenges of Cultural Diversity, Human Resource Management International Digest